D1116956

A COLONIAL AFFAIR

A COLONIAL AFFAIR

COMMERCE, CONVERSION, AND SCANDAL IN FRENCH INDIA

DANNA AGMON

CORNELL UNIVERSITY PRESS

Ithaca and London

This book was published with the aid of a grant from Virginia Tech (Office of the Executive Vice President & Provost, College of Liberal Arts & Human Sciences, and University Libraries).

Copyright © 2017 by Cornell University

All rights reserved. Except for brief quotations in a review, this book, or parts thereof, must not be reproduced in any form without permission in writing from the publisher. For information, address Cornell University Press, Sage House, 512 East State Street, Ithaca, New York 14850.

First published 2017 by Cornell University Press

Printed in the United States of America

Library of Congress Cataloging-in-Publication Data

Names: Agmon, Danna, 1977– author.
Title: A colonial affair : commerce, conversion, and
    scandal in French India / Danna Agmon.
Description: Ithaca : Cornell University Press, 2017. |
    Includes bibliographical references and index.
Identifiers: LCCN 2017008830 (print) | LCCN 2017010561
    (ebook) | ISBN 9781501713064 (epub/mobi) |
    ISBN 9781501713071 (pdf) | ISBN 9781501709937
    (cloth : alk. paper)
Subjects: LCSH: Puducherry (India : Union Territory)—
    History—18th century. | French—India—Puducherry
    (Union Territory)—History—18th century. |
    Compagnie des Indes orientales—History.
Classification: LCC DS485.P66 (ebook) | LCC DS485.P66
    A34 2017 (print) | DDC 954/.86029—dc23
LC record available at https://lccn.loc.gov/2017008830

Cornell University Press strives to use environmentally responsible suppliers and materials to the fullest extent possible in the publishing of its books. Such materials include vegetable-based, low-VOC inks and acid-free papers that are recycled, totally chlorine-free, or partly composed of nonwood fibers. For further information, visit our website at cornellpress.cornell.edu.

For Eli and Ido

CONTENTS

ILLUSTRATIONS

ACKNOWLEDGMENTS

So many people have had a role in the writing of this book, and it is a joy to have an opportunity to finally thank them.

I am deeply indebted to the dozens of people, not all of whom can be listed here, who read the manuscript at various stages and so generously shared their insights with me; their good ideas profoundly shaped this work. For these efforts, I thank Richard Allen, Ned Alpers, Daniel Birchok, David William Cohen, Joshua Cole, Alexandre Dubé, Nafisa Essop-Sheik, Héloïse Finch-Boyer (who deserves a very special note of thanks for first suggesting that I might want to look into French India as a research topic), Malick Ghachem, Federico Helfgott, Daniel Hershenzon, Jennifer Heuer, Steve Hindle, Maya Jasanoff, Paul Christopher Johnson, Lloyd Kramer, Tamara Loos, Jessica Marglin, Aliocha Maldavsky, Jessica Namakkal, Minayo Nasiali, Brian Owensby, Jennifer Palmer, Sue Peabody, Bhavani Raman, Natalie Rothman, Stephen Sparks, Robert Travers, Fredrik Thomasson, David Washbrook, Ellen Welch, Gary Wilder, Matt Wisnowski, Laurie Wood, Akhila Yechury, and Tal Zalmanovich.

I have presented this work in various works-in-progress settings and benefited tremendously from doing so. For this I thank the members of the Anthropology and History Workshop at the University of Michigan, the Historians Writing Group at Virginia Tech, and the Huntington Library Long-Terms Fellows Working Group. I was also aided by the comments made by participants at the North Carolina Research Triangle French History and Culture Seminar and the George Washington University Medieval and Early Modern Studies Institute. Special thanks go to the group of anthropologists who let me into their stimulating and productive work-in-progress group: Laura Brown, Elana Buch, Monica Patterson, and Bridget Guarasci. I am also grateful to the two anonymous readers who so deeply engaged with the manuscript, the sharp insights provided by my editor Mahinder Kingra, and the terrific staff at Cornell University Press.

In various archives, in Aix-en-Provence, Puducherry, Paris, and Nantes, I have received the help of thoughtful professionals. Special thanks are due to the staff at the wonderful Archives nationales d'outre-mer in Aix-en-Provence and to Mme. Brigitte Appavou of the archives of the Missions étrangères de Paris, Mme. Cécile de Cacqueray of the Bibliothèque Francisicane des Capucins in Paris, and Père Robert Bonfils of the Jesuit archives in Vanves. I am grateful to the American Institute of Indian Studies and especially to Purnima Mehta in Delhi for her assistance, which made possible my time at the archives of the Record Centre, Puducherry. There Mr. M. Murugesan, the assistant archivist, was exceptionally helpful.

I consider it the greatest piece of good luck to have been trained in the joint program in anthropology and history at the University of Michigan. The intellectual curiosity, passion, and generosity that characterized everyone involved with the program, far too many people to name here, taught me so much and continue to inform my work. I have been extremely fortunate to have a group of dedicated and brilliant mentors, who support me professionally and intellectually. Most important, Dena Goodman, Diane Owen Hughes, and Sumathi Ramaswami have been the most insightful readers and the fiercest advocates, and my gratitude for their wisdom and constant efforts on my behalf is immense. In Ann Arbor and Paris, I was able to enlist, respectively, Webb Keane and Ines Županov as my marvelous mentors, and since I arrived at Virginia Tech, I have been helped by the ongoing collegial support offered by Mark Barrow, François Debrix, and Helen Schneider.

Institutional support for this project made possible travel to archives in France and India and funded precious time to write. I am grateful for financial support provided at the University of Michigan by the Rackham Graduate School, a Barbour Scholarship, and the Center for Medieval and Early Modern Studies. A Bourse Chateaubriand from the French government, a fellowship from the Center for European Studies, a Franklin Research Grant from the American Philosophical Society, and several grants from Virginia Tech's College of Liberal Arts and Human Sciences also funded archival and writing time. Most crucially, at key junctions of the development of this work, yearlong fellowships provided not only time to write but also an inspiring community of fellow writers—first, at the Institute for the Humanities at the University of Michigan, and more recently at the Huntington Library in San Marino, California, where a Barbara Thom long-term fellowship enabled me to complete the manuscript. Both institutions provided a setting that advanced this work in myriad ways and helped to convince me that even individual scholarship is best pursued in fellowship. I've acted on this belief by writing most of this book in a variety of daily writing groups and partnerships. Two of my writing partners deserve special thanks. Bridget Guarsci in Ann Arbor and later Dale Winling in Blacksburg heard me talk about Nayiniyappa more than was perhaps fair, and their insights and generous engagement were extremely helpful. For their camaraderie, steadfastness, and shared commitment to the pomodoro writing system, I also thank Carmen Gitre, Melanie Kiechle, Elizabeth Mazzolini, Xotichl Ruiz, and the Huntington Fellows daily writing group, especially Tawny Paul, Daniel Immerwhar, Martha Rust, and Alice Fahs.

For their love, patience, and unwavering boosterism from across the sea, my thanks go to my parents, Ora and Tamir Agmon, and my sister, Tal Elazar. My deepest words of gratitude go to Dan Simundza, whose wisdom, good humor, and unfailing, abiding support have strengthened and sustained me.

Portions of chapter 2 were first published in Danna Agmon, "The Currency of Kinship: Trading Families and Trading on Family in Colonial French India," *Eighteenth-Century Studies* 47, no. 2 (2014): 137–55. Copyright © 2014 Johns Hopkins University Press. Portions of chapter 5 were first published in Danna Agmon, "Intermediaries on the Move: Mobility and Stability in the Making of Colonial Go-Betweens in Eighteenth-Century India," in *Intermédiaires Culturels/Cultural Intermediaries: Séminaire International des Jeunes Dix-Huitiémistes*, ed. Vanessa Alayrac-Fielding and Ellen R. Welch (Paris: Honoré-Champion, 2015), 217–36. Copyright © 2015 Editions Honoré-Champion.

THE ACTORS

The Accused

Nayiniyappa: Chief commercial broker to the Compagnie des Indes in Pondichéry, 1708–1716

Nayiniyappa's Family and Associates

Guruvappa: Nayiniyappa's eldest son

The Widow Guruvappa: Guruvappa's wife, Nayiniyappa's daughter-in-law

Tiruvangadan: A merchant of Madras, and Nayiniyappa's business associate and brother-in-law

Ramanada: Nayiniyappa's business associate.

Ananda Ranga Pillai: Nayiniyappa's nephew, Tiruvangadan's son, and chief commercial broker to the Compagnie des Indes, 1748–1761.

French Trader-Administrators

Guillaume André Hébert: Governor of Pondichéry 1708–1713; Général de la nation, 1715–1718

Hébert *fils*: The governor's son and a junior employee of the Compagnie des Indes

Pierre André Prévost de La Prévostière: Governor of Pondichéry, 1718–1721

Nicolas de La Morandière: Pondichéry councillor, author of several appeals filed by the accused Indians

The Missionaries

Guy Tachard: First superior of the Jesuit mission in Pondichéry

Jean-Venant Bouchet: Second superior of the Jesuit mission in Pondichéry

Père Esprit de Tours: Capuchin missionary and parish priest to Europeans in Pondichéry

Jean-Jacques Tessier de Queralay: Representative of the Missions étrangères de Paris.

The Interpreters

Manuel Geganis: A French-speaking Tamil Christian, son of the Jesuits' chief catechist (religious interpreter)

Père Turpin: A Tamil-speaking Jesuit missionary

Cordier: A French man born in India to a company employee

A COLONIAL AFFAIR

Introduction

When three French merchant ships arrived in 1714 in the port of Pondichéry, on the Coromandel coast of India, the disembarking sailors found themselves in the midst of a massive celebration.[1] The town was marking the marriage of the son of Pondichéry's chief commercial broker, a Tamil man named Nayiniappa.[2] Ten thousand guests, Tamil and French, took part in the event. The party went on for days, with elephants, fireworks, lavish feasts, religious rites, and dance performances—including one that took place in the house of the commander of the French fort. The scribe of the French merchant fleet devoted several pages of the ship's journal to the description of the event, clearly dazzled by the wealth, influence, and authority on display.

The host of the wedding celebration, Nayiniyappa, was the most important Indian employee of the Compagnie des Indes orientales, the French trading company governing Pondichéry.[3] The town-wide celebration reflected his place and power in the colony. Yet only two years later this same man was alone in a prison cell; for days he was held without even knowing the charges against him. On June 6, 1716, the French colonial court convicted Nayiniyappa of the crimes of tyranny and sedition after finding him guilty of abusing his power and organizing an employee uprising that had taken place the previous year. He was taken to the town's main bazaar and received fifty lashes of the whip in front of a watching crowd. All of his vast wealth, accumulated over decades of doing business with French traders—the land, houses, jewels, elephants, cash, and goods—was stripped from him, and his three sons were banished from Pondichéry in perpetuity. He was sentenced to serve three years in prison, but just a few months later he died in his cell under somewhat mysterious circumstances.

Three years after this solitary death, in 1720, a young Tamil man would kneel to embrace Christianity in the ornate chapel of the royal family in the Palais Royal in Paris. No less a personage than Philippe d'Orléans, the regent of France, would serve as his godfather. French missionaries hosted the young foreigner in their Paris headquarters. A few months after that he knelt again, this time to receive a French order of knighthood. The pendulum had swung back for Nayiniyappa's family, for the kneeling man was his eldest son, Guruvappa.[4] It was likely Guruvappa's own wedding that the ship's scribe had depicted in his journal six years earlier. Nayiniyappa's son returned to India ennobled, the banishment rescinded, with a new name honoring his royal godfather and the young King Louis XV: he was now the Chevalier Charles Philippe Louis Guruvappa.[5] He assumed the position that had been his father's: chief commercial broker to the Compagnie des Indes in Pondichéry. The event known in both France and India as *l'affaire Naniapa*—the broker's rise, fall, and posthumous rehabilitation over the course of a decade—had come full circle as Nayiniyappa's son returned triumphant to the colony.

These radical reversals of fate were an essential feature of the Nayiniyappa Affair, the event at the center of this book. And as the Nayiniyappa Affair was litigated, investigated, and contested, the involved actors all articulated their vision of French empire in the East and debated the role of local intermediaries like Nayiniyappa in Pondichéry. An investigation of the affair and the fault lines it revealed shows that conflicts between and within the projects of trade and religion were a defining characteristic of French empire in South Asia.

The French Crown and its agents were engaged in two central efforts in India in the first decades of the eighteenth century: building the town of Pondichéry into a prosperous trading hub and converting local men and women to Catholicism, the religion of the French state. The two efforts at the heart of the French presence in South Asia—making money and making Christians—shared important characteristics. French colonial trade and Catholic religious mission were both concerned with creating and propagating a colonial vision of order, authority, and morality. However, they differed in the specifics of this vision, and the intersection of the two efforts entailed significant instability and friction. Although the French state chartered, funded, and to a large measure directed both of these projects, merchant-administrators and missionaries could not agree on what kind of colony—and *colonie* was the term consistently used by contemporaneous sources to describe the settlement of Pondichéry—they were creating.

Traders and officials of the Compagnie des Indes sought to sustain the very profitable status quo and to insert themselves into long-standing Indian Ocean trading networks. French missionaries, on the other hand, espoused an ideology of disruption and radical change in an effort to reconfigure the local spiritual and social hierarchies. The book's central argument is that commerce and conversion in French India were simultaneously symbiotic and fundamentally in tension with one another. Would the traders' vision of a profitable status quo prevail, with the French newcomers seamlessly inserted into the established networks and markets of the Indian Ocean world? Or would the missionaries' transformative agenda emerge triumphant, with a Catholic order replacing the multiple religious practices in the region?

The complexities of internal colonial rivalries and the imbrication of local networks within these rival efforts shaped the French experience in South Asia. The creation of sovereignty in French India, I argue, required distributed authority. Local intermediaries shared in the mechanism of distributed authority, effectively sidestepping the binary of collaboration or resistance that has informed so much of the scholarship on colonial encounters. The first decades of French rule in Pondichéry, and especially during the course of the Nayiniyappa Affair, revealed with particular clarity the stakes of such distributed authority.[6] The actors most intimately involved in the Nayiniyappa Affair understood the case as hinging on precisely the intersection of mediation and sovereignty.

What, then, was the Nayiniyappa Affair, and why should it matter for the histories of colonialism, France, and South Asia? The remainder of this book is devoted to teasing out the affair's multivalent and layered meanings, but its twists and turns were the stuff of high drama and can be briefly summarized. Nayiniyappa came to Pondichéry as a young man, and over several decades of involvement with the Compagnie des Indes he became one of the richest and most influential men in the French colony. In 1708 the French governor, Guillaume André Hébert, appointed him to the highest position a local man could hold: courtier to the company and "head of all Malabars." Nayiniyappa and Hébert worked closely together for several years, trying to build the colony's trade and reputation. Five years into Nayiniyappa's tenure as chief broker, Hébert was removed from office because the directors of the company in Paris were unhappy with his management of the colony, and he was sent back to France.

But Hébert wanted to return to India, where a man could make a lot of money quickly. Hébert's rivals told an unflattering story about the governor's agenda and methods; according to Nayiniyappa and his allies, Hébert cultivated the powerful Jesuits, who had the ear of some of the most important actors in the French court. In return for the Jesuits' support—so goes the story according to Nayiniyappa's supporters—Hébert agreed to help the Jesuits in Pondichéry bring about Nayiniyappa's downfall. The Jesuits strongly objected to Nayiniyappa as chief broker because he refused to abandon his local religion, which we would today term Hinduism, in favor of Christianity.[7] The Jesuits wanted a Catholic Indian as chief broker.

We cannot know whether Hébert and the Jesuits struck a deal. But in 1715 Hébert was sent back to Pondichéry, and a few months later he ordered Nayiniyappa's arrest. Two of Nayiniyappa's close associates, his brother-in-law Tiruvangadan and a man named Ramanada, were arrested as well. Nayiniyappa's trial attempted to answer the question, how central a role in the colony's rule was it possible, permissible, or desirable for a local intermediary to fill? His conviction was an effort to curtail the influence of local actors. But after Nayiniyappa's conviction, a global mobilization effort on his behalf ensued—by missionaries who were rivals of the Jesuits, traders who were rivals of Hébert, and an association of merchants from St. Malo with trading interests in India, who relied on Nayiniyappa to keep their ships full and their journeys profitable. Nayiniyappa died before he could benefit from these efforts on his behalf, but he was exonerated posthumously. Hébert was removed from office, sent back to France in disgrace, and ordered to pay damages to Nayiniyappa's heirs.

This bare-bones account of the affair does little, however, to reveal its multiple and contradictory meanings and implications for the history of French India. An inquiry into Nayiniyappa's life, downfall, and rehabilitation starkly reveals the fissures between the commercial and spiritual branches in Pondichéry, especially between the Compagnie des Indes and the Jesuit missionaries. We see here conflicts at multiple scales and intersections, with institutions fracturing against each other and internally: traders against missionaries, traders against traders, missionaries against missionaries. The Nayiniyappa Affair pitted government officials and traders on the one side against Jesuit missionaries on the other, but it was also the site of even more internal face-offs: current administrators of the Compagnie des Indes battling their current and former colleagues; traders in France against traders in India; Jesuits against rival Catholic religious orders, the Capuchins and Missions étrangères de Paris (MEP) missionaries, a society created in 1658 expressly for conversions in Asia.[8] It is worth reiterating that all these actors purportedly shared a single cause—the prosperity of Pondichéry in the name of God and king. The Nayiniyappa Affair thus reveals the fractured nature of the colonial effort.

Historiographies of both France and South Asia have largely neglected the history of French India, albeit for different reasons. In colonial South Asia, the shadow of the British Raj has loomed so large as to obscure the neighboring French as well as Dutch and Danish colonies in both the Tamil region and Bengal, site of the French holding in Chandernagore. Even as the historiography of India in the eighteenth century has been growing, it is still, to a large extent, devoted to unraveling the origins, processes, and consequences of British rule.[9] The study of the Indian Ocean more broadly has grown enormously in recent years, but the French experience within it has similarly garnered surprisingly little attention. French historians, on the other hand, have only relatively recently begun to study empire, owing to what has been described as a "fit of collective imperial amnesia" following the French loss of colonies in Asia and Africa in the twentieth century.[10] Late twentieth-century efforts to reckon with the war in Algeria and its ongoing impact on France in the modern era have been central in the turn toward colonial history, meaning that the bulk of the work on French colonialism has been devoted to France's Second Empire, of the nineteenth and twentieth centuries.[11] Work on France's First Empire, in the seventeenth and eighteenth centuries, on the other hand, has by and large focused on the Atlantic. Historians have marginalized the French colonies in India and the Indian Ocean and dismissed them as failures and thus insignificant.[12] Yet French experiences in the early modern Indian Ocean—precisely because they do not follow the trajectory of more familiar, later imperial histories—enhance our understanding of the conflicts, challenges, and contradictions inherent in colonialism.

This book integrates ongoing debates about colonial mediation on the one hand and the making of imperial sovereignty on the other by situating the Nayiniyappa Affair at the heart of an account of French colonialism in India. In the first decades of the eighteenth century, across the empire, French actors and populations newly under French rule negotiated mutual working orders. This period saw debates over practices of enslavement, cultural blending and miscegenation, trade and smuggling, and the relationship between metropolitan vision and colonial enactment.[13] At the heart of most of these debates was an attempt to determine the contours of French sovereignty in colonial locales.[14] The Nayiniyappa Affair illuminates this phenomenon with particular clarity, since in the course of the affair debates about mediation and its limits morphed into explicit claims and counterclaims about both the desired ambition and the possible reality of French sovereignty.

Cultural mediation, and more specifically the work of native intermediaries in colonial settings, has been shown to be pivotal in the making of emerging empires.[15] Scholars have demonstrated how colonized subjects, especially elites, could come to have crucial roles in the creation of political and administrative ties between the intermediaries' communities of origins and the sometimes far-flung colonial cities where official power was concentrated.[16] These investigations, however, have focused almost exclusively on the bridge these go-betweens provided between European newcomers and indigenous populations. Historians have only recently turned their attention to the role local intermediaries filled within European political and institutional settings, to examine how they provided an opportunity for colonial actors to grapple over their different approaches to governance, trade, and religion.[17] In Pondichéry, native colonial intermediaries acted *within* the European imperial structures, mediating, highlighting, or benefiting from conflicts among European groups as much as from the differences between new arrivals and local populations. The focus on intermediaries in Pondichéry reveals both that intra-European conflict was a defining feature of colonialism and that intra-Tamil conflict, particularly between rival families of local brokers, similarly informed colonial decision making.

Scholars have also attempted to uncover the mechanisms by which imperial sovereignty comes into being.[18] Yet this work, Mary Lewis has suggested, focuses on the unitary, categorical whole of empire, to the neglect of the local specificity of colonial politics.[19] Much attention has been paid to resistance on the ground to colonial sovereign rule, but sovereignty itself is often described as stemming from political and intellectual trajectories that are conceptually separate from the actual experience of colonialism.[20] By theorizing sovereignty in early modern empires as a construct imported from Europe, this literature obscures the role of local agents, including the significant role of the intermediaries on which colonial rule relied.[21] The spatial and temporal categorizations that posit that concepts of sovereignty arrived with colonists aboard European ships or were developed in later, more hegemonic imperial settings do not do justice to the historical record. Agents of the French state in Pondichéry neither wholly conceived sovereignty in advance nor fully held it in undivided fashion. French sovereignty had to be constructed in Pondichéry and thus incorporated local actors, conflicts, and practices.

Puducherry to Pondichéry

The French were the last to arrive of all the Europeans who established trading posts and colonies in India, following the Portuguese, Dutch, English, and even the Danes. The Compagnie des Indes orientales, created in 1664, was the first durable vehicle for French commerce in India. Unlike the merchant-led Dutch and English companies, the French endeavor was an explicitly royal project, imagined and executed by Jean-Baptiste Colbert, Louis XIV's minister of finance.[22] The creation of the company was of a piece with Colbert's broader mercantilist vision, according to which control of foreign trade was crucial for the state's well-being.[23] Earlier scholarship has tended to consider the early efforts of European charter companies in the East as "mere" merchant capitalism; more recently, scholars have demonstrated how these mercantile efforts acted in state-like ways, with territorial and cultural ambitions informing their decisions, such that the distinction between "purely" or "merely" commercial projects and political, state-like, imperial, or colonial ones holds little water.[24] After all, every European trading company depended on its relationship with the state that provided its charter.[25] If it is true that the early British East India Company presence in India was in many ways that of a state, as Philip Stern has cogently argued, this was much more the case in the French experience, since the French company, as scholars have recently argued, was a "state concern . . . rather than a truly merchant-run trading organization."[26] The French case is distinctive, not least because the involvement of various missionary orders, explicitly charted by the French king and sent to support commercial efforts, demonstrates that the French in Pondichéry were engaged in an effort to transform the spiritual, cultural, and political landscape, alongside their attempts to insert themselves into established commercial exchanges.

The company's structure bore witness to its royal origins: a Paris-based *chambre générale* of directors appointed by the Crown managed it, under an official who reported directly to the king.[27] Most of the capital that established the company was raised from the royal family, government ministers and other members of the court at Versailles, and financiers. Both Louis XIV and the powerful minister Colbert were major shareholders in the company, with the king providing more than three million livres of the original capital subscription to the company, roughly half the initial capitalization.[28] Once established in India, the Compagnie des Indes, like other European charter companies, administered towns, made laws and dispensed justice, minted money, commanded troops, built fortifications, and supported conversion efforts.[29] But in this case the French state was the explicit planner and director of its actions, making the imperial dimension of this commercial project central to the company's development.

The French first tried to establish themselves in Surat, a bustling and well-established port in Gujarat on the west coast of India, where the French founded a trading post in 1668, but they quickly encountered difficulties.[30] Too many rivals, too little room for newcomers. It was in the town of Pondichéry, almost a decade after the Compagnie des Indes orientales was first formed, that the French would gain a measure of political sovereignty, but it was a somewhat haphazard affair at the outset. In the 1670s the company's traders turned south from their failed effort in Surat to the Coromandel coast of India. In an unexpected turn of events, Sher Khan Lodi, a local Indian governor appointed by the sultan of Bijapur, suggested the French might like their own establishment in the region, and he gave the French representative Pondichéry as a gift.[31] The village was not far from English and Dutch holdings, and its Tamil name—Puducherry—meant "new town."[32] The newness of Pondichéry also meant that almost all its residents—French and South Asian–born alike—were effectively newcomers and that French rule in the town was not displacing an earlier form of Tamil sovereignty. The French company also made a concerted effort to cast a broad geographic web in India, founding satellite trading posts (comptoirs) in Karikal, Yanaon, Mahé, and Chandernagore, and it maintained its lodges in Surat and Masulipatam. Beginning in 1701, Pondichéry served as the administrative, political, and military center of the French presence in the subcontinent (figure 1).

Pondichéry's survival and prosperity depended on trade. Trade in India radiated across a wide-flung web of ports, out from the coastal cities of the subcontinent to Asia and the Indian Ocean. From Pondichéry, trade routes fanned out both east—to Aceh, Mergui, Pegu, Batavia, Manila, and China—and west—to Mocha, the Maldives, and the islands of Île Bourbon and Île de France in the Indian Ocean. In all these ports, French traders competed not only with the Dutch, English, and Portuguese but with the commercial communities of Gujratis, Jews, Muslims, Armenians, and others that had preceded them.[33] Cross-cultural trade, in the Indian Ocean as elsewhere, depended on trust, familiarity, and reputation, as merchants tried to establish a stronghold far from home and relied on credit to carry out transactions.[34] French traders would have been intimately acquainted with the absolute centrality of credit for doing business, since credit structured economic and social life in early modern Europe.[35] For Europeans who arrived in the Indian Ocean, the solution for their lack of credit and entry was dependence on local actors. The French were by no means unique in their reliance on intermediaries, since the practice was widespread across early modern imperial settings.[36] But those empires that managed to transform themselves into more hegemonic powers—and the British Raj is the most pertinent example—obscured this reliance.[37]

It is surely no coincidence that the span of the Nayiniyappa Affair corresponded to a difficult period for French officials on two fronts: first, the instability of the French state, and second, the shaky finances of the Compagnie des Indes. The instability at the level of the French state was the result of ongoing war—the War of Spanish Succession in 1701–1714, with its resulting

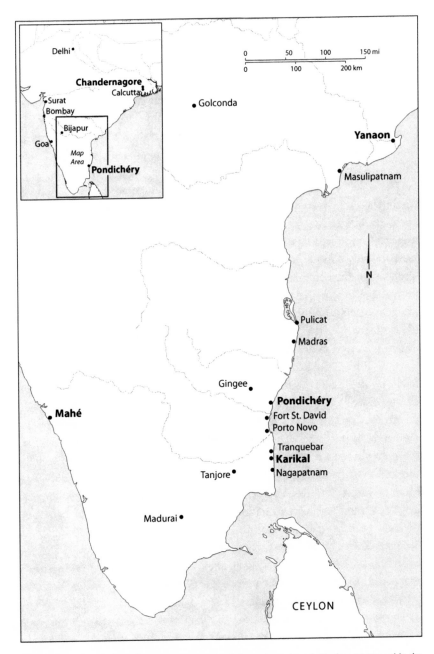

FIGURE 1. The Coromandel coast of India in the eighteenth century. In the large map and in the inset, the five French *comptoirs* are in bold font. Map by William L. Nelson.

financial crises—and the Regency period during Louis XIV's minority, dating 1715–1723.[38] The war and its repercussions continued to reverberate throughout the French colonial world, in both the Atlantic and the Indian Ocean, long after the end of fighting. In the resulting debt crisis, showy trials against individuals deemed culpable for France's unstable financial system were a common feature both in the colonies and in the metropolis, where a special tribunal, the *chambre de justice* of 1716, was charged with assigning blame for financial disorder within the monarchy's finances.[39] Similarly, when Nayiniyappa was sentenced to pay the Compagnie des Indes an enormous fine upon his conviction, the inflow of cash supported the always cash-strapped company.

There were multiple reasons for the financial difficulties of the Compagnie des Indes. French merchants and financiers were reluctant to invest in the company, preferring regional opportunities; the company had high operating costs; and the occasional capture of French ships and subsequent heavy losses posed a serious problem. As a result, the company relied on the sale of one load of cargo to finance its next Asia-bound voyage. It also saw multiple reorganizations in the seventeenth and eighteenth centuries. This institutional upheaval and the persistent shortage of capital lay behind many of the political struggles that characterized Pondichéry's administration in the first decades of the eighteenth century.

If the French political context was one of uncertainty and flux, the same held true in the Indian subcontinent, where the states that surrounded Pondichéry were in a state of ongoing war for much of the first part of the eighteenth century.[40] With battles between the Deccani sultanates of Bijapur and Golconda, tension between the Maratha armies and the Mughal empire, the general decline of Mughal power, and intra-European rivalries about their relations with local patrons, the political landscape in South India was extremely volatile. Given the fact that one of Nayiniyappa's roles as chief broker was to mediate political relations with local rulers, the uncertainty of local political systems made the position of chief broker more crucial than ever. Taken together, the French and South Asian political uncertainty on the one hand and the financial difficulties of the Compagnie des Indes on the other would inform the debates that animated the struggle over Nayiniyappa's conviction and subsequent acquittal.

Despite this fraught context, the first half of the eighteenth century was a period of significant growth in Pondichéry, in both its urbanization and its demographics (figures 2 and 3). In this period, Pondichéry was transformed into an important regional center, with several thousand Frenchmen and tens of thousands of mostly Tamil-speaking inhabitants and a growing trade reliant on the export of textiles.

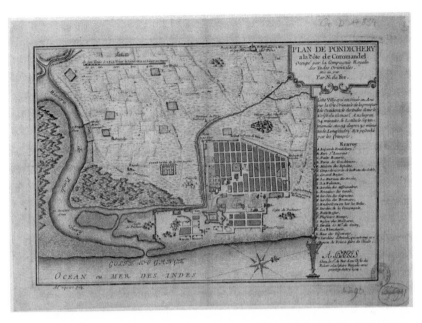

FIGURE 2. A 1704 map of Pondichéry exhibits the city's grid and highlights its religious diversity by noting Jesuit, Capuchin, and numerous local places of worship, described as "pagodas." "Plan de Pondichéry à la côte de Coromandel occupé par la Compagnie royale des Indes orientales/ mis au jour par N. de Fer—1704." Bibliothèque nationale de France, département Cartes et plans, GE D-17834.

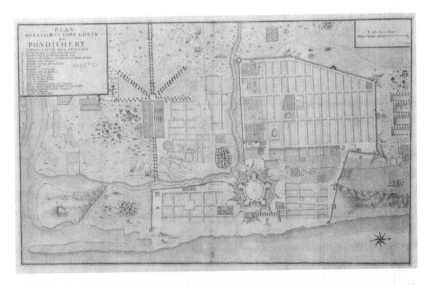

FIGURE 3. This 1716 map, drawn by Nayiniyappa's ally, the engineer Denyon, shows the growth of Pondichéry in the first two decades of the eighteenth century. "Plan des ville et fort Louis de Pondichéry par M. Denyon." Bibliothèque nationale de France, MS-6432 (1BisA).

The town's physical setting was a crucial feature of its commercial and demographic success in the first decades of the century. During much of the year the town's port was relatively sheltered from the monsoons, and a river flowing into the sea, navigable by small, flat-bottomed boats, made it an attractive spot for trade.[41] The port did not allow for the anchoring of large ships, so the town had no wharves; instead, small vessels darted through the water, loading and unloading merchandise.[42] The fort on the water's edge where Nayiniyappa was held was meant for the town's protection, but it also was used as Pondichéry's commercial and administrative center, with the Compagnie des Indes's offices and chambers of the Superior Council housed within.

French ships left Pondichéry carrying a dizzying array of textile products, cotton, silk, and wool in well over one hundred different varieties.[43] The volume of trade in textiles over these years was quite variable; in general, however, the first three decades of the eighteenth century were a period of steady expansion of French investment in Pondichéry.[44] Nevertheless, the French company got a smaller share of trade than the English and Dutch companies, and ships sent by the Dutch East India Company and the English East India Company consistently outnumbered French ships heading to the East.[45]

The exact demographic makeup of Pondichéry's population in the first decades of the eighteenth century is difficult to determine, since the first existing census dates from 1769.[46] At the time of the Nayiniyappa Affair, the French population of Pondichéry is estimated to have been only 1,000 to 2,000 souls, among a general population numbering in the tens of thousands.[47] The French residents were mostly employees of the Compagnie des Indes—traders, clerks, soldiers, sailors, doctors, engineers, and the like—but some French residents arrived there independently, lured by the opportunity to trade on their own account. The non-French population made up the vast majority; in 1740, a French writer estimated Pondichéry's population to have grown to 120,000.[48] Roughly one-third of these residents were weavers, who manufactured the cotton textiles that were the central commodity of French trade in India, and their presence in the colony was therefore of paramount importance. Throughout this period, when textile workers in South India enjoyed significant mobility, weavers and merchants migrated to Pondichéry, as the company was engaged in labor-intensive projects of fortification, acquired several villages surrounding Pondichéry, and grew its textile production operations.[49] The new residents were mostly practitioners of local religion (what today would be glossed as Hindu) and diverse in caste.

The fact that they formed the town's majority would figure prominently in the Nayiniyappa Affair, as traders and missionaries tried to decide precisely what place a non-Christian broker should play in the town's commerce and politics. The town's judicial and administrative records, as well as maps from the period, also attest to the presence of a much smaller population of local converts to Christianity, a small community of Muslims,[50] and a handful of Armenian merchants, as well as new arrivals from other parts of India beyond the Coromandel coast. Many French households also held Indian domestic slaves, both Christians and Hindus.[51]

The town's spatial layout was segregated, separated into so-called White Town and Black Town. In this, the town was organized according to urban plans conceived by the Dutch during the brief period late in the seventeenth century when Pondichéry was under their control.[52] White Town was adjacent to the water, encompassing the port and the fort, and the larger Black Town lay mostly to the west, in the area of higher elevation, but the line between the two was a porous one.[53] Despite the town's explicitly segregated layout, French and Indian actors who came together at Pondichéry's founding in the late seventeenth century attempted to paint it as a religiously and culturally diverse and cosmopolitan locale, a location that would be both a port of departure and a point of destination. By the beginning of the eighteenth century, the residents of Pondichéry were indeed a fairly cosmopolitan bunch. The marriage and death records, kept by the Capuchins who acted as the Catholic population parish priests, revealed that the town's residents hailed from all over the globe: various locales in South Asia, the Indian Ocean island colonies, Bagdad, Isfahan, Ireland, England, Germany, Venice, and as far afield as Canada.

Religious Tensions in a Commercial Town

In 1708, Pondichéry's colonial officials issued a proclamation on behalf of the company's board of directors. It proclaimed in Tamil, French, and Portuguese that merchants of every nation should pursue commerce in Pondichéry and would not be disturbed.[54] The 1708 proclamation promising a welcome haven for all, on the one hand, and the cityscape's grid of racial and religious segregation, on the other, reveal an unresolved tension that lay at the heart of the French presence in Pondichéry. The goals of French officials to make the town both a place in which authority took a Catholic form and a commercially successful city in a landscape that was emphatically non-Christian seemed at times to be mutually exclusive. The ongoing conflicts about the integration of commercial ambitions and missionary agendas tried but did not succeed in resolving this tension.

When the Compagnie des Indes was created, its charter charged the company not only with commercial profit making but also with propagating and supporting Christianity in the territories under its control.[55] The relationship between religious mission and the state in early modern colonial projects was hugely variable, with different fault lines appearing in different contexts. French India not only highlights this variability but also reveals the challenges that religious agendas posed to commercial and political efforts in newly established colonial settings with existing strong local state systems. Such challenges were much less visible in cases where political, cultural, and religious hegemony was achieved.[56] In Pondichéry, the multiple agendas of rival missionary groups made the bifurcated nature of French empire in India—the simultaneous mandate to advance both commerce and Christianity—all the more difficult to achieve. Missionaries of different orders all sought to advance conversion agendas through cooperation with the state and state-supported commercial projects. French missionaries of different orders in Pondichéry were thus adversaries vying for resources and influence. Nayiniyappa's body was a site for the unfolding of this battle.

In the seventeenth century and early in the eighteenth century, Christian missionary work in South Asia was the exclusive domain of Catholics. The missionaries who made Pondichéry their base were Frenchmen of three separate Catholic orders: Jesuits, Capuchins, and members of the Missions étrangères de Paris. The Capuchins, an offshoot of the Franciscans, were the first to appear in the colony, arriving in Pondichéry in 1674 and serving as both parish priests to the European Catholics and missionaries to the local population. From the very earliest days of the Compagnie des Indes's presence in India, the Capuchins often positioned themselves as allies to and participants in the royal commercial project. The collaboration between the company and the Capuchins both stemmed from and exacerbated the Capuchin rivalry with the Jesuits—a rivalry so pronounced that some locals once asked a Venetian living in Pondichéry whether he worshipped the God of the Jesuits or the God of the Capuchins.[57]

The Jesuit-Capuchin conflict originated with the arrival of the Jesuits in Pondichéry in 1689, when the ambitious newcomers compromised the Capuchins' position as sole religious providers. Upon the Jesuits' arrival, Governor François Martin divided the spiritual field, declaring that the Capuchins would serve as chaplains to the European parish, and Jesuits would tend to the flock of indigenous Christians and potential Christians. This compromise suited neither side. Internal divisions and bitter exchanges between the groups would figure prominently in the Nayiniyappa Affair. The squabbles between the Jesuits and the Capuchins consistently unfolded before both ecclesiastical authorities and the institutions of the French state.[58]

The deepest and most persistent struggle between Capuchins and Jesuits in French India revolved around the form of religious ministration to neophytes and potential converts. Conflicts between Jesuits, members of other Catholic orders, and the church hierarchy writ large were by no means limited to Pondichéry, manifesting as the "Malabar Rites" controversy in South Asia and the "Chinese Rites" controversy in China. In both sites, Vatican officials and rival orders objected to the Jesuits' conversion practice and ideology known as "accommodation," which allowed new converts to maintain local customs (for example, those pertaining to marriage and burial rites) after conversion to Christianity. The Jesuits' opponents argued that accommodation diluted Christianity.[59] This controversy had higher stakes in Pondichéry, which was ruled by Catholics, unlike, say, Madurai, the Tamil city where Jesuit accommodationist practice in India was developed. Contestations over accommodation led to bitter conflicts between missionaries of different orders. But the debate also informed the conflict between the Jesuits and officials of the Compagnie des Indes because while the Jesuits were willing to accommodate their converts in an effort to bring them to Christ, they saw no reason why the company officials would reward and advance those local residents, such as Nayiniyappa, who refused to convert to Christianity.

The Second Empire of the nineteenth and twentieth centuries would feature frequent conflicts between a state seeking anticlericalism and colonial ventures dependent on missionary labor, as J. P. Daughton has shown.[60] No such inherent conflict underlay the struggles in French India early in the eighteenth century that would explode in the course of the Nayiniyappa Affair. Administrators and religious workers were sent to India long before the invention of laïcité, the secular nature of the state, as a French ideal. Commercial and religious agents alike were acting on behalf of a divinely ruling king, the head of the Gallican church, and were furthering the ambitions of a state explicitly and timelessly Catholic. Colonial officials and traders in the early eighteenth century would therefore have shared many of the goals and attitudes of their missionary contemporaries. Yet the repeated struggles in Pondichéry among lay and religious agents indicate that the ideal of a shared commercial-religious agenda, manifest in both the charter of the company and missionary texts, remained elusive in practice. As the French in India tried to enhance their commercial, administrative, judicial, military, and spiritual position, the bifurcated nature of a colony in which traders and missionaries were struggling over control hampered their efforts.

The Nayiniyappa Affair as a Prism for Empire

Tensions about the interpenetration of secular and religious authority drove the Nayiniyappa Affair, and an examination of the affair sheds new light on their significance. Using the Nayiniyappa Affair as a prism for French empire more generally makes possible a new understanding of both. Yes, the Nayiniyappa Affair was in part a battleground for powerful Jesuits, their missionary rivals, and factions within the French commercial venture. But if we simultaneously consider the broader imperial context and the local struggle for prominence in Pondichéry, a fuller understanding of events emerges. The Nayiniyappa Affair was neither French nor Indian but a Pondichéry affair. It grew into existence in the landscape of the colony, and thereby it inevitably wove together strands both local and metropolitan, French and Tamil. The affair brought together the interests of the town's petty shopkeepers and its wealthiest traders, the highest echelons of French officialdom with illiterate Tamil widows, well-connected missionaries born in France, and multilingual children of the Jesuits' local employees. The Nayiniyappa Affair also affords a unique entry into the life of an indigenous actor and his social, familial, religious, and commercial milieu. *Affaires*, the scandalous and well-publicized trials that were a feature of public life in the Old Regime, were also common in the colonies.[61] Yet the Nayiniyappa Affair stands out for having an indigenous actor at its center, one who is doubly exceptional for having managed to attract significant advocacy to his cause and overturn the decision against him.

This study, then, considers the contested and unstable aspects of imperial claims, and of French claims in India in particular. It situates the agency of indigenous actors, and especially brokers and intermediaries, at the center of these contestations and as a result at the very center of the colonial experience. Imperial sovereignty had to be continually constructed, and in this period it was never fully achieved. The example of French India demonstrates how early imperial formations relied on dispersed and fractured authority, shared and contested among agents with diverse agendas, backgrounds, and political and religious allegiance, whose hierarchical relations to one another were in a state of flux.

Chronology soothes as it smooths, its unfolding coming to seem inevitable and logical. In the following chapters, I resist a chronological narrative of the affair, instead opting for a prismatic history, returning to the same details and events in each chapter, slightly shifting the analytic lens in each one to go over the same narrative material. The thematic approach aims to excavate the overlapping layers of the Nayiniyappa Affair, to show that it cannot be reduced to a tidy event, one with a linear narrative, heroes and villains, or unitary meaning. The metaphor of the prism is especially apt here. As a prism reflects, returns, and refracts light in multiple directions, so the documentary richness distributed by the Nayiniyappa Affair in archives in France and India sheds new light on the role of trade and religion in the making and unmaking of colonial authority.

French colonial administrative records of the Compagnie des Indes form the central archive on which this book relies, but it also draws on a diverse set of materials held in archives in France and India, including missionary letters, court records, notarial records, and personal diaries. While most of the source material was written in French and collected by French institutions, its authors are both Frenchmen and South Asian–born residents of Pondichéry.[62] Surely, Tamil and other Indian actors appear in this archive with their voices refracted through multiple processes of translation and often with French coauthors; but their involvement in the production of these archives—an issue explicitly taken up in greater detail in the book's final chapter—means that local intermediaries played an important role in the construction of the French colonial bureaucratic and judicial record. Bringing together these authors, genres, and modes of archival production is a crucial methodology of the prismatic history that follows. The result is both a microhistory of the Nayiniyappa Affair and a broad consideration of French imperialism in this period. As a French imperial history that pays close attention to the fine details of a largely forgotten local affair, this study draws out the intricate negotiations that situate empire in place.[63]

The book is composed of three parts. The first part examines the reliance of both trader-administrators and missionaries in the newly established colony of Pondichéry on local intermediaries and discusses the social, political, and commercial structures in which French colonists, missionaries, and intermediaries all intersected. Chapter 1, "The Elusive Origins of a Colonial Scandal," provides multiple answers to a deceptively simple question: Why was Nayiniyappa arrested? Chapter 2, "Kinship as Politics," considers the role of family networks, both French and Tamil, in the development of French empire in India.

The second part centers on Nayiniyappa's days in court and the details of his investigation, appeals, and the reinvestigation of the affair. Chapter 3, "The Denial of Language," serve as a corrective to the tendency in European imperial history to overlook the centrality of polylinguistic scenarios in colonial encounters. It examines the relationship among French, Portuguese, and Tamil in colonial politics of commerce and conversion and in the unfolding of the Nayiniyappa Affair. Chapter 4, "Conflict at Court," examines the affair as a court case, addressing the judicial setting in which it took place and the legal questions it attempted to resolve.

The third part considers the repercussions of Nayiniyappa's conviction, death, and posthumous rehabilitation. Chapter 5, "Between Paris and Pondichéry," focuses on mobility in the Indian Ocean and between France and India. Chapter 6, "Archiving the Affair," describes the archives in which traces of the Nayiniyappa Affair are sedimented and reveals the agentive processes by which these archives and subsequent historical narratives were created. The book's epilogue reflects on how Nayiniyappa's role in the imperial project in Pondichéry shaped his life and in turn shaped the politics of the colony. In other words, it inquires into the effect of empire on individual lives and the impact of individuals on the development of empires.

PART ONE

The World of the Affair

CHAPTER 1

The Elusive Origins of a Colonial Scandal

When he was twenty years old, Nayiniyappa, a merchant of Madras, moved to the newly established French colony of Pondichéry. Forty-three years later, in 1717, he died in a prison cell in Fort St. Louis, Pondichéry's center of French administrative and military power in India. At the time of his death he had served three months of a three-year prison sentence for the crimes of tyranny and sedition, having been removed from his post as the colony's chief commercial broker and head of the town's indigenous population, a position the French referred to as *courtier* and *chef des malabars*. As Pondichéry's chief commercial intermediary, Nayiniyappa had amassed considerable property, but the French confiscated all his wealth, including precious gems, horses, elephants, and several houses. In a rite of public humiliation, he was whipped with fifty lashes in Pondichéry's main bazaar. Had he lived out his prison term, he and his entire family would have been banished from the colony forever. None of these details are contested. The meanings of the scandal that came to be known in India and in France as *l'affaire Nayiniyappa* are not nearly as straightforward.

The Nayiniyappa Affair has a haunting quality. Fort St. Louis no longer stands, so Nayiniyappa's ghost hovers instead in the archives. Officials of the Compagnie des Indes in Pondichéry maintained detailed yearly logs of their doings, as well as copies of all their correspondence.[1] The logs for most years contained exhaustive and meticulous descriptions of changes in personnel, new building projects, and discussions of the political situation surrounding Pondichéry. But a large portion of the records for the years 1716 to 1724 is devoted to Nayiniyappa's conviction, the subsequent appeals on his behalf, and the resulting official investigations. The wealth of documentation attests to the imaginative pull Nayiniyappa's downfall exerted, as more and more actors in India and in France participated in the analysis, reinvestigation, and interpretation of the events surrounding his arrest. Nor was this interest limited to Nayiniyappa's contemporaries. When the colonial exhibition of 1931 was mounted in Paris, officials in Pondichéry sent a small handful of documents to represent the history of French India.[2] They selected three that concerned the Nayiniyappa Affair.[3]

Why was Nayiniyappa arrested? No easy answer to this deceptively simple question exists. Several of Nayiniyappa's contemporaries debated the story of his plummet from Pondichéry's pinnacle of power, as did he himself. Different groups of actors—French government officials in both the colony and metropole; missionaries of various Catholic orders; friends and relatives of Nayiniyappa; traders employed by the Compagnie des Indes and trading associations in Brittany; and, later on, historians of French India—have interpreted Nayiniyappa's investigation, conviction, and posthumous exoneration differently and provided divergent explanations for the origins of the affair.

Through the juxtaposition of these competing interpretations of the affair's commencement, a picture of the colony emerges. The different origins ascribed to the Nayiniyappa Affair reveal starkly different understandings of colonial authority; the relation among metropolitan center, periphery, and colony; and the role of local intermediaries in the French overseas project. These parallel and contradictory versions of events, I argue, created a point of condensation that enabled different groups to articulate their own vision of the imperial project in relation to the Nayiniyappa Affair.

While each of the four interpretations of the affair's origins examined here offers a different version of the unfolding of events, they all shared an underlying concern. Missionaries, colonial officials, Indian employees, and metropolitan traders all attempted to offer solutions to a vexing question: What was the basis for colonial authority and sovereignty? The issue was especially troubling in the early decades of the eighteenth century, when Pondichéry was a relatively new and unsettled seat of French power, facing constant threat of military attack and financial collapse. Its sovereignty was a very fragile construct, its hegemony more aspiration than reality. Michel-Rolph Trouillot has argued that success is a matter of continuous historical articulation rather than fact.[4] Colonial empires of the nineteenth century narrated themselves as inevitably successful. But early French and Indian concerns about the justifications for European sovereignty and the limits of authority offer a different tale, one that sheds light on the conditions in which colonial projects come into being and their subsequent historical and political retellings. Rather than presenting a teleological narrative of hegemony, the tensions driving the Nayiniyappa Affair and those that erupted in its multiple retellings allow for a more complicated understanding of authority in colonial settings. The affair reveals shifts and uncertainties in the distribution of authority, particularly in how forms of kinship, exchange, and belonging, both local and imported, supported and supplemented the state. The juxtaposing of the four accounts of the origins of the affair recounted in this chapter is what makes such shifts legible and knowable.

Where Do Go-Betweens Go? Commercial Brokers in South Asia

When employees of the French trading company and Catholic missionaries first arrived in Pondichéry in the 1670s, they found a region roiling with political upheaval and mighty military struggles, among both European and Indian polities, and the political landscape was in a state of bewildering flux. The commercial world posed a different challenge to French newcomers: the maritime trading associations of the Indian Ocean world were well established, cemented by centuries of contact and exchange and based on the familiarity of kinship and religious affiliation. Scholars of Indian Ocean trade have shown that European involvement in the region was less transformative of these networks than previously assumed. The preexisting structures were sustained throughout most of the eighteenth century, with European traders trying to position themselves within these structures rather than displacing or transfiguring them.[5]

One scholar has argued that to the extent to which the Indian Ocean was an integrated world system, it relied on the work of commercial brokers.[6] And while it was not only Europeans who employed commercial brokers to facilitate trade, European trade companies in the Indian Ocean had no established networks of kinship or origin upon which they could draw for support and thus depended even more heavily on their brokers.[7] In both commercial and political spheres, therefore, Europeans in general and French newcomers in particular, since they were the last of the European powers to arrive in India in the seventeenth century, needed to negotiate a place for themselves in densely populated and often confusing realms. To do so, they relied on the services of local intermediaries, who either introduced them into new markets or acted on their behalf. Commercial brokers—such as Nayiniyappa—who were employed by the Compagnie des Indes and by individual traders filled this function.

The many terms used to refer to these actors—intermediaries, go-betweens, middlemen, cultural brokers, middle figures, marginal men, *passeurs culturels*—are an indication of a certain murkiness inherent in the category. Arguably, anyone in a cross-cultural encounter acts as an intermediary, but such a definition renders the category too vague to have much analytic purchase. My own use of the term "intermediary" is intentionally narrow: Pondichéry's intermediaries were men—and it was exclusively men who were appointed to these positions—whom French traders and missionaries retained as paid employees, as either commercial brokers or religious interpreters, known as catechists in the Catholic terminology. They thus intentionally and self-consciously acted as go-betweens. Nayiniyappa himself reflected on the meaning of the position and described it as a fundamentally public role at the center of the colony. He wrote, "For there to be communication between the Frenchman and the Indian, there is need for an intelligent man, who will act as an ambassador between the two nations. He is called the *chef des malabars* and is a public man. The [governor] addresses only him, and he alone is known by the Indians. It is a very distinguished position in this land."[8]

The issue of nomenclature of commercial brokers in Pondichéry is a surprisingly thorny one. In Madras, Pondichéry's neighbor to the north, these brokers were known as "dubashes"—according to one etymology, meaning "men of two languages."[9] Although South Indian historiography frequently uses the term "dubash" to refer to these actors, French sources of the period do so rarely. The French equivalent term, usually rendered *daubachy*, does show up in French documents but not in the first decades of the eighteenth century. In the first three decades of the eighteenth century in Pondichéry, several different terms were used to refer to the Tamil men who enabled French trade. One term was "modeliar," which stems from the Tamil word for "first" (*mudal*); it is commonly used to designate a Vellala caste group to which many of these men belonged. A second term often used to refer to brokers is the French word *courtier*. Most often courtier referred to those, like Nayiniyappa, who had obtained the highest rank of commercial brokers, hired by the Compagnie des Indes as the most senior Tamil employee in the colony; the term was typically joined to *chef des malabars* (head of all Malabars).[10]

The double title, *courtier et chef des malabars*, points to two different aspects of these men's position at the crossroads of two cultural systems and their ability to act at the intersection of needs. As courtiers, they were enmeshed in a French system of service, with a commitment to furthering the agenda of the French company and the Crown. But simultaneously, they were *chefs des malabars*, local leaders of the Tamil community and therefore responsible also for representing the interests and voices of local merchants and workers back to the company. This double positioning at the heart of both the French and the Tamil commercial and social infrastructure in Pondichéry enabled commercial brokers to become such central figures of authority. This double-sourced authority also motivated French anxiety about the repercussions of intermediaries' power and influence in the colony and beyond.

The services commercial brokers provided were diverse; under French employment, their main task was to ensure that enough merchandise would flow into French hands, so that the ships leaving Pondichéry's port would be fully stocked with the cloth and other commodities that were then sold in European markets. To this end, brokers negotiated with regional merchants who supplied goods but also set up both farming operations and artisanal centers, where raw materials were produced and transformed into commodities. In return, brokers received a percentage of the sale they had made possible—generally between 2 and 4 percent. They were also able to extend credit, to the French trading company, to individual French traders, and to their Asian partners. Well-positioned intermediaries not only supervised and made possible the flow of goods into company ships, but they also managed diplomatic relations with local rulers by writing letters, leading delegations to courts, and arranging for the exchange of gifts. In addition, they were responsible for local labor markets. In Pondichéry, this meant recruiting and managing the highly skilled textile workers (mostly weavers and dyers) who produced the colony's most important commodity. As Shubhra Chakrabarti has noted in the context of Bengal, artisans and producers owed their allegiance and commitment not to the European company but to the local brokers and intermediaries who hired them and provided them with orders and capital.[11] This was also the case in Pondichéry, where the chief broker was charged with managing relations with local artisans, either directly or through a subordinate group of merchants who acted as intermediaries for him. But intermediaries were also involved in other labor markets. For example, hired intermediaries recruited and managed Indian seamen, or lascars, to serve on the ships of the English East India Company.[12]

Commercial brokers made the trade of the company possible, but they also enabled the private trade of French traders who were employed by the company but were eager to take advantage of opportunities to trade on their own account. This meant that every single employee of the Compagnie des Indes in Pondichéry, from the governor on down to the lowliest sailor at the port, had a strong, personal incentive to see the colony's commerce in the region flourish and continue to grow. The fact that the Nayiniyappa Affair engendered such committed and passionate involvement from so many was a result of this shared investment in Pondichéry's commercial prospects. In his role as chief commercial broker to the French company in Pondichéry, the job Nayiniyappa held from 1708 to 1716, he held the general responsibility for creating a robust market in Pondichéry, drawing capital-rich merchants to settle in the town, ensuring the timely production of textile goods, and generally enhancing French commercial reputation in the region. Nayiniyappa made money in the colony flow. Arresting and convicting him, argued his diverse supporters, jeopardized the colony's commercial success and by extension its very existence. Nayiniyappa's importance for the success of Pondichéry was a feature of the position of brokers in India in the seventeenth and early eighteenth centuries. As Michael Pearson has noted, in the early modern Indian Ocean "relations between brokers and their clients were by and large ones of equality rather than (as became the case later) of domination and subordination."[13] The Nayiniyappa Affair, then, gives rise to the following question: In exchanges between French traders and missionaries and their local intermediaries, who was the patron and who was the client?

The French reliance on intermediaries in India did not begin in Pondichéry but dated back to Surat, a cosmopolitan and prosperous port in Gujarat where the Compagnie des Indes first tried to established itself. A French *comptoir*, or trading "factory," was established in Surat in 1666. For centuries, Surat had occupied an important place in the maritime trade of the Indian Ocean, with a bustling local trade spreading across Asia and to Africa, a wealthy Armenian trading population, and English and Dutch factories. A French Jesuit, Father Guy Tachard, who arrived in Gujarat late in the seventeenth century, described Surat as "the most beautiful, the wealthiest, and largest commercial city I have seen in the Indies, not even excepting Batavia or Goa."[14] Indian cities such as Surat drove the image of an ideally cosmopolitan town that French administrators later sought to achieve in Pondichéry. Brokers facilitated and managed the diversity such cosmopolitanism entailed. It was the attempt to reconcile commercial and cultural diversity with Catholic authority that later became so divisive for traders and missionaries in Pondichéry.

The status of the French as late arrivals in Surat did not appear initially to be a great impediment, thanks to aid the French received from local brokers. In 1666, the Mughal emperor Aurangzeb granted the French a *firman*, a royal decree, that allowed them the same trading privileges in Surat as the Dutch and the English had, and in 1669 the French were granted a firman by the court in Golconda to establish a factory in Masulipatnam on the Coromandel coast. This latter success largely depended on the connections and efforts of an Armenian go-between, Martin di Marcara Avachintz, who acted as a broker and diplomatic emissary for the French in the 1660s.[15] Marcara had been born in Isfahan, in present-day Iran, and possessed many of the most desirable traits of a broker: he was well connected in a variety of ports, spoke many languages, and had traveled extensively between India, Persia, and Europe, settling for a while in the Italian port of Livorno before heading to Paris.[16] He set sail to the East in 1666 as part of a French fleet that went first to Madagascar, then to Surat. From Surat he was sent to advance French interests on the eastern coast of India, but he soon fell out with François Caron, the director of the French initiative in India. Caron had the Armenian broker arrested in 1671, following the spread of rumors that Marcara had poisoned a French colleague and mishandled French shipping interests. The arrest led to a drawn-out legal battle that traveled back to France, where, after Marcara was released from prison in 1675, he demanded restitution for losses he had sustained.[17] The differences between Marcara and Nayiniyappa are significant—not least among them Marcara's Christianity. But much as in the case of Nayiniyappa's downfall, Marcara's success as a broker proved dangerous. His history with the Compagnie des Indes demonstrates both the deep roots of French reliance on Indian Ocean brokers and the tendency of these relationships to transition from intimate dependence to acrimonious legal struggles.

Scholars have debated how the rise of European power in the subcontinent and the Indian Ocean impacted the position of mediating men like Marcara, Nayiniyappa, and others. In Ashin Das Gupta's account, the powerful individual brokers of the first half of the eighteenth century gave way to a class of men who were subservient to colonial masters in the second half of the century, in a process that was replicated in Bengal, the Coromandel, and Gujarat.[18] Shubhra Chakrabarti has argued, on the other hand, that a class of local commercial brokers remained both crucial to and powerful in British East India in Bengal well into the late eighteenth century, and reliance on these intermediary figures did not decline as European political power grew.[19] This was certainly the case in French India, where political power outside the confines of Pondichéry—and sometimes even within it—remained more notion than reality for much of the eighteenth century.

Before the Fall: Nayiniyappa in Pondichéry

Nayiniyappa arrived in the French colony about 1674 as a young man and traded with the French long before he was appointed chief broker. He originally came from the environs of English-ruled Madras. His migration to Pondichéry was part of the ongoing French attempts to draw prominent and well-connected merchants to the town. Such residents were much sought after, since the French hoped that their credit and reputation would convince others to conduct trade in the town and with the French company. Nayini-yappa himself, according to a history written by one of his descendants in the late eighteenth century, persuaded his brother-in-law to join him and relocate from Madras to Pondichéry.[20]

We know little of Nayiniyappa's daily life in Pondichéry prior to his arrest—his social encounters, preferences, and day-to-day activities. Luck-ily, Nayiniyappa's nephew—a man of the same family, class, and caste, who filled the very same position of chief commercial broker to the Compagnie des Indes—kept a minutely detailed account of his own life for twenty-five years. The diary written by this man, Ananda Ranga Pillai, is renowned as the first work of Tamil prose in the genre.[21] His journal offers a window into the lives of Pondichéry's commercial brokers. As chief commercial broker, Ananda Ranga Pillai kept a close eye on French commercial dealings, both the appointments of company employees and the comings and goings of French ships. He had daily contact with French administrators—both the governor and lower-ranking officials who kept him abreast of developments—and he had up-to-date knowledge of the proceedings in the Superior Council's chambers. Even as Ananda Ranga Pillai was deeply involved in the minutiae of company trade, he remained intimately invested in his own business as well, packing up pieces of cloth and visiting his warehouses daily. Like him, Nayiniyappa also maintained his private business while serving as chief bro-ker. The level of detail with which the diarist followed the life of the French governor—Joseph Dupleix for much of his tenure—was minute; on one occa-sion the broker described the outfit that the governor wore to sleep.[22] He kept close tabs on the broader political landscape, particularly the military and commercial dealings with the English in Madras—the area from which Nayiniyappa and Ananda Ranga Pillai's family had originated and where they still had close connections. The diary also reveals a very tightly knit familial circle, with significant space devoted to family events celebrated, the broker's concern about his brother, and the future of his children. Ananda Ranga Pillai was also active in the town's cultural and spiritual life, commissioning poetry and donating to temples, as well as participating in religious rituals regularly, and there is every reason to assume Nayiniyappa did the same.

Over several decades of living in the French colony, Nayiniyappa rose to fill the influential and profitable post of chief commercial broker of Pondi-chéry. He first appears in French records already involved with the commer-cial doings of the French company but not yet its employee. In 1704 his name appears in the deliberations of the Superior Council of Pondichéry: "The council has awarded the farming of tobacco and betel leaf to Naniapa for two years," noted the minutes.[23] Four years later, in 1708, the council again discussed its business dealings with Nayiniyappa and considered putting a large provisioning contract in his hands but ultimately decided to choose a group of merchants with whom it was more familiar.[24] Even though Nayiniyappa did not win this contract, he must have made a good impression on the members of Pondichéry's council and the French governor. He was appointed to the post of head commercial broker, replacing a Christian broker who had bungled a business deal that the always cash-strapped French company was eager to undertake.[25] The replacement of a Christian, even an inept one, with a Hindu, was unusual.[26]

The Jesuit missionaries objected to Nayiniyappa's appointment in 1708 on religious grounds and continued to do so until the broker's ultimate arrest in 1716. In 1711, the Jesuits petitioned the king for a series of measures meant to boost the number of Christian conversions in the town.[27] The petition itself was a testament to their ongoing difficulties with proselytizing. Following orders received from France, the Superior Council of Pondichéry gathered in March 1714 to discuss the possibility of granting these Jesuit requests. The council discussed two requests at length. First, the Jesuits asked that Hindus be allowed the use of only two temples. All other temples in Pondichéry should be barred shut and allowed to fall into disrepair. Second, the Jesuits argued that in order to attract new converts, they must be able to give converts marks of distinction. Accordingly, only a Christian should hold the post of chief broker, and Nayiniyappa must be immediately dismissed.

The sitting governor, Pierre Dulivier, was willing to entertain the Jesuits' demands only grudgingly. The council's deliberations, probably written by Dulivier himself, clearly reflect his reluctance. The councillors noted that both measures—the closure of Hindu temples and the dismissal of Nayiniyappa—could have dangerous consequences, which might lead to the "complete ruin of this establishment."[28] The council argued that there was not a single Indian, Hindu or Christian, who was as capable as Nayiniyappa at filling the post of chief broker.[29] Nevertheless, Dulivier and the council offered a compromise of sorts. First, the council appointed a Christian Tamil cobroker to serve alongside Nayiniyappa. This man, Chavoury (Tamil: Savari), was, according to council documents, expected to act "conjointly and in concert" with Nayiniyappa and was endowed with the same "powers, honors, prerogatives and preeminence attached to the post, without any difference or distinction between the two."[30] Chavoury was also tasked with protecting the interests of Christians, advancing Christian faith in Pondichéry, and making sure that Nayiniyappa would not impede these aims.

Second, the council members declared that they had given Nayiniyappa six months in which to be instructed in the mysteries of Christianity and convert. If at the end of this period he insisted on remaining a Hindu, they promised he would be removed as head broker and replaced with a Christian. It was to be hoped, the council wrote, that the force of the Gospel and the good example of Christians would attract Nayiniyappa to the Christian faith. Given the fact that Nayiniyappa had by that point been living around Christians for several decades, this hope seems to have been misguided. Indeed, six months later, Nayiniyappa was still a Hindu and still serving as head broker.

In a letter that Governor Dulivier sent in July of 1714 to Jérôme Phélypeaux, Comte de Pontchartrain, the French minister in charge of the Compagnie des Indes, he advocated for the compromise of the Christian cobroker instead of Nayiniyappa's dismissal and explained why Nayiniyappa was irreplaceable: "This gentile [Nayiniyappa] knows everyone, as your Grace has already been informed, and is one of the most capable of men in India in the art of negotiation. His correspondents are everywhere, there is no service he is incapable of providing, even when the need is most pressing."[31] Dulivier explicitly linked the dismissal of Nayiniyappa with the restrictions of religious practice also advocated by the Jesuits, writing that acquiescence to these demands could have tragic results for the future of Pondichéry.[32]

Complaints about the dearth of suitable candidates were a constant in the colonial administrators' correspondence with the directors in Paris. In 1719, in the midst of the Nayiniyappa Affair, the directors wrote from Paris to Pondichéry, listing the kinds of qualities they hoped to find in their courtier in India: "We suggest, in the strongest possible terms, that you choose a courtier who is wise, loyal, experienced, and well-listened to, and impress upon him that he must keep as absolute secret the management of the company's workings," they wrote. In a response dated two years later, the colonial administrators in Pondichéry somewhat peevishly wrote back that this was easier said than done. "We haven't yet settled on a choice for courtier; the talents and qualities that the company desires to find in the man are absolutely essential, but not easy to find in this country, if we find someone who accords with the company's wishes, we will appoint him."[33]

Ananda Ranga Pillai, a successful broker himself, offered his own account of the elusive combination of traits that made for a good commercial intermediary. In discussing the possibility that his own brother might be considered for the position, the diarist first described the characteristics that might suit him for service in the company. "My brother—who is close to thirty-five— [is] . . . naturally possessed of the gifts of high culture, excellent parts, guarded temper, winning manners, handsome presence and fortunate birth." Despite these attributes, however, he did not think his own brother was well suited to fill the role of go-between. The reason: he was "not blessed with the courage and spirit of enterprise which is indispensable for raising oneself to distinction." His brother's lack of drive was the central problem, or so Ananda Ranga Pillai believed: "He has no desire to acquire wealth and no ambition to figure conspicuously in the service of the company. Further he is too retiring to hold any intercourse with the Europeans."[34]

Difficulties with finding suitable Christians to appoint to the position of chief broker in Pondichéry did not conclude with the Nayiniyappa Affair. In Ananda Ranga Pillai's diary, in an entry written before he was appointed to the position himself, he described a conversation on this topic he had had with a French trader, who urged him to seek out the appointment. The Frenchman told Pillai in 1746: "There is no one at present as competent as yourself. If there were any individual amongst the Christians who could command the confidence of the public, the situation would, no doubt, be offered to him. But as matters stand, the Christians of this city are all paupers, and are of such condition that people are scarcely inclined to give them even alms."[35] The difficulty of finding a Christian man who was accredited, well connected, and influential enough to fill the role of chief commercial broker stood at the heart of the struggle over Nayiniyappa's fate. If not he, then who else?

"Tyranny and Sedition": The Contradictory Accusations against Nayiniyappa

Despite the Jesuits' 1711 request to dismiss Nayiniyappa and his refusal to convert in 1714, Nayiniyappa remained in his position as chief broker. This changed suddenly in 1716, when he was arrested. He faced two charges: sedition and tyranny. The first of these, sedition, stemmed from an event that had taken place in 1715, in which local Hindu weavers, laborers, and traders threatened to abandon the town because of encroachments on religious freedom. In a colonial context, with a tiny French community, the fear of population loss was never far from the councillors' minds. Accusing Nayiniyappa of orchestrating an employee walkout thus resonated with ongoing and broad French concerns about the viability of their efforts in India.[36] The crime of tyranny was a more diffuse signifier. Different observers saw the charge differently. Governor Hébert accused him of general abuse of power against Indians. The Jesuits suggested he had committed religious persecution against the town's largely poor and less powerful population of Tamil Christians (an accusation discussed in greater detail below).

At first glance, it might seem strange and even contradictory for one man to stand accused of sedition against French rule and tyranny against colonial subjects. The charge of sedition refers to an attempt to overthrow the current order and supplant it. The charge of tyranny, on the other hand, implies authority, an ability to use the system and its hierarchy to one's own advantage. Why would a tyrant wish to overthrow a system that supplies him with his power? This apparent contradiction speaks to the fact that Nayiniyappa's French employers found his position in the colony unsettling. The greater Nayiniyappa's value to his employers, the more his authority grew, and the more threatening he became because of their reliance on him. This contradiction helps explain Nayiniyappa's rise to prominence, his downfall, and his subsequent posthumous rehabilitation.

Nayiniyappa on the Origins of the Nayiniyappa Affair

In the brief period between his arrest in 1716 and his death in prison in 1717 Nayiniyappa participated in the creation of two documents appealing his conviction. He signed the first, which was written in Portuguese and translated into French, on December 20, 1716. The second was printed in Paris in 1717. The complex authorship of these documents is discussed in more detail later—Nayiniyappa had French coauthors—but he did personally participate in the writing of these documents, which are presented as his point of view. Both appeals display knowledge of the biographical details of his life and discuss at length details from the broker's multiple interrogations, when only Nayiniyappa, Governor Hébert, and a Tamil interpreter were in the room. Taken together, the two appeals offer Nayiniyappa's own understanding of the reasons for his arrest.

The first document opens by noting the peculiar difficulties of appealing to Parisian officials from the colony. "A process so unjust, striking, and evil . . . obliges Naynapa [sic], as far away as he is, to put himself at the feet of your Majesty, and those of the Company, to reclaim and demand justice."[37] In Nayiniyappa's tale of the origins of his plight, his service to the company was distinguished by a series of satisfied employers, a flourishing trade, and a colony beloved by its people: "In this state M. Hébert found this place the first time he arrived here." The golden days continued during Hébert's first tenure as governor (1708–1712), and the appeal noted Hébert's satisfaction with the broker's "good and agreeable services and fidelity, which attracted the affection [of the colony's administrators]."[38]

When Nayiniyappa tried to explain why Governor Hébert had turned against him in 1716, he turned toward Paris for an explanation, citing the official's brief return to France from India. Once back in France, Nayiniyappa conjectured, Hébert no longer had the strength of character to ignore the "false persuasions" of troublemakers. He described those same meddlers—obviously the Jesuits, though they remain unnamed—as "those who, having become masters due to their adulation of those in power, followed no rule, and did not hesitate to take any means, even the most unjust . . . to achieve their ends."[39]

Lured by these "seditious voices" and a desire to amass riches made more pressing, Nayiniyappa wrote, by a financial loss Hébert had suffered due to a shipwreck, Hébert sided with the Jesuits. The use of the term "seditious" is significant. Here the appeal used the same accusation levied at Nayiniyappa against the Jesuits, implying that their actions were those that posed a real threat to the colony and to long-term French sovereignty. Since Hébert owed his reinstallation in Pondichéry to the Jesuits, claimed Nayiniyappa, the general began "believing that he may not refuse them anything, regardless of what injustices may accompany their requests." Once Hébert returned to India as *général de la nation*, according to the broker, he "executed absolutely all of [the Jesuits'] desires, even the most unreasonable, and would not forgive anyone whom he suspected or presumed of being their enemies." Nayiniyappa pleaded ignorance of why the Jesuits considered him an enemy, saying there was no "possible reason for this, since he had always provided services to them and to their Christians."[40]

Nayiniyappa framed the period following Hébert's return to Pondichéry as an abandonment of the old ways that had functioned smoothly in his first governorship: "From the moment of Hébert's return to Pondichéry . . . everything changed in an instant: virtue became a crime, the innocent became the culprit, and Naynapa, until that point honored, praised, endowed with a position of confidence . . . became nothing more than a victim, suitable to be sacrificed to those whom he had displeased."[41] This account starkly evoked the complete and utter semiotic confusion created for all involved in the Nayiniyappa Affair, the sense that signs and established modes of communication had lost their purchase: nothing was as it seemed, nothing was as it should be.

The issue of unwarranted, inexplicable change was central to Nayiniyappa's understanding of his own downfall. Thus he summed up one of his appeals: "Naynapa was innocent during the first government of Hébert but became guilty upon his [Hébert's] return to India in 1715. . . . This was the price of [Hébert's] new post as general. After forty-three years of innocence and good conduct, Naynapa was no longer the same man in the eyes of a man changed by ambition." The affair, as Nayiniyappa's appeals presented it, was divorced from any action he himself had taken. The primary moment was a decision to accuse him, while the content of that accusation was of only secondary importance. To this end his interrogations at Hébert's hands, Nayiniyappa suggested, were a predetermined performance leading to his inevitable conviction: "It was the entire life of a man, all his actions, all his steps that they wanted to examine, in order to find something with which to accuse him. This was a man they wanted to condemn, sacrifice and deliver to his enemies at any price. . . . Where is a just man who could escape such a rigorous examination?"[42] No man, the appeals suggested, could emerge innocent from the kind of performative interrogation to which Nayiniyappa was subjected.

In Nayiniyappa's version of events, Pondichéry was a tranquil place, where money was made and relationships fostered. Problems did not originate in Pondichéry—French ships brought them there. Thus, his own troubles originated in France and not in India. This claim has two implications. It presented the French metropole as a place that was near—near enough that deals that supposedly took place behind closed doors in Paris reverberated quickly and profoundly in Pondichéry. It also created a moral hierarchy, in which Pondichéry ranked higher than Paris, since evil deeds and projects filtered down from the European metropole toward the colony. This hierarchy of moral goodness did not, however, overturn the more fixed hierarchies of justice. Thus Nayiniyappa sent his appeals back to France, in an attempt to fix a wrong at its place of origin. Finally, by stressing the fact that the affair began in France and was imported to the colony, Nayiniyappa positioned his adversaries as usurpers, robbing the colony of its formerly established harmony. Presenting himself as a partner in the colonial project in Pondichéry, he sought to reclaim the influence stripped from him.

The Nayiniyappa Affair as a Jesuit Crusade

Lettres patentes given by the French Crown in 1695 established the Jesuits in India as emissaries of Louis XIV.[43] The French Jesuits in India were therefore in a unique position compared with other members of their order because they had been sent to the mission field directly by the French king rather than by the Society of Jesus or the pope. The first task of the Jesuits, as this text described, was the propagation of the Christian faith, but that was not their only task: the Jesuit Fathers, "as distinguished for their erudition as for their piety," were to report back to France in order to further "the perfection of the arts, sciences and navigation." The Jesuits were also exhorted to support French commercial efforts in India. This caused a split in institutional allegiance between the Society of Jesus and the French Crown. Ultimately, though, in spite of rifts between company officials and Jesuits, the Jesuit mission was without a doubt a part of the French imperial project in India.

Nayiniyappa blamed the Jesuits for instigating the investigation against him. The Jesuits would gladly have accepted responsibility for Nayiniyappa's downfall—a fully merited downfall in their view. Jesuit missionaries had attempted to turn Pondichéry into an exclusively Christian town ever since their arrival in the colony in 1689. Their repeated efforts to curtail public religious practice by Hindus largely failed.[44] But in the second decade of the century, Jesuit leaders took on Nayiniyappa instead, a much more circumscribed—and embodied—target. They objected in principle to Hindus filling positions of prominence in the colony, including other company posts, and agitated for Christians to fill these roles. Their reasoning was twofold. First, having a Christian in a prominent post would have boosted the status of Christianity in the colony, thereby making the task of conversion easier. Second, the post of chief broker relied on family networks and benefited members of those networks. Having a Christian broker would have been a boon to the Christian community as a whole and would likely have attracted more converts and therefore resources. The utopian Christian homogeneity the Jesuits wanted to erect in Pondichéry was clearly out of reach, at least for the moment, but they still tried to persuade the French government to present an unequivocally Catholic front. The Jesuits' argument was that as a Christian company, running a town with explicitly Christian ambitions, with the support of a Christian king anointed by God, the Company of the Indies should not have a Hindu man as its most senior and most visible Indian employee in Pondichéry.

The Jesuits themselves relied on a whole cadre of local employees to act as their own intermediaries—the catechists, or native religious interpreters who served Jesuit missionaries in mission fields around the world. Therefore, it was not the act of mediation itself that they found problematic, but the person of the mediator. The Jesuits accepted the fact that the Compagnie des Indes would rely on the services of a broker, but they demanded that a Christian like their intimate Pedro, who would later indeed become Nayiniyappa's replacement, get the job.

The Jesuit attack on Nayiniyappa could be seen as both strategic and symbolic: the removal of Nayiniyappa would have advanced the Jesuit agenda by placing a Christian in a powerful position, with favors to dispense. But a Christian *courtier* would have more broadly symbolized the desired dominance of Catholics in the colony. Nayiniyappa's role as chief broker was highly public. His own description of himself as a "public man" demonstrated this fact.[45] His position was evidence of non-Catholic power in Pondichéry and therefore grated on the Jesuits. While they sought to abolish local religious processions and limit worship in temples, they also agitated to remove Nayiniyappa from his post. All these efforts in concert contributed to a single aim: the transformation of Pondichéry into a Christian enclave, or at least the creation of a Christian façade.

The Jesuits first requested Nayiniyappa's removal in 1711. Three years later, Governor Dulivier wrote that "the matter which most concerns the Fathers is that of Naniapa."[46] In 1715 they attacked Nayiniayppa for his involvement in an event they described as an act threatening to Christian—and by extension, French—authority. Nayiniyappa's crime, in the Jesuit telling, was committed in an unexpected setting: the giving of alms to Pondichéry's Christian poor, an event Nayiniyappa hosted in his house over the course of several days in February 1715. The broker invited several hundred of the town's most needy residents and provided them with food, pieces of fabric, and Catholic prayer rosaries. It is not clear whether only Christians were invited to the almsgiving or whether the correlation between Christianity and low social status meant that an event targeted at the poor would draw a mostly Christian crowd. In hosting this event, Nayiniyappa was following a tradition of gift giving by affluent Indian merchants. As Douglas Haynes has noted in his study of Surat, such acts of patronage were meant to transform financial capital into symbolic capital.[47] Other Tamil brokers in the region similarly performed acts of patronage, specifically in Madras.[48] Officials of the Compagnie des Indes also engaged in elaborate acts of ritual gift giving with local Indian rulers.[49] But for the Jesuits, the event was an example of Nayiniyappa's tyranny.

This apparent act of goodwill, argued the Jesuits, was in fact a cruel and mocking masquerade. They claimed Nayiniyappa had given the food in a manner meant to humiliate and degrade the Christian recipients of his so-called charity. The Jesuit superior, Jean-Venant Bouchet, wrote a letter of complaint to Governor Dulivier, claiming that Nayiniyappa had treated Christians "like dogs" and in so doing offered the Hindu residents of the town a spectacle, "a comedy." Beyond the vague allusion to dogs, no information was provided on what made the almsgiving disgraceful. Father Bouchet asked the governor to use his authority to "put a stop to such disgraceful acts . . . so that you will not be blinded by the false appearance of a good work, and thus set straight those who would be inclined to canonize [Nayiniyappa] for this."[50] It seems likely that the goodwill and reputation Nayiniyappa's acts of patronage and charity earned him among the Christian converts exacerbated Bouchet's outrage. For Bouchet, the event was part of a series of assaults Nayiniyappa had committed on Christianity. Bouchet named a number of Christians who had suffered religious oppression at Nayiniyappa's hands and claimed the broker had forbidden the conversion of several Hindus to Christianity and had, with promises and threats, convinced several Indian converts to become apostates.

Bouchet dispatched his written complaint to the Superior Council even as the almsgiving was taking place, and when the members of the council gathered to discuss the complaint, on February 20, 1715, Christians were still receiving Nayiniyappa's largesse.[51] The council sent the newly appointed Christian cobroker, Chavoury, and an Indian Christian named Pedro (quite likely the same man who would serve as the chief commercial broker after Nayiniyappa's arrest) to find witnesses to the events. The four witnesses they found, members of the Christian community in Pondichéry, came to the council's chambers directly from Nayiniyappa's house. According to the council's official report, they testified that they had gone to Nayiniyappa's house of their own free will because they had heard that the broker was providing "food to the poor, and all those who wished to come would be welcomed; this is why they went there." They told the council that three hundred people were taking advantage of the broker's offer, Christian and non-Christian alike. In the compound, they were given food and cloth with which to cover themselves. The witnesses went on to say that nothing had been done to belittle the Catholic religion, and "if anything had been done to deride our religion, [we] would not have stayed there."[52] They added that Nayiniyappa had also given them three hundred rosaries, asking them to dispense them among the Christian population.[53]

Following the testimony of the four Christian witnesses, the council summoned Nayiniyappa himself and questioned him briefly. They asked him why he had held the event, and Nayiniyappa stated that it was an act of charity and that he was in the habit of giving charity every year. They also asked how Nayiniyappa had procured so many rosaries—he said he had purchased them from a sailor, although they were widely sold by both Christian and Hindu vendors in the bazaar. While the interrogation of the participating Christians had been lengthy, the questioning of Nayiniyappa consisted of only these two questions. The council dispatched a letter to the directors in Paris saying that if the Jesuits were not ordered to "leave everyone alone," all the company's principal Tamil employees would abandon it.[54]

Nayiniyappa's gifts, particularly the cloth and the rosaries, were symbolically laden objects. Cloth in particular would have held special resonance with the local recipients and French observers alike, both because trade in textiles was the central interaction between Indian merchants and French traders and because of the rich symbolic and spiritual meanings of cloth in both societies.[55] The Jesuits' fury was mostly directed, however, to the distribution of rosaries. Father Bouchet singled out this gift as an act meant to abuse the naïveté of poor Christians, who presumably would not understand that they were being used as the tools of their own humiliation. The council in its investigation also paid special attention to the matter of the rosaries, not only asking Nayiniyappa about them but also asking the witnesses, for whom they produced an "authentic" European rosary, whether they had received a similar object. The witnesses confirmed that they had.

The dismay of French observers at Nayiniyappa's distribution of rosaries should perhaps be understood in light of French memory of the Wars of Religion, which had raged in France in the late sixteenth century. Familiar with stories of the brutal bloodbaths Catholics and Protestants had inflicted on one another over matters of Christian dogma, French colonists and missionaries must have found Nayiniyappa's act of religious cross-gifting downright inexplicable. Yet in the South Indian context, where a measure of religious syncretism was the norm, a Hindu giving out Christian prayer implements would not have been so shocking.[56] The distribution of rosaries, succor for the soul, was of a piece with the distribution of cloth and food, succor for the flesh. The broker class to which Nayiniyappa belonged had no horror of Christian practices such as the missionary writers evinced in relation to "pagan" religious practice. Ananda Ranga Pillai, Nayiniyappa's relative and chief broker in Pondichéry under Dupleix in the mid-eighteenth century, blithely described his travels in pursuit of Christian-oriented tourism: "I intend to stay at Ariyankuppam for a day," he wrote in his diary, "to see the festival there, which the Christians celebrate for ten days in magnificent style."[57] Furthermore, the gifting of the rosaries was not the first occasion on which Nayiniyappa himself had engaged with the artifacts of Christianity in an apparently benign fashion. In the appeal Nayiniyappa's sons put forth, they noted in passing that at one time, prior to the affair, Nayiniyappa had given Governor Hébert a cake as a gift to celebrate the governor's saint's day.[58]

The indignation over the rosaries is an instance of what I term semiotic confusion: Nayiniyappa and his French employers ascribed different meanings to the same sign—in this case the rosaries—with resulting conflict. Both parties would have understood the gift as an act of patronage, with a resulting obligation.[59] But what Nayiniyappa likely considered a desirable gift struck the Jesuits as a subversive attempt to take over Catholic authority, a hijacking of signs from the Jesuits' symbolic economy to enhance his own standing.

The Jesuits' ongoing difficulties in the mission field in India would have worsened their outrage. Despite having the support of institutional and military authorities in Pondichéry, their success in making new converts was slim. Several decades after Pondichéry became a French colony, only several thousand of the town's population of fifty to sixty thousand were Christians.[60]

In spite of concerted efforts, they had gained even smaller penetration in other towns in the Tamil country, where Hindu or Muslim rulers dominated. The Jesuits likely saw Nayiniyappa's act of almsgiving as calling attention to their superfluity in Pondichéry. By taking on a role they would have liked to fill—that of a munificent and powerful patron—Nayiniyappa strengthened his own already-strong position at the Jesuits' expense.

Nayiniyappa's charity, then, challenged the Jesuits' position at a time when they had accomplished little in the colony. The ongoing struggles between Jesuits and Capuchins in Pondichéry, a drawn-out battle over spiritual turf, only compounded the Jesuits' sense of being vulnerable. The Capuchin order had a venerable tradition of charity, and the Capuchin missionaries in town raised no complaint about Nayiniyappa's assistance to the poor. Tending a desperately poor flock of converts made the Jesuits vulnerable, in stark difference to their position in Europe and even some locales overseas, such as China, where Christianity was in vogue among powerful elites. Nayiniyappa's almsgiving thus had the effect of encroaching on territory the Jesuits were having difficulty claiming.

The accusation that Nayiniyappa had fed the poor Christians as if they were dogs spoke to an even more insurmountable difficulty the Jesuits faced. Because so many converts were from the lower castes and so-called pariahs, Christianity had come to be seen as a lower-caste religion. French Jesuit commentators blamed this on the first Portuguese to arrive in India, arguing that because the Portuguese did not respect the caste system, they had acquired a bad reputation among all Indians, and thus greatly damaged the cause of Christianization in the subcontinent. The Jesuit missionaries went to great lengths to disassociate themselves from Europeans and even attempted to "pass" for Brahmans because of the low status of *Paranguis*, the pejorative term used to describe Europeans in India, but at the time their flock largely remained desperately poor.

According to Indian social norms at the time, receiving Nayiniyappa's largesse in itself signified depressed status.[61] When Nayiniyappa gave alms to Christians, he drew attention to the very fact that so many of the town's Christians were indigent. By allegedly giving them food in a degrading manner, Nayiniyappa, in the Jesuit account, was also ensuring that Christians remained objects of pity and Christianity a religion to be shunned. The act of almsgiving, as both a mimicry and mockery of Christian charity, crystallized for the Jesuits their ongoing difficulties and the bleak prospects for the project of Christianizing India. The fact that their humiliation had taken place in a town where they should have been in control, and at the hands of a man they thought unsuitable for the position of head broker, only made their predicament more maddening and their crusade against Nayiniyappa more pressing. Even worse, Nayiniyappa was effectively using the Jesuit practice of accommodation by incorporating Christian symbols into his realm of authority, thereby besting the Jesuits at their own game.

The Jesuits' subsequent persecution of Nayiniyappa therefore located the almsgiving, and specifically the gifting of the rosaries, as the moment when Nayiniyappa committed a crime meriting his dismissal and arrest. By focusing on this very public moment, which the Jesuit missionaries framed as undermining the position of Christianity in Pondichéry, Father Bouchet and his brethren were making a claim for the Catholic nature of the colony and positioning Nayiniyappa as a dangerous enemy of the faith and even the French state. Examined from the Jesuit perspective, the gifting of the rosaries dangerously juxtaposed non-Christian munificence and Christian practice. In essence, Nayiniyappa was modeling for the town's poor a powerful hybrid alternative to what the Jesuits offered. Where the Jesuits tried to claim that conversion entailed submission to the authority of the church and its agents, Nayiniyappa offered a middle ground to avoid an irrevocable choice between Christianity and non-Christianity. This, in Jesuit eyes, made him a dangerous foe indeed.

Governor Hébert and the Politics of Governing

Pondichéry was administered by a governor appointed by the directors of the Compagnie des Indes in Paris. The governor was accountable both to company directors and, as in older, more established settings like Canada, to the secretary of the navy. Between 1716 and 1723, a period that corresponds exactly to that of the Nayiniyappa Affair, the governor would have been accountable to the Naval Council, as a result of the regency system known as the polysynody, in which councils replaced ministers. This system came to an end with Louis XV's majority and the appointment of the Comte de Maurepas as naval minister, charged with management of the colonies.[62] In this period of administrative instability, colonial governance in Pondichéry was similarly volatile.

If the Jesuits' attempts to remove Nayiniyappa from his post were of long standing, the fact that Governor Hébert turned against his employee in 1716 was more unexpected. Governor Hébert had been the one to first appoint Nayiniyappa to the position of chief broker, in 1708, and had repeatedly rebuffed Jesuit requests to dismiss him. It is therefore surprising that when Hébert returned to India in 1715 after several years in France, he became a steadfast Jesuit ally and Nayiniyappa's primary accuser. Almost immediately after securing a new appointment to India, under the new title of *général de la nation*, he opened the investigation that resulted in Nayiniyappa's conviction and subsequent death.

Nayiniyappa's appeal suggested that the alliance between Hébert and the Jesuits was a startling change; it is indeed one of the most peculiar aspects of the Nayiniyappa Affair. During his first term in India, Hébert was often at cross-purposes with the Jesuit missionaries. In a letter he sent to the Jesuit superior Tachard in 1708 Hébert offered a stern rebuke, demanding that the Jesuits cease interfering in government affairs: "You are so accustomed to meddling in the affairs of the company, notwithstanding the fact that I have asked you repeatedly to leave us in peace," he scolded. "You have often put the previous governors in an awkward position with your importunities and your constant threats of writing to the king, so that they were obliged to give in to you in all matters."[63] On another occasion the governor went so far as to accuse Tachard of lying to him, saying that the Jesuit had come to him to complain about various matters on twenty-five different occasions, yet every time Hébert inquired into the matter he found that there was no truth to the complaints.[64] Even the Missions étrangères missionaries, who would become some of Hébert's harshest critics, came to the governor's defense when the Jesuits attacked him as a hindrance to Christianity in 1711.[65] One MEP missionary in Pondichéry wrote that Father Tachard was sending extraordinary libels against Governor Hébert back to France, bluntly describing the Jesuits' complaints about the governor as lies, as part of their "disastrous plan to ruin the reputation of this honest man."[66]

When Hébert left Pondichéry after his first appointment ended, Dulivier was installed as governor. However, when Hébert returned to India as *général de la nation*, he was Dulivier's superior.[67] Hébert objected to Dulivier's management of the colony in his absence. In a letter sent to Paris early in 1716, shortly after Hébert's return to India, he complained that "since my arrival . . . I found everything here in a state of disorder, due to the weakness of M. Dulivier." He described a colony that had run amok: "Everyone wants to be the master, so there are as many governors as there are subjects."[68] In a letter posted a few months later, Hébert presented a picture of a town rife with internal tension and strife. According to Hébert, Dulivier did everything possible to vex and annoy him, "goaded into this by people who seek only trouble and division."[69] Dulivier, on his end, wrote a letter to his supervisors in Paris in which he described himself as "mortified" by the decision to send Hébert back to India.[70]

Hébert linked his criticism of Dulivier to his own about-face in regard to Nayiniyappa—the same man he had appointed to the highest-ranking post of any Indian in his government. He argued that Nayiniyappa had changed his ways and had committed various crimes and evil deeds while Hébert was away in France. He blamed Dulivier's weakness as governor for exacerbating Nayiniyappa's misbehavior. Hébert also claimed that the broker had bribed Dulivier to let him keep his job—a charge Nayiniyappa denied in his own appeal.[71]

Hébert wrote that he had received bad reports of Nayiniyappa soon after his return from France and that these reports had surprised him. He had no choice but to investigate Nayiniyappa: "Every day I received new complaints from the inhabitants, I finally had to decide to have him arrested." In Hébert's narrative, his decision to arrest the broker was a heroic and paternalistic act of liberation for the town's Indian population. "Right away all the tribes, or castes as they are called here, came to see me in order to thank me, saying that I had rescued them from the tiger [i.e., Nayiniyappa] that had destroyed and devoured them with his great teeth."[72]

Hébert's letters provided few specifics to justify these metaphors. He mentioned that some said that Nayiniyappa was responsible for fomenting the employee uprising of 1715. He cited the Jesuit claims that Nayiniyappa was impeding Christian conversions. But he insisted that it was the people's complaints of Nayiniyappa's "embezzlements, malpractices, and other crimes" that had moved him to arrest the broker. "I can truthfully declare, as if I were about to appear before God, that the principal motivation that made me decide to go to this extreme [of arresting Nayiniyappa] was the wish to render justice to the people who submitted for so many years to the tyranny of this miserable man."[73]

In this formulation, Nayiniyappa brought about his arrest through his abuse of power. This abuse manifested itself in the cruel mistreatment of the town's Indian population, Hindu and Christian alike. Thus, in Hébert's view of the affair, Nayiniyappa's crime represented a threat to the political stability of the colony. His actions were presented as a challenge to French sovereignty, and his arrest and conviction were an opportunity for Hébert to affirm his sovereign role and cast himself in the role of a savior. French authority, it appears, was a fragile proposition, a construct that could be compromised and required vigilant protection. The council members' admission in a letter penned several years before Nayiniyappa's arrest that they did not wish to dismiss the broker because he held "the key to all the company's secrets" reveals the dangerous dynamic at play. The letter acknowledged that if the company fired Nayiniyappa and he chose to go live in a settlement controlled by the Dutch, English, or Mughals, the consequences for the company and the colony would be dire, since the advantage to the rival might lead to the demise of the French project.[74] The council, or at least Hébert, would eventually come to believe that imprisonment was a better way to neutralize the threat. Hébert attempted to eradicate any future claim to authority on Nayiniyappa's behalf while enhancing his own position of power.

A Metropolitan Intervention: A View of India from St. Malo

Nayiniyappa's arrest was of concern to Frenchmen and Indian actors in the colony, but it was also of vital interest to a group of merchants from St. Malo in France, who provided their own origin story of the affair. The St. Malo merchants came to have a role in the affair as a result of the continual capital crises of the Compagnie des Indes. There were multiple reasons for this plaguing shortage of capital: French merchants and financiers were reluctant to invest in the company, preferring regional opportunities; the company had high operating costs; and Louis XIV's European wars at the end of the seventeenth century gave birth to a dire financial crisis in both the metropolitan center and the colonies.[75] In this period, the company was so devoid of funds and the necessary capital outlay for Asian voyages was so high that the company could simply not afford to finance any voyages to India.[76]

The company had already farmed out some portion of its shipping to an association of merchants from St. Malo in Brittany, a region with strong connections to the maritime trade of the Indian Ocean, in the years 1707, 1708, and 1709. The St. Malo association took over the company's privilege of trading in India on a temporary basis in 1712, and this arrangement was reconstituted on a permanent basis in 1714.[77] In return, the Compagnie des Indes received 10 percent of the value of sales. Until 1719—when the company was restructured by John Law and united with the Company of the West Indies, bringing an end to the arrangement with the St. Malo merchants—the deal helped the company resolve much of its crushing debt, bringing 4,500,000 livres into its coffers over the term of the agreement.[78] For both the officials of the Compagnie des Indes and the St. Malo merchants, the timely acquisition of goods in India was of paramount importance to ensure each voyage would be profitable.

At the time that the Compagnie des Indes handed over its trading monopoly in India to the St. Malo association, Nayiniyappa filled the crucial role of agent on the ground, the man most responsible for ensuring that French ships—now financed by the St. Malo merchants instead of the Compagnie des Indes—would return to Brittany laden with valuable goods. Even though he was an employee of the Compagnie des Indes, it was Nayiniyappa's role to keep the St. Malo voyages profitable, since retaining the agreement and the attendant portion of the profits was absolutely crucial if the colony was to remain a viable commercial endeavor.

However, even as the Compagnie des Indes could not outfit its own ships, it still retained its position as the governmental authority of Pondichéry, with the right to tax goods flowing through its port, and it therefore held significant sway over the commercial success of the St. Malo merchants. The fact that the Nayiniyappa Affair erupted precisely at the time of this transition in power is surely no accident. In this period the company's raison d'être, its central identity as a commercial concern, was called into question. The leasing out of the trading monopoly especially unsettled the position of Governor Hébert, who found himself charged with managing the commercial well-being of the colony but without the opportunity to direct the trade that was the fundamental feature of life in Pondichéry. With directors in Paris, administrators in Pondichéry, and merchant capitalists in Brittany all jostling for influence, Nayiniyappa's case became a site for the articulation of struggles over the basis of French authority in India and the conditions that made such authority possible.

When the St. Malo merchants found out that Nayiniyappa had been arrested, they sent a lengthy complaint to the directors of the Compagnie des Indes in Paris. The Nayiniyappa Affair stands at the heart of the 1717 St. Malo complaint as the chief exemplar of Hébert's vengeful misman-agement of the colony, which, in turn, imposed diminished profits on the St. Malo traders. In retelling the story of Nayiniyappa's fall from grace, the St. Malo merchants identified an action that Hébert had taken as a defin-ing event: namely, a tax hike. During his second term in India, wrote the merchants, Hébert had decided to raise the tax on the Indian merchants in Pondichéry, from the previous 4 percent to 5 percent. In order to recoup their losses, all the merchants in town promptly either raised the price of the merchandise they sold to the St. Malo traders or substituted goods of lesser quality for their offerings.[79] Crucially, the information about the tax hike and the subsequent rise in prices arrived in Brittany not through the conduits of French officialdom but through Nayiniyappa himself. As a com-mercial broker employed by both the French company's administration and the St. Malo merchants in India, he provided this information to the captain of a St. Malo ship. The captain passed the information on to the partners in the St. Malo association, who thus learned of Hébert's deci-sion and the harm done to their commerce in India.[80] The St. Malo com-plaint posited that Hébert had turned on Nayiniyappa precisely because he divulged this information to the Malouin captain and that Nayiniyappa's arrest was therefore an elaborate vendetta orchestrated by Hébert.

The St. Malo merchants demanded Hébert's return to France and Nayiniyappa's reinstatement. The complaint began with a threat, very clearly couched: "The directors of the St. Malo Company of the Indies humbly inform his Majesty that they will be forced to abandon their contract . . . if it does not please his Majesty to immediately recall M. Hébert . . . and his son, who committed [in Pondichéry] all sorts of injustices, persecutions, and even inhumanities, and who do not cease to disturb the commerce of the supplicants."[81] The merchants claimed a clear and direct interest in the events in India: "We will not enter here into the details, which would make you tremble with horror; the supplicants speak here only of that which concerns them."[82] This interest was the result of the merchants' dire need of a broker's services. Nayiniyappa's access to knowledge in Pondichéry and his unique position at the crossroads of several routes of information were necessary to make remote commerce possible. Indeed, the St. Malo merchants lavished praise on Nayiniyappa throughout the text, describing him as "a man very wise in the ways of negotiations, and almost the only one whom [we] could trust . . . [a] loyal and intelligent courtier . . . [a] zealous and capable man who had served better than anyone else, [and] the best and most highly regarded servant of the company."[83]

The St. Malo complaint was very likely a decisive factor in the ultimate decision in favor of Nayiniyappa, or rather his heirs. High-ranked Parisian officials appear to have been, from the very beginning of the Nayiniyappa Affair, inclined to side with the local broker, partly in an attempt to appease the St. Malo merchants. The Marine Council, the body that supervised the Compagnie des Indes, appeared reluctant to lose Nayiniyappa's services. In a marginal note responding to a report from Hébert written just as the process against Nayiniyappa was gathering force, the record noted, "Supposing that Naniapa were to be found guilty, according to the rules of justice, the Council would not want to prevent such justice from being carried out. But if he is found innocent of the crimes of which he is accused, given that this man seems very useful for commerce, and *is agreeable to the Company of St. Malo* [emphasis added], he must be reestablished in his duties, and given a Christian adjunct."[84] Employees of the Compagnie des Indes who were stationed in St. Malo also advanced Nayiniyappa's cause on behalf of the St. Malo association, arguing in letters they sent from Brittany to Paris that Hébert was destroying Pondichéry's prospects of prosperity.[85]

The complaint presented by the St. Malo merchants demonstrates that access, information, and the justification for acting authoritatively and profitably in India were the most important services provided by professional intermediaries like Nayiniyappa. However, for metropolitan actors standing at the battle lines drawn by the Nayiniyappa Affair, the event also functioned as a threat to such claims for authority. The fact that Nayiniyappa, and other Tamil employees like him were necessary for the daily functioning of the colony compromised the position of French actors in India by exposing their limited knowledge. By positing that Nayiniyappa's arrest occurred because the broker had divulged sensitive commercial information, the St. Malo merchants argued that Nayiniyappa made possible a difficult endeavor: the ability to act knowledgeably in India, even from afar.

Historians, working their way from the present back into the past, tend to focus on conclusions and outcomes. How did things turn out? But while the Nayiniyappa Affair had a relatively clear conclusion—the man's death and subsequent exoneration—pinpointing a point of origin is trickier. Did the affair begin with the accused's greedy abuse of power or with his conscientious efforts to carry out his duty? Was he cruelly mocking Christians, or were the Jesuits neglecting their mission to persecute an innocent man? By focusing on multiple and seemingly contradictory origins presented by Nayiniyappa and his contemporaries, the productive tensions that made the affair so contentious and prolonged are revealed. The Nayiniyappa Affair provided French and Tamil actors alike with opportunities to make bold statements about colonial rule and commercial and religious interaction in the French empire.

The issue of the origins of the Nayiniyappa Affair, with which this chapter has been concerned, speaks to the multiplicity of roles and functions filled by professional intermediaries. The fact that so many competing explanations of Nayiniyappa's actions and motivations could be plausibly put forth stems from the variety of positions intermediaries occupied. As the most dramatic example of the explosion of tensions between Indian intermediaries and French employers, the Nayiniyappa Affair demonstrates the political and emotional stakes invested in these relationships. The implicit narrative framings, inclusions, and exclusions in these four different versions of events shed light on the agendas and motivations that drove the different groups involved in the case, the tellers' understanding of their role in the colony, and their vision of the project of French empire in India, in which they all participated.

These actors, and more generally the groups they represented, offered various answers to the question, what kind of place should Pondichéry become? Nayiniyappa, with his strong roots in Madras and connections in the villages surrounding Pondichéry, presented the colony as a place deeply imbricated in the local and the regional, and he attempted to downplay the role of the metropole in the colony's development. Jesuit missionaries propagated the position that Pondichéry should be, above all else, a Catholic space. Governor Hébert put forth a vision of a city controlled by unshakable French authority, presaging the French paternalism of later imperial efforts. The merchants from Brittany who became involved in the affair chose to adhere to a vision of the colony as a commercial space, where the logic of profit making would trump affinities of nation or religion. The Nayiniyappa Affair was precipitated by these clashing visions of the colony, was a site for the articulation of these different frameworks, and resulted in the deepening of the crevices that ran through the French colony. These tensions divided French lay and religious institutions, members of different religious orders, colonial and metropolitan trading companies, and Indians and Frenchmen.

CHAPTER 2

Kinship as Politics

In the course of the Nayiniyappa Affair, three different sets of fathers and sons filled crucial roles in advancing Nayiniyappa's arrest, prosecution, and ultimate posthumous rehabilitation. These were Nayiniyappa and his sons, the French governor and his son, and the Jesuits' catechist (religious interpreter) and his son. These fathers and sons, who together engaged in legal, political, and religious maneuvering, demonstrate the inextricable connections between the familial and the institutional, both in the evolution of the Nayiniyappa Affair and in the administration of colonial Pondichéry in general. They offer a microcosm of the forces grappling for control in the affair. While other types of familial ties—consanguinity, marriage, and godparentage—all characterized the bonds at work in Pondichéry, the coincidence of three father-son teams playing such a central part in the Nayiniyappa Affair reflects the working of family ties in the evolution of the colony. French and Tamil agents alike were eager to bring together the intimate and institutional facets of their lives. By examining these fathers and sons, we can see the familial workings of both the commercial and missionary projects in French India.

This chapter argues that the family was a nexus for the enunciation of various agendas in the governance of Pondichéry. It utilizes the prism of the Nayiniyappa Affair to reveal the interpenetration of family and colonial rule. Extended families, both French and Tamil, worked together to further their aims, taking advantage of the loyalty and commitment afforded by the ties of kinship. The benefit of an extended family network derived from the fact that long-standing familial ties enabled actors to extend relationships across time and space, securing support through successive generations and in different locales. For example, this meant enjoying the boomtown opportunities of Pondichéry while also drawing on the established trade of Madras. The ability to create relations across a diverse group of actors and the efficacy of couching such relations within a shared idiom of kinship were very much on display in Pondichéry early in the eighteenth century. Public performances of kinship, inscribed in colonial archives, served as a central tool for the negotiation and articulation of power in the colony.

The small body of work on the Nayiniyappa Affair has largely focused on the interreligious nature of the affair and the attendant power dynamics, with the Jesuits taking down a Hindu actor.[1] But an analysis that makes room for the family in colonial politics can offer a different view. The Nayiniyappa Affair in fact occurred in part because of a rivalry between two local families—Tamil dynasties of commercial brokers who served the French for over a century, one of which happened to be Hindu, and one of which was Christian. The Nayiniyappa Affair was therefore partly the result of an ongoing local feud that both predated and followed French preoccupation with Nayiniyappa. Local agents took advantage of the way their own agendas dovetailed with those of the French and vice versa. The decades-long rivalry, and French involvement in it, reveals the connections between the structures of the family and those of the colonial project.

Kinship and Imperial Politics

While histories of empire had long neglected the study of family life, it is now at the center of scholarly debates. More recent scholarship has shown that the structures of family underlay early modern European state building and highlighted the familial and gendered commitments of mercantile families that went into the making and governance of early modern states in the Netherlands, France, and England.[2] In the imperial setting, "patrimonial power"—the exertion of power by rulers when this power is based on kin and personal relationships—has illuminated the making of sovereignty overseas.[3] Scholars have shown how European colonizers used the bonds of kinship and other intimate ties as a technology of colonial rule, particularly in the Atlantic world.[4] This work demonstrates that a history of a particular family can serve as a revealing account of global empire, in which the traces of kin, connection, and the quotidian both mirror and underlie the structures of imperial ambition.[5] It also reflects anthropologists' long-standing arguments that we should seek out kin relations and kinship practices not only in affinities undergirded by the ties of biology but in more constructed and contingent formulations of the family.[6]

In a colony as new and unstable as Pondichéry was at the beginning of the eighteenth century, families provided an especially crucial context and site for claims making. It is worth noting again that since Pondichéry had been little more than a sparsely populated fishing village before it was given to the French in 1673, nearly everyone in the town was a relative newcomer. This heightened the ability to forge new connections, and the idiom of kinship was rich ground for making such connections. The commitments of family, whether consanguineous or created, were crucial in the making of colonial authority, and Indian, Creole, and French families played a role in the French expansionist project in Pondichéry.[7]

Because French colonial authority in India was much more aspiration than reality in the late seventeenth century and early eighteenth centuries, French administrators of the Compagnie des Indes and missionaries alike depended on access provided by their local brokers. In the context of this dependence, family—biological, fictive, and metaphorical—served as a shared and legible framework for local and French actors. Claims of relatedness could be made across ethnic, religious, and geographical difference, pointing to the existence of what has been termed "vernacular kinship."[8] That is, in the early encounter between French and indigenous actors in Pondichéry, as repeatedly demonstrated in the French archive, the family was a conceptual and practical resource in constant use.

The linkage between family and statecraft would have been familiar in France and India alike. In sixteenth- and seventeenth-century France the careful construction of familial commitments was key for political and professional success.[9] Much as dynastic tradition in France brought together the institutions of the family and the state, in India state formation and family formation were also complementary projects.[10] In both India and France, the family was a nexus for the definition of personhood and an anchor for communal history and commitment.

While the history of the family has been central to French historiography for several decades, the same cannot be said for the historiography of South Asia.[11] In this historiography, caste has served as a central structuring analytic in discussions of both intimate and official power relations, a focus stemming in part from the much-commented-upon centrality ascribed to caste in and by the nineteenth-century British Raj. While the caste position of local Tamil actors held some importance for French employers, kinship offers an alternative prism in Pondichéry. It was the ties of family, more than caste, that emerged as a crucial shared component in the interactions between French-men and local actors.[12] The concept and practice of family, rather than of caste, were ripe for mutual exploitation in cross-cultural encounters in India, since this was a conceptual framework French and Tamil actors alike could use. Where the analytic focus on caste highlights the ways in which "colo-nizers" and "colonized" differed from one another, the emphasis on kinship makes visible the shared world that existed in Pondichéry at this early stage of European empire in the Indian Ocean.

The Broker and His Sons

The events of the Nayiniyappa Affair hinge on family. While Nayiniyappa would not live to see the lengths to which his sons went in order to clear his name and restore their family's fortune and position, his posthumous good name at least benefited strongly from the special loyalty of fathers and sons. His three sons—Guruvappa, Moutiappa, and Vingatachelam—were respon-sible for two of the appeals submitted on his behalf, and after his death his eldest son traveled to France to plead with the Crown to restore Nayini-yappa's fortune. In these efforts, the sons (and the Frenchman who assisted them in writing appeals and letters of support) highlighted the familial ties that motivated their efforts, referring throughout their texts to "our father" instead of the more impersonal "Nayiniyappa."

The sons' intense efforts involved their own interests, of course. Their father's position provided tangible benefits, while his arrest carried with it dire consequences for them. Even before Nayiniyappa was appointed chief commercial broker in 1708, the benefits of his engagement with the company had trickled down to his family members. In 1706, the Superior Council of Pondichéry awarded to "Gourvapapullé" (almost certainly Nay-iniyappa's eldest son) a tax farming privilege.[13] Conversely, when Nay-iniyappa was first arrested, on February 13, 1716, his sons were arrested alongside him.[14] According to Nayiniyappa, the French governor Hébert menaced him by saying, "If I had witnesses to this [wrongdoing], I would send you and your sons to the Mascarenes," the French islands in the Indian Ocean where the French held slaves.[15] The banishment imposed on Nay-iniyappa and his family in 1716 affected his sons. After their father's arrest, all three sons relocated to "the lands of the Moors";[16] the fact that they resettled in the French colony as soon as a new governor was appointed after Hébert's removal in 1718 suggests that leaving Pondichéry imposed significant costs on them.

Collectively, the appeals on Nayiniyappa's behalf pointed to the varying kinds of damage the sons had inherited as a result of their father's conviction. For fiscal compensation, they requested monetary restitution of forty thousand pagodas, since this was the value of Nayiniyappa's confiscated goods at the time of his arrest, and an additional one hundred thousand pagodas in damages.[17] Reflecting the fact that the family's good name had been damaged by their father's conviction, they also asked that his good reputation be reestablished in the broad context of French India and the Tamil region, writing, "[We ask you to order] that his good name be restored, and that the decree doing so shall be read, published, and posted in the city of Pondichéry, and in the lands of the Company."[18] Clearing Nayiniyappa's name rehabilitated the family as a whole. And reflecting the importance of family on both sides of the imperial divide, they asked the Crown to punish Governor Hébert's son as well as the official himself.

Broker Dynasties in Pondichéry

The appeals sent following Nayiniyappa's conviction reveal that the conflict pitted two local families against one another. In Pondichéry, for nearly a century only members of these two competing families had enjoyed the benefits of the post of chief commercial broker. The hereditary nature of the position was not unique to Pondichéry: in the French holding of Chandernagore, in Bengal, the family of one Indranarayan Chaudhuri held the post of broker for decades. The position was also hereditary in Ceylon, where Europeans employed local men in a similar position, and in the important commercial center of Surat on the west coast of India two rival dynasties also fought over the rights of brokerage.[19]

Tamil nomenclature does not assign family names as in the European tradition, but for convenience, I will refer to Nayiniyappa's family as Pillai and their rivals as Mudali. French sources usually refer to the families with Europeanized versions of these names: Poullé and Modeliar. The term *modeliar*, derived from the Tamil word for "first," was also a synonym for the position of chief broker in Pondichéry. Both terms are titles associated with the Vellala caste group, high-ranking agricultural landlords.[20] The two families competing for the highest post available to Indians in the colony were of the same caste, though the Pillais were Hindu and the Mudalis Christian.[21] In the Pillai family, Nayiniyappa was the first to be appointed *courtier et chef des malabars*, in 1708. At least three of his relatives would hold the position subsequently: his eldest son, Guruvappa (chief broker in 1722–1724); his nephew Ananda Ranga Pillai (1746–1761); and his likely great-nephew Tiruvangadan (1790s).

The Christian brokers employed by the French, the Pillais' rivals, had a history of service that stretched back even earlier, to the very first days of the colony's existence as a French holding. The founder of this dynasty was Tanappa Mudali (Modeliar), also known by his Christian name, André.[22] He arrived in Pondichéry on January 17, 1674, at the express invitation of the town's first governor, François Martin.[23] His son, Lazare Moutiappa, followed him as courtier; Nayiniyappa replaced him in 1708. His grandson was Kanakarâya Pedro Mudali (Modeliar). Pedro then became chief broker when Nayiniyappa was arrested. The council ousted Pedro when Nayiniyappa was cleared of charges, establishing Guruvappa in the post. However, when Guruvappa died of dropsy two years later, in 1724, the council reappointed Pedro to the post, and he served until his death in 1746. Ananda Ranga Pillai ascended to the post at this time. It is possible that the French deliberately pitted one family against the other, with the position strategically made to oscillate between the two.

Just as the Jesuits had been agitating against Nayiniyappa for years prior to his arrest, the rivalry between the Pillai and Mudali families long predated Pedro's assumption of the position of broker. The removal of Lazare and his replacement by Nayiniyappa in 1708 marks the beginning of the rivalry.[24] At that time, Governor Hébert lambasted the Jesuits for their support of the Christian broker whom Nayiniyappa had replaced. A letter he wrote to the Jesuit superior, Father Tachard, read, "Ever since my arrival in Pondichéry, I have been astonished that we employ Lazare as modelier, since he has so little ability, and so little credit in the town."[25] Hébert dismissed the claims of family in Lazare's case, although he acknowledged that he had retained "André's son," emphasizing kinship over individuality, because he respected the choices made by his predecessor, Governor Martin. Had Lazare been at all capable of filling the post, continued Hébert, he would rather have employed him than anyone else in the town, seeing that he was "a Christian of good caste and high rank."[26]

After Nayiniyappa's son Guruvappa died unexpectedly while serving as chief broker, the Pillais sought to retain the post in their family. French correspondence devoted to the struggle between the two dynasties shows that colonial officials were uncomfortably aware of the power and influence that the post bestowed on local men. The contours of this struggle, as well as the very fact of its inscription in the French colonial archive, demonstrate that the French were well versed in the details of these families' lives. Both French and Tamil actors made their claims with reference to kinship, suggesting there was a clear link between the institutions of the colonial state and the practice of local family life.

The French governor at the time of Guruvappa's death, Beauvollier de Courchant, deemed Nayiniyappa's brother-in-law Tiruvangadan, one of the candidates for the job of chief broker, too ambitious.[27] Another candidate was Nayiniyappa's second son, Moutiappa. Moutiappa had the support of his widowed sister-in-law as well as the support of missionaries of the Missions étrangères. But the French governor opposed Moutiappa as well, writing to Paris, "I feel obliged to alert you that he is the Black here who seems to me least suitable to being a modeliar [courtier]." He claimed that Moutiappa had stolen money and jewels from his brother. Also "he is a young man of very poor physiognomy, of ill regard, who is hated by everyone. . . . In short, we don't see any talents in him. Furthermore, he is too young, and he would never want to become a Christian."[28] The governor's remarks suggest an intimate acquaintance with squabbles within the Pillai family. While the charge of stealing from his brother may or may not have been accurate, Moutiappa could not be an effective courtier without the strong support of a family network of connections and commitments. Intrafamilial rivalry could be just as important as interfamilial rivalry in encounters with the French administration.

Correspondence between the company directors in Paris and the council in Pondichéry in 1725 reveals that the Parisian directors wanted to dismiss the Christian broker Pedro a year after his resumption of the post following Guruvappa's death and replace him with another courtier as part of a number of personnel shake-ups. But the council resisted this directive, claiming that Pedro's dismissal would significantly harm the company's commercial interests. Council members lavished praise on Pedro as "an honest man, who is wise, loyal, experienced, one who is listened to and enjoys good credit, always providing signs of his zeal to serve, his docility, the care he takes of alerting us to all movements among the blacks."[29] The Pondichéry council described Pedro as "beloved by the blacks." Added to this, his family connections made him eminently suitable for the post. "We also remembered his father, who was an excellent courtier, much loved by everyone; his uncle was also a modeliar and a very honest man."[30] While this memory belied Hébert's assessment of Pedro's father, it reflects the importance of kinship. The Pillai family would not take the post again until Pedro's death in 1746, when the council selected Ananda Ranga Pillai over Pedro's younger brother.

The rivalry between Pillais and Mudalis was long-standing, but the Nayiniyappa Affair was nevertheless a crucial juncture in the struggle over the profitable and powerful position of the colony's chief broker. Nayiniyappa's interrogation and subsequent appeals reveal that the tension between the two courtier clans directly influenced the investigation. An example is the testimony of a man who had been Nayiniyappa's servant. A few years prior to his arrest, Nayiniyappa had accused this servant of stealing from him and complained of this theft to Governor Hébert. Hébert ordered that the man's house and goods be sold and that the profits be given to Nayiniyappa in restitution. When Nayiniyappa stood accused of tyranny and sedition, the council called this servant as a witness against him, and he gave, as Nayiniyappa's sons wrote in one of their appeals, "a horrible declaration against our father." The sons accused Pedro and his brother-in-law of pressuring the witness into testifying.[31] In fact, a number of witnesses against Nayiniyappa held grudges against him, for reasons that had little or nothing to do with the charges against him. As well as this servant, a group of shopkeepers who had been involved in a business dispute with Nayiniyappa testified against him.[32] The sons accused Pedro of also influencing this group of witnesses.

Whether or not Nayiniyappa's sons were right to accuse Pedro and his extended family of meddling with witness testimonies, the accusation reflects the importance of the broker clans and the tension between them. Nayiniyappa's sons clearly understood the crusade against their father in a familial framework set against the world of local Tamil Christians, as well as the Jesuits. Their appeal alleged, "It was the Jesuits who crushed our father, they who instigated false testimony, the servant for this being Moutapen, their catechist, Pedro the modeliar, Raphael his brother-in-law, Darnacheraon his uncle, and other Christians known for their scandalous lives and their dishonesty."[33] In this account, the Jesuits were able to undertake their persecution of Nayiniyappa only with the assistance of a deeply familial network of accomplices—Pedro, his brother-in-law, his uncle, and their coreligionists, among them the catechist and his son the interpreter. In fact, a likely telling of the Nayiniyappa Affair would cast the Jesuits as the tools of the Mudali family, rather than the other way around.

Certainly the French fully understood the importance of local familial networks. A 1702 letter from Pondichéry's Superior Council to the directors in Paris exposes further detail about the family ties that undergirded hiring decisions in the colony. The council conceded that the Jesuits had reproached French authorities for preferring to hire non-Christians (usually referred to in French sources as gentiles) over Christians for company positions. The council members halfheartedly denied the charge and justified their hiring decisions in terms that highlighted the familial. "The principal jobs suitable for local people . . . are held by an old Christian family, who began serving the king in St. Thomé under M. de La Haye in 1672, and have been employed by your company ever since," wrote the council, referring to the Mudali family.

The letter went on to name specific examples of Tamil Christians who held prominent positions in the company's ranks, calling attention to the fact that brokers, interpreters, and laborers at the docks were all related: "The most important interpreter, the people who work on the waterfront assisting in the reception and departure of merchandise . . . are all of this family."[34]

As this description reveals, working as a commercial broker had immediate benefits for members of one's extended family, providing employment opportunities. The council's premise that it was the family's shared Christianity that ensured them all jobs should not be taken at face value. Rather, it seems just as likely that it was the familial association—regardless of confessional standing—that would have made the jobs travel across and between generations of a single family, with one relative securing a position for another. The fact that the Pillai family enjoyed similar benefits, despite its continued Hindu practice, indicates as much.[35]

The Widow Guruvappa

The centrality of familial relations in the Nayiniyappa Affair is emblematic of the centrality of family to colonial governance in French India. The bonds between fathers and sons played a particularly visible role in the Nayiniyappa Affair. But one Tamil woman, Guruvappa's widow, made a surprising impression in the French record of the affair. The archives of the French colony refer to her only as "the widow Guruvappa." Her first name is never mentioned.[36] Her experience reminds us that the bonds of kinship could enable all kinds of actors to advance their political, economic, and social agendas.

The correspondence of the widow Guruvappa with various colonial and metropolitan French institutions in the 1720s demonstrates how family members of Indian employees in Pondichéry were able to insert themselves into the sphere of influence of the French establishment and to successfully make claims on rights and rewards due to them by drawing on the language of kinship. The fact that such claims could be made by a woman, one who was illiterate in French and likely in Tamil as well and still repeatedly received favorable hearing, is an indication that the Compagnie des Indes was willing, and at times even eager, to draw extended familial networks into the complex calculus of its decision making in the colony.[37]

In the years following her husband's death in 1724, the widow Guruvappa lobbied extensively to receive support from French institutions, writing to the company's directors, to the directors of the MEP seminary in Paris, and, it seems safe to assume, also contacting the council in Pondichéry and the Missions étrangères missionaries living in the colony.[38] In a letter to the seminary, she explicitly attempted to evoke the familial relationship she enjoyed with the missionaries in Pondichéry, writing that they had bestowed on her "the honor of receiving her and treating her as your child in your house."[39]

In her communication with French interlocutors, the widow pursued two goals: she tried and succeeded to secure financial support for herself, and she advocated unsuccessfully for her husband's brother Moutiappa to be appointed chief broker after Guruvappa's death. Her letters offer a rare example in the archives of French India of a woman speaking in the first person.[40] One of the letters in which the widow Guruvappa speaks in the first person concludes with the note "This is the mark [here an X appears] made by the widow of the Chevalier Guruvappa, who does not know how to write her name."[41] It is extremely unlikely that she spoke the French in which her letters were composed. She was also very young, only fourteen years old in 1723, when her name first appears in the records of Pondichéry's état-civil. But although the letters were certainly coauthored by a Frenchman, there are indications the woman herself was intimately involved in the production of these first-person texts. One of the letters contains information about her childhood, which suggests her involvement. The fact that the widow found it necessary and expedient to make her claims in French, using the French terminology of kinship, reveals that effective claims making in French India necessitated navigating various affiliations and idioms.

Even though Guruvappa's widow had powerful relatives who had long been in the habit of conferring with the colony's highest-ranking French officials, she intimated in one of her letters that her act of writing to the directors of the company in Paris was a surprising one, perhaps even a transgressive one. "What will you say of the liberty I take in writing you," she began a letter of August 12, 1724. "I admit that it is a great temerity on my part to thus abuse your patience and importune you, but as I think of the equity and justice which have made you so admired among all nations, I dare to flatter myself, messieurs, that you will have the goodwill to forgive me and cast compassionate eyes upon a poor, afflicted widow."[42] This letter was written shortly after her husband's death of dropsy and implied that the widow had a right to expect assistance from the company, since her husband had served as courtier to the great satisfaction of the Superior Council. Her claim on the directors' time and effort was also couched as depending on a long trajectory of family loyalty, mentioning the decades of her husband's father, Nayini-yappa's, involvement with the company. The widow Guruvappa had very specific ideas about the ways in which the company should assist her. "I am honored to prostrate myself at your feet and beg you to honor me with your protection, and to appoint my brother-in-law Moutiappa to the position held by his brother, my husband. I dare to hope that he [Moutiappa] will not prove himself unworthy of the grace that you will grant him."[43]

The widow positioned herself as a stakeholder in the company's hiring practices on more than one occasion. In a letter she wrote in 1726 to the Missions étrangères missionaries, she involved herself directly in the ongoing rivalry between the Pillai family and Pedro, the broker who had been appointed to replace Guruvappa. She proclaimed that Pedro should be "chased out of the office of modeliar," since he did nothing except under the direction of the Jesuits.[44]

The widow Guruvappa's attempts to create an alternative or supplementary kin network with the French might have been influenced by her precarious position within the Pillai family after her husband's death. French records (as well as the widow's letters to Paris) attest to the fact that after Guruvappa's death, the family was involved in an inheritance battle, and a widowed woman would have been vulnerable. In a letter to Paris dated August 15, 1725, the council mentioned the internal squabbles in the Pillai family: "Ever since the death of the Chevalier Guruvappa, his widow is fighting with the deceased's heirs, we have awarded her this revenue for her subsistence for the duration of her life."[45]

The two requests in the letters—a job for her relative and a pension for herself—speak to different approaches to the benefits of kin networks. In the widow's request that the post of broker be given to her husband's brother, she was clearly attempting to bolster the position of her kinsmen in the colony, and by extension her own. That is, the protection she solicited from the company was configured and accessed through preexisting networks of family and marriage. But simultaneously, she worked to establish a fictive kin relationship with French institutions so as to enable herself to draw on their support and commitment by positioning herself as a child entitled to their protection. Her efforts were successful, as evidenced by the company decision to grant her a lifelong pension.[46]

The rhetoric of the widow's letters appears, at first glance, to conform to the colonial fantasy of a submissive and childlike native requesting the protection of a paternal, colonial master. But a closer reading reveals that the widow Guruvappa drew on the currency of kinship strategically. Her engagement with French officialdom demonstrates how local inhabitants could participate in the administrative and political work of colonial governance through public and inscribed performances of kinship. The strategy of the widow Guruvappa, who both drew on the access afforded by her network of kin and attempted to forge new, kin-like relations with French newcomers, reveals how the local reality of kinship in India could intersect with the French idea and practice of family. She advanced her position and that of her relatives in

Pondichéry through the idiom of kinship and mobilized support among Missions étrangères missionaries and company officials in both Pondichéry and France. By using affect-laden language, she demonstrated ingenuity, creativity, and strategic bonding in her interactions with colonial institutions. Her efforts relied on utilizing lines of communication long established between members of her family and the French authorities.

The ability of commercial brokers in South India to draw on their family ties to accrue profit and power, or what the historian Bhavani Raman has called the "lucrative tie of kin and cash," has drawn some scholarly attention.[47] But less remarked upon is the ability of European colonizers to similarly benefit from the bonds of kinship, and to this the next section turns.

The Governor and His Son

The extent to which administrators of the Compagnie des Indes both sought to capitalize on local Indian family networks and accepted that their local employees brought with them both the advantages and the responsibilities of familial entanglements should not surprise. French imperial action—from the French Crown, itself a familial institution, on down—relied on the family as both a politicized concept and a daily practice. The same was true for the commercial sphere in France, in which reliance on credit extended through personal and familial relationships, making the family "of key importance in the commercial culture of the Old Regime."[48] The fact that the Compagnie des Indes was itself an institution in which advancement often relied on the associations of kinship is equally pertinent.[49] Much as Tamil men could inherit the position of chief broker, French traders maintained and benefited from family connections within the institutional setting of the company. The company was, by some measures, a familial body: having a father who was a company employee virtually guaranteed a post for the son.[50] This was true in the lower ranks of the company as well as in its highest reaches: when a director of the company in Paris died or withdrew, a relative would often fill his spot.[51] In fact, beginning with Colbert's creation of the Compagnie des Indes in 1664 to the days of the Nayiniyappa Affair, the ministers in Versailles charged with overseeing the company were composed of two sets of fathers and sons.[52] Governor Dupleix, one of the colony's most well-known governors in the mid-eighteenth century, was the son of one of the directors of the company.[53] Employment in the company was a true Dupleix family business, since his brother also became one of the Parisian directors.[54]

Frenchmen treated the bonds of both godparenthood and marriage as means to expand and strengthen their family networks. By forging new kin relations, they could cross the borders of origin in order to affiliate with powerful people.[55] The highest-ranking officials in the colony and their wives frequently appear in the Pondichéry notarial and religious record as godparents to French and Tamil Christian children born in the colony; it seems likely these designations offered a measure of economic benefit to the children and their parents.[56] The *état-civil* record marking the birth of Jeanne Albert, a woman born to a Luso-Indian family who would become Governor Dupleix's wife, exemplifies the uses of godparenthood. When Jeanne was born, her godparents offered the newborn support from both the ranks of the French company and local families in Pondichéry. The birth record written by a Capuchin missionary described the event: "Today, June second 1706, I baptized a girl named Jeanne. . . . The godfather was M. François Cuperly, a trader of the Royal French Company, and the Godmother Madame Jeanne de Castro."[57] While Jeanne's godfather, Cuperly, solidified the Albert family's position as members in good standing in the company's town, the choice of her grandmother and namesake as the baby's godmother—a local Christian woman who was the widow of a Portuguese man—suggests the family's long-standing involvement in the regional landscape. Jeanne was a social force to be reckoned with in the colony when she became Dupleix's wife and was herself a popular choice of godmother for Pondichéry's newborns.

French parents' choice of godparents created alliances with influential Tamil actors as well. The great-grandson of Governor François Martin's wife, a child whose father was a powerful Pondichéry councillor, had in 1706 the "Armenian merchant, a resident of Madras," Pedro Sacaria, as his godfather.[58] Although the baby died in infancy in 1707, Sacaria provided the parents, the Hardencourts, and their circle a tangible connection to two worlds.[59] First of these was the wealthy and well-connected Armenian diaspora, important players who provided French newcomers with entry into Indian Ocean trade. Second, he provided entry to the community of merchants in Madras, the prosperous English-ruled town where an Armenian might find an easier place for himself than a Frenchman.

Moving beyond the French sphere also allowed parents to create cosmopolitan horizons for their locally born children. Niccolaò Manouchi (Manucci), a well-known Venetian who had married a half-English woman from Madras and had spent years in the Mughal court, served as godfather to the children of several powerful families.[60] With connections to multiple religious, linguistic, and political networks, he would have been a useful connection to his godchildren. Frenchmen in Pondichéry's society may also have viewed being selected as a godparent as a symbol of arrival, an indication that one was a significant actor in the colony. Governor Hébert likely saw it that way when, upon his first arrival in India in July of 1708, he was almost immediately chosen to serve as the godfather to a son born in September to Claude Bruno, the port's captain.[61]

Godparenthood also created horizontal links among the godparents, although that didn't stop Governor Hébert and then councilor, later governor La Prévostière from becoming bitter adversaries in the course of the Nayiniyappa Affair. Governor Hébert and Marie Desprez, La Prévostière's wife, had both served in 1709 as godparents to the same infant, six years before the explosion of the Nayiniyappa Affair.[62] Nor was this the only such conflict or even the most recent one that Hébert experienced in relation to the affair, since in 1718 he became the godfather to the son of M. Delavigne, the general director of commerce in India for the Company of St. Malo, which intervened on Nayiniyappa's behalf and called for Hébert's removal. The baby's godmother was the wife of Dulivier, Hébert's archenemy and competitor for the role of governor.[63] We can only conjecture about Delavigne's motives in asking Hébert to serve in the role a year after his company had called for the governor's removal. He may have been seeking to mend fences between the St. Malo Company and bickering Compagnie des Indes officials.

While godparental relations may have complicated Governor Hébert's role in the affair, it was his paternal ties that were implicated in his turn against Nayiniyappa in 1715, when he returned to India for his second term with his adult son accompanying him. According to Nayiniyappa's sons, both Héberts craved a return to India as a means to repair a dire financial situation: they were saddled by debts that they were unable to pay.[64] Nayiniyappa's sons claimed the official had promised to attack Nayiniyappa, long an object of the Jesuits' animosity, in exchange for their support. Hébert the younger stood to inherit his elderly father's debts and may have influenced the governor's decision to reverse his former loyalties, supporting the Jesuits and attacking Nayiniyappa. Nayiniyappa himself thought so, and in one of his appeals he referred to Hébert's "seditious son."[65] In this he leveled at his enemy the same accusation he had suffered.

In fact, Hébert fils took on an outsized role in the affair, even though he was only a junior employee of the company, a *second du commerce*.[66] According to Nayiniyappa's sons, the younger Hébert carried out queries that might have been embarrassing for the governor of the colony to undertake himself. They claimed that he had promised the Jesuit superior, Father Bouchet, that the governor would support a persecution of Nayiniyappa.[67] Nayiniyappa's sons were, of course, a partisan source, but there is no reason to doubt their claim that the son made the initial overtures, since this rendition of the affair is actually less damaging to Governor Hébert, removing some of his agency in Nayiniyappa's persecution.

The sworn testimony of Manuel, the Tamil interpreter used to translate in most of Nayiniyappa's interrogations, also suggests that Hébert fils played a crucial role in the Nayiniyappa Affair. The interpreter Manuel stated that Hébert the son, not the father, reviewed the testimonies of the witnesses against Nayiniyappa.[68] Nayiniyappa's sons referred to both Héberts, father and son, as the de facto governors of the colony, writing that their avarice had led them to conspire with the Jesuits, so that "they could retain the government of Pondichéry."[69] It appears the governor and his son made little effort to hide the fact that they were operating in concert, furthering a shared agenda in their pursuit of Nayiniyappa and his allies. The younger Hébert was present in some of Nayiniyappa's interrogations by Governor Hébert, and according to Nayiniyappa's appeal, Hébert fils intimated that he would accept a bribe to ameliorate the broker's punishment.[70]

It was not only Nayiniyappa and his sons who claimed that both generations of Héberts conspired together. Nicolas de La Morandière, a company bookkeeper who was involved in drafting Nayiniyappa's appeals, also viewed father and son as one operational unit. In a letter he wrote from India to the directors of the company in France in 1719, La Morandière said that when he looked into the books kept by the Héberts, an action he took in his capacity as company bookkeeper, he angered both father and son, and the two men together threatened to ensure he lost his job with the company.[71] La Morandière also revealed that Hébert fils was in the room when the judges confronted Nayiniyappa before his sentencing. He described Hébert the younger (who was a junior employee and thus not technically qualified to serve as one of the judges) addressing the prisoner with authority: "You are a thief, we know you well."[72] La Morandière stressed the culpability of both Héberts: "I make no distinction at all, Messieurs, between father and son, and you must be entirely convinced that the crime of one is the crime of the other, with this difference: that the father is infinitely more culpable, because the authority of the government resides in his person."[73] The other judges also mentioned the younger Hébert's' presence in the room when they were interrogated in 1718 about their decision to convict Nayiniyappa.[74]

The Catechist and His Son

The third father-son pair in the Nayiniyappa Affair, apart from Hébert and his sons and Nayiniyappa and his sons, was composed of a father employed as a catechist and a son who was a company interpreter. The father was Moutiappa, the Jesuits' head catechist (religious intermediary). His son, Manuel Geganis, served as the central interpreter in Nayiniyappa's investigation—he was the interpreter for five out of a total of seven interrogations. He was also charged with arranging for the translation of witness testimonies from Tamil to French. Manuel was, like his father, a Christian and an intimate of the Jesuits. The first mention of him in the French archives dates to 1705, when he was arrested along with several other native Christian men.[75] The Jesuits had long tried to bring about the closure of a large Hindu temple located right next to the Jesuit compound. An incident in connection with this had turned violent, when several of the Jesuits and their local Christian supporters stormed the temple and vandalized it.[76] When Manuel was arrested, his father was already acting as the missionaries' most trusted employee, and the arrest of the son suggests he was also closely affiliated with the Jesuits. On one occasion, Governor Dulivier explicitly referred to him as a catechist, the position also filled by Manuel's father.[77] Further, Manuel worked with the Jesuits prior to becoming an interpreter for the Compagnie des Indes, traveling to France with a Jesuit missionary. By 1715, the French company in Pondichéry employed Manuel as an interpreter, but Nayiniyappa's supporters emphasized instead his father's connection to the Jesuits, referring to him as "the catechist's son" and not by his given name. Nayiniyappa's sons wrote in their 1720 appeal, "The other interpreter is named Geganis, and is the son of the Jesuits' catechist, which makes the matter even clearer," as evidence that the proceedings were politically driven.[78]

Manuel's role arranging for the translation of witness testimonies from Tamil to French allowed him to draw on his familial networks to advance the case against Nayiniyappa. Manuel provided Governor Hébert with easy access to a whole set of Christian actors involved in the production of evidence against Nayiniyappa, both Tamil and French: Moutiappa; the Christian Pedro, who was to replace Nayiniyappa as broker and was the central figure in Pondichéry's Christian community; and the Jesuit fathers.

The council solicited testimonies from Tamil witnesses in Moutiappa's house, and Manuel ferried the documented testimonies from place to place. As the catechist's son, though not himself an employee of the Jesuits, Manuel was just close enough—but not too close—to serve as a perfect intermediary for interactions between Hébert and the Jesuits. His experience is yet another example of the imbrication of family in colonial governance.

Conversion and the "Ties of Blood"

Moutiappa and Manuel's involvement with the Jesuits was of a piece with the missionaries' broader strategy. Much like commercial brokers and French traders, Catholic missionaries and their native catechists, or religious intermediaries, relied on kin, family, and caste community to further the French missionary project of proselytization. Conversion to Christianity by French missionaries relied on the familial relations of their catechists. The importance of family relations was thus paramount for catechists, much as it was for commercial brokers. Conversion could move along family maps that the Jesuits had not charted but that instead followed lines of blood, caste, and familiarity.

The experiences of French Jesuits in the mission field away from Pondichéry thus demonstrate that much as the traders depended on the familial contacts of their commercial brokers, missionaries relied on the kin networks of their catechists. However, a crucial difference between traders and Jesuits was their response to this dependence on local family structures. The traders and administrators of the Compagnie des Indes were willing to accept this dependence, while the Jesuits were actively engaged in an effort to replace and supplant these kin relations with a membership in the family of Christ.

Many French Jesuits were themselves members of powerful and influential families, and the importance of family in professional advancement in French India would have been a familiar practice. But their training would have predisposed the missionaries of the Society of Jesus to shy away from too-heavy a reliance on the worldly ties of family connections. Upon entering the society, candidates were required to perform the *Spiritual Exercises* devised by the society's founder, Ignatius of Loyola. The exercises were meant, suggests one scholar, to lessen the hold of ties outside the society, such that the community of the order would supplant the support and affective relationships of family.[79] Although many individual Jesuits maintained close connections with their kin, the official position of the society discouraged this. Loyola was explicit about this in the *Constitutions of the Society of Jesus*: "Everyone who enters the Society . . . should leave his father, mother, brothers, sisters, and whatever he had in the world."[80] Missionaries in India had chosen to replace the connections of natal responsibility and reciprocity with spiritual brotherhood. How galling, then, to find themselves utterly reliant on the ties of kin in India to spread the word of God. Even more upsetting would have been the position of Jesuits within these family networks. Not only did Jesuits depend on the familial relations of their native converts, but they were not even allowed to enter as equals, let alone superiors, into the networks on which they now relied. Jesuit missionaries thus found themselves denied membership in an association—that of the temporal family—toward which they were ambivalent at best.

Despite the Jesuits' best efforts to insert themselves into such networks, albeit temporarily, their own stories demonstrate that most successful conversions in Pondichéry and beyond were achieved by the connections of catechists and other converts rather than by Jesuit persuasion. Father Pierre Martin told the story of a lady of the Indian court in Madurai named Minakchiamal, who was raised in the palace from a young age and given the task of administering to consecrated images of the deities that were worshipped there. After her marriage, she occasionally ventured out of the palace and made the acquaintance of several newly converted Christians. One of these, a woman with whom Minakchiamal had close relations, acquainted her with a "pious and wise catechist."[81] In this account the catechist told the new and highborn convert "about the grandeur of God whom we adore, and inspired in her, by his speeches, a high regard for our sainted religion."[82] Father Martin himself elsewhere admitted he lacked the ability to make such inspiring speeches in Tamil.[83] Further, unlike the catechist, he could not produce the clincher: "It also came to pass during their many talks, that they discovered that they were quite closely related. The ties of blood intensified [her] esteem and confidence."[84] The catechist was thus able to offer the woman a conversion that did not entail a severing of all links to her community. The catechists' ability to draw on ties of consanguinity was both a central offering they could make to the Jesuits and a durable source of their success in conversion.

The Jesuits drew on a long Christian tradition when they described their converts, and especially their catechists, as their spiritual children. In the preface to the ninth volume of the *Lettres édifiantes et curieuses*, the editor, J. B. du Halde, used an image that illustrated the intimate, corporeal relation the missionaries envisioned themselves to have with their employees the catechists. He wrote, "A missionary is multiplied in strength several times in distributing these catechists in various locations of the missions."[85] This image situated the catechists as emerging from Jesuit bodies, much like fathers creating sons. The catechists enabled the missionary to multiply himself, sending pieces of his body away, in a form of celibate generation. But this metaphorical kinship had its limits. The successes the Jesuits gained in the Nayiniyappa Affair depended more on paternal-filial ties built on consanguinity, such as that between Manuel and his catechist father, than on spirituality kinship.

Before Governor Hébert allied with the Jesuits, in a letter he penned on February 5, 1710, he pointed to the limits of relationships of fictive kinship. "One Christian Father leaves upon his death ten Christian children," wrote Hébert, but he observed that the commitment Jesuits were able to inspire in their converted "children" in Pondichéry was of a more fleeting nature. "For at the end of ten years, you can scarcely find even one who still adheres to the true religion."[86] The benefit of an extended family network was that it enabled passing power and connections down through the generations. The spiritual family that Jesuits tried to construct in the subcontinent did not prove quite so enduring.

For catechists to succeed in their mission, they had to occupy positions of some authority among local communities, yet Christianity was a taint on one's social standing in South Asia in this period. The problem created by their close association with the European missionaries was extreme for catechists. Missionaries paid catechists to devote themselves to being an example of faith to be followed, but their association with the missionaries could make them degraded and tainted men to be avoided. The difficulties surrounding the marriage of one of the missionaries' catechists demonstrated this conundrum. This young man, who came from a family of "good caste," had served the Jesuit missionaries from an early age in an unnamed coastal city—perhaps Pondichéry. Although the text does not explicitly refer to this man as a catechist, his close and intimate association with the missionaries as a member of their household makes it likely that he served them in this capacity. In the course of his life with the missionaries, he had on many occasions eaten with the Jesuits. When the missionaries decided it was time for him to be married to a young woman of his caste, "according to the custom," it was quite difficult to find a bride of the right caste, because he had been tainted by sharing food with the missionaries, who, being Europeans, were of course not of his caste. "Nevertheless, after much effort," recounts an eighteenth-century missionary account, "a family of gentiles [Hindus] that was much pressed by poverty agreed to give their daughter, and to have her instructed in [Christian] religion and baptized."[87] Alliance with the Jesuits was clearly quite costly in social terms.

Nor did the difficulties end once a bride was found. The missionaries went to considerable expense and hosted a large banquet to celebrate the marriage, inviting Christians of the young man's caste and other guests. Yet even the Christians among the guests were loath to accept the invitation, being reluctant to eat with the missionaries and consume food prepared by European hands. They explained that the gentiles (referring to practitioners of local religion) would cast them out if they did so.[88] These converts had remained active and respected members of their extended families and larger Tamil community, and their refusal to eat with Jesuit missionaries was emblematic of the Jesuits' continual rebuff in their attempts to carve out a respectable foothold in the local landscape.

When the Jesuits tried to find a bride for their young protégé, they were attempting to use him as a stand-in for their own participation in these social and familial affiliations. The difficulties they faced speak to the limits of the use of intermediaries. Catechists could, on occasion, afford the Jesuits entry into local networks, but the missionaries inevitably came across barriers that could not be traversed. Because marriage meant the linkage of lineages, the Jesuits—with their murky and problematic social status and background—would have made for problematic and undesirable affines.

The missionary related the story of the Jesuits' difficulty in arranging a marriage for their catechist in an aggrieved and accusatory tone. The Jesuits' insistence on hosting a feast for their guests—disregarding the fact that sharing food with Europeans was at the root of the problems with securing a bride—suggests they hoped that their exclusion from local networks of celebration and conviviality would disappear if they simply refused to acknowledge it. The act of trying to arrange for the marriage suggests a usurpation of the familial role, and even the local Christian community—the very same people the Jesuits hoped would treat them as their spiritual fathers—refused to grant them this status. As Jesuits tried to supplant the networks provided by local families, the paths of conversion still flowed through families, thereby forcing Jesuit missionaries to participate in social settings in which they had little place.

This chapter has traced the efficacy of kinship in the Nayiniyappa Affair in order to demonstrate that a description of the politics, commerce, and conversion of colonial Pondichéry must account for the families of Pondichéry. The diary of the broker Ananda Ranga Pillai recounted an interaction he and an Indian friend had with the French colonial official Dumeslier in 1737. The entry highlights the centrality of kinship in the view of both French traders and their local intermediaries. Ananda Ranga Pillai wrote, "We both asked M. Dumeslier whether he meant to stay in India, or return to Europe. He replied that he did not see what advantage he could gain when he was separated and far away from his parents, brothers, sisters, and kindred. Alluding to his earnings in this country, he asked us whether we did not think that he could obtain the same on his own. He said that it was better to earn ten pagodas in one's own land, than 100 in a foreign one, as in the former case a man need not give up friends and relatives."[89]

Dumeslier's plaintive summary of his position points to an important feature of colonial governance in Pondichéry: in the absence of local family networks, French newcomers depended on local employees like Nayiniyappa and Ananda Ranga Pillai. Ananda Ranga Pillai relayed this anecdote with a clear sense of his enviable position, given his secure access to a vast network of family and acquaintances and a close friend by his side.

French and local actors in Pondichéry drew on the shared idiom of kinship to strategically advance their political, commercial, and religious agendas. It is worth noting that both French and Tamil fathers and sons in the colony used kinship for political aims. Kinship was not cordoned off by European newcomers as a system that was primordial, immutable, or the domain of so-called natives. Rather, the efficacy of kinship cut across different systems of classifying relatedness, different religious affiliations, and different genders. Even though French and Tamil inhabitants of Pondichéry held different conceptual and practical understandings of familial relations, kinship was a shared idiom and the foundation of many of their most productive encounters. Scholarship on British India has shown how reliance on familial networks greatly strengthened the hierarchical authority of British company officials in South India while simultaneously providing subordinates with power over local inhabitants.[90] The example of French India is markedly different in that working relations between French administrators and moneyed commercial brokers, and between Jesuits and their catechists, did not allow for such clear hierarchical distinctions. Affiliation with the French company or with missionaries did not necessarily entail subordination, and therefore French reliance on local family networks did not always position European newcomers as patrons. French trader-administrators, cognizant of their profound dependence on local markets and patterns of familial obligation and patronage, largely refrained from attempts to restructure or displace these patterns, as was common in later colonial projects.

In the Nayiniyappa Affair and beyond it, the action and theory of kinship were enmeshed within the practice of statecraft and bureaucracy, of commercial transactions, and of religious conversion. In the colony, French and Tamil families—both actual families and different conceptions of the family—collided and colluded. Familial relations sustained, enhanced, and shaped imperial projects in India.

A result of French reliance on local familial networks was that commercial and spiritual dealings with the French did not necessarily entail alienation from natal kin. On the contrary, the French desire to access such connections could even lead to the strengthening of these ties, as professional go-betweens and other local actors took advantage of these opportunities to bolster their standing in their family circles. Local, mostly Tamil agents who came into contact with the French at both the highest reaches of power and more humble spheres could leverage their employment by the French to strengthen their position in natal and affinal networks by using their authority in the colony to act as patrons and protectors. Such strengthening of kin ties was also a result of French strategies of trade, conversion, and employment. French officials, traders, and missionaries were all intensely aware of the importance of local associations of kin and caste. In their hiring of local employees, they attempted to insert themselves and their interests into such networks, albeit with only partial success.

The dependence on local familial networks was a site where trader-administrators and missionaries articulated the persistent conflict between projects of commerce and conversion. Religious and commercial agents took different approaches to dealing with this dependence. Trader-administrators were, by and large, comfortable with their reliance on the familial networks that their brokers made accessible, being accustomed to traveling along similar paths of advancement in French institutions. But Jesuits, while just as dependent as the traders on the local entanglements of their employees, were loath to accept this fact and instead attempted to provide an alternative kin network for their converts.

PART TWO

The Unfolding of the Affair

CHAPTER 3

The Denial of Language

Several men came into Nayiniyappa's prison cell, in the fort on Pondichéry's waterfront, and without a word of explanation took him away.[1] It was March 13, 1716, exactly one month after his arrest, and he still did not know the charges against him. He was taken to an office where three men were waiting for him: Governor Hébert, the governor's secretary, and the Tamil interpreter Manuel Geganis. The sight of the interpreter must have made a puzzling situation all the more confusing: Nayiniyappa's position, wealth, and success as the chief commercial broker of the Compagnie des Indes in Pondichéry stemmed from his ability to mediate and interpret, from his facility in crossing linguistic, commercial, and cultural boundaries. For years he had conversed fluently with French traders but not in French; rather, he used the lingua franca of the region, Portuguese. Yet from the moment of his arrest to his death in prison in 1717, French officials insisted on speaking French to him. The reliance on an interpreter, an intimate of the town's Jesuits and a man one of Nayiniyappa's appeals would later describe as "a bad interpreter of the truth," was galling to Nayiniyappa and his allies.[2]

Even after more than forty years as a resident of the French-ruled colony and a subject of the French Crown, Nayiniyappa did not speak French because he had never needed it, relying on Portuguese in his exchanges with Europeans.[3] Hébert, like other French administrators, needed to be fluent in

Portuguese to do his job, and Nayiniyappa described Portuguese as "a language known to both the accused and the judge equally."[4] The French were by no means the only Europeans to rely on Portuguese to communicate with South Asian employees and subjects. For example, after the Dutch conquered Sri Lanka, they also used Portuguese to communicate with local inhabitants; as late as 1757, during the Battle of Plassy, Robert Clive spoke with his native troops in Portuguese.[5] This policy changed over the course of the eighteenth century; the presiding chief broker, Pedro, still testified before the Pondichéry Council in Portuguese in 1729,[6] but later in the eighteenth century professional intermediaries regularly spoke French.[7]

Despite the long use of Portuguese between Nayiniyappa and his French employers, throughout the interrogation the questioners addressed Nayiniyappa in French, Manuel repeated the questions in Tamil, and the interrogators made Nayiniyappa respond in Tamil. Forced to use a language that no one in the room but Manuel understood, he answered very briefly in Tamil, often responding to lengthy questions with an unelaborated yes or no. Nayiniyappa's appeals described the use of French in the interrogation room as a travesty: "They all had a common language, which is Portuguese. . . . The accused clearly cried out that he had a natural right to use a language intelligible to both the judge and the accused, and to the secretary, but they did not want to listen to him. They decided to violate all rights. The investigation continued as it had begun: the interpreter, a devotee of the accused's enemies [the Jesuits], interpreted as he wished, and the accused [Nayiniyappa] was forced to sign that which he had neither heard, nor understood."[8]

Reliance on linguistic mediation performed by local employees had been the norm in Pondichéry from its earliest days as a French colony in the late seventeenth century and had by no means abated even after several decades of French rule. By contrast with the policy of Francophonie of nineteenth- and twentieth-century French empire, neither French traders nor missionaries in India early in the eighteenth century pursued the goal of making French the language most commonly spoken by the local inhabitants of Pondichéry. Like many Indian locales, large swathes of metropolitan France,[9] and virtually all colonies, Pondichéry was a polyglot city with a diverse and complex linguistic economy, with linguistic registers of various value, purchase, and potential for exchange.[10] However, traders and missionaries had different responses to this linguistic diversity: French officials adopted Portuguese, while French missionaries sought to master Indian languages.

Frenchmen of the Old Regime, accustomed to a polyglot homeland rich in languages and regional dialects, from Breton to Occitan, would have felt right at home in India's multilingual environment. French traders and missionaries alike relied, respectively, on local brokers and native catechists, but these parties used categorically different linguistic strategies. French traders and their employees in South India regularly used Portuguese as their common language, following a norm common to merchant maritime communities across the Indian Ocean, from China to Goa to Africa, and stemming from the former importance of Portuguese ships in the region. Even as Portuguese power in India declined in the seventeenth century, the Portuguese language remained essential for French traders in doing business. The unstable political context in Pondichéry late in the seventeenth century and early in the eighteenth century also contributed to the continued use of Portuguese. When the Dutch took control of Pondichéry in the late seventeenth century, the colony's new rulers, themselves fluent in Portuguese, could communicate with the town's Portuguese-speaking population. When a treaty signed in Europe restored control of the colony to the French in 1699, the linguistic transition was just as smooth.

French Jesuits and other missionaries in Pondichéry highly valued the use of indigenous languages and sought to acquire new languages as they moved between different mission fields. Therefore, they relied on catechists but sought to learn their languages and ultimately render the catechists unnecessary. A French missionary reflected on the Portuguese linguistic legacy in a letter sent to France. He described the lingua franca as "corrupted Portuguese which the Portuguese have left behind in all the parts of India from which they have been driven out."[11] He lamented, "This jargon is perpetuated among the Indians, so that the other nations of Europe are forced to learn it."[12] However, he likely sought to speak local languages, as many missionaries did. All three of the orders active in Pondichéry—Jesuits, Capuchins, and the MEP missionaries—prioritized learning South Indian languages.

This chapter considers the import of polylingualism in Pondichéry—the mixture of French, Tamil, and Portuguese in both commercial and religious settings and in the course of the Nayiniyappa Affair.[13] The problems of communication and interpretation in the affair were epistemological, revolving around the proper and just conditions for actionable knowledge. In the early, unstable days of the colony, French *colons* sought to obtain reliable information upon which to act and to communicate with the colony's population in the most effective way. Nayiniyappa's appeals emphasized language and communication precisely because, as a professional go-between, he had devoted his whole career to solving this problem. Religious catechists ("native" religious interpreters employed by Catholic missionaries) and linguistic interpreters also addressed the communicative gap, and like commercial brokers they could selectively dispense information to further both their own agendas and those of their employers. Yet after Nayiniyappa had addressed the communication problem for years, French officials deployed this communicative gap against him in the course of the affair. The deployment of language to prevent understanding in the Nayiniyappa Affair—the choice of French and the denial of Portuguese—was therefore a departure from long-standing practice in the colony. The insistence that Frenchmen would speak and understand French alone in Nayiniyappa's case prefigured the diminishing role of local intermediaries in the later decades of the eighteenth century.

Writing of communication in colonial regimes, Johannes Fabian noted that exchanges such as those that made it possible for the company to function in Pondichéry depended on "a shared communicative praxis providing the common ground on which unilateral claims could be imposed."[14] But the Nayiniyappa Affair was an event that changed the rules of the game, and therefore Tamil and French supporters of the jailed broker alike considered it a scandal. In other words, the affair hinged on communicative exchanges that left little or no room for previously established bilateral claims or agreements rooted in shared language.

Up to the time of the broker's arrest, when Nayiniyappa and all the French trader-administrators he worked with used Portuguese, both sides had to adapt to mastering, remaking, and manipulating their cultural and linguistic position in a language that was not native to them. By making French the official language of the affair, Nayiniyappa's adversaries made a new claim for their jurisdiction and authority over him.[15] Language became a means of denying communication. Nayiniyappa and his allies recognized the turn away from Portuguese as a violent act, an attempt to replace a colonial regime based on mutual understanding with one based on subordination.

Saving Language: Catechists and Missionaries

For the Jesuits, language acquisition was a global project, since they believed direct communication with potential converts was crucial to conversion. Accommodation, the conversion practice developed by Roberto di Nobili in India and Matteo Ricci in China, which relied on the comprehension and affinity a joint language can engender, contributed to this belief. Therefore, Jesuits prized the skill of learning new languages, and Jesuits in India who were sent to difficult inland missions, away from the more Christianized coastal areas like Pondichéry and Goa, were handpicked on the basis of their demonstrated academic prowess and linguistic faculty.[16]

The life of the Jesuit Pierre Martin embodied this belief in linguistic agility. A missionary who moved between the Indian-ruled city of Madurai and

French Pondichéry, Martin could speak and read Turkish, Persian, and Arabic, which he was convinced saved him from death when he was captured by Muslims at sea on his way to India. Upon his arrival in India, he sought to learn Bengali and Tamil.[17] Not all Jesuits were so eager to learn new languages. Father Guy Tachard was reluctant to move from Pondichéry to Chandernagore in Bengal because he could, he wrote, "confess, catechize, as well as read and understand the books of the area" in Tamil, while in Bengal he would have to undertake the study of a new language, "not an easy task when one is sixty years old."[18]

Other Catholic orders also pursued proficiency in Indian languages. When the Jesuit superior Tachard argued that the Jesuits should have the right to minister to the Malabar Christian parish in Pondichéry because none of their rivals, the Capuchin missionaries, spoke Tamil, the Capuchin father Paul Vendôme was outraged. He wrote in 1703 that the Jesuit Tachard was a liar and attached testimonies to his letter attesting that the Capuchin Father Esprit, "who has been living in Pondichéry ever since the town was given to the Royal Company, both preaches and catechizes in the Malabar language [Tamil]."[19] The seminary of the MEP, the third French missionary order active in Pondichéry, also wanted to employ missionaries who were fluent in native languages, but they sought to address the problem by developing a native clergy. In a statement made in Paris in 1700, the directors of the seminary declared that "it will be difficult for Europe to go on forever supplying priests, who take a long time to learn the language."[20]

Both Jesuits and Capuchins admitted that they found the study of Tamil extremely taxing. A Capuchin writer described Tamil as "harsh, crudely fashioned, unpleasant, and repelling, especially in its pronunciation. It is only a zeal for the propagation of faith which makes it possible to learn this language."[21] Fluency in Tamil was neither universal nor complete among European missionaries, and local catechists constantly served at the missionaries' side, preaching sermons, catechizing new converts, even on occasion listening to confessions. One Jesuit missionary admitted that "one can do almost nothing in this country without the help of the catechists."[22] Another missionary writer blamed the intemperate weather in South India for making missionaries lethargic, rendering them the equivalent of convalescents in Europe. The only task the newly arrived missionaries still took on, despite their sorry state, was the study of languages—a priority that could not be forsaken, regardless of one's health.

The catechists could enthrall the locals in a way that eluded the foreign missionaries. Jesuit Father Jean-Venant Bouchet described how this worked before a crowd: "The catechists, seeing this multitude of people, profited from the occasion in order to announce [to the crowd] the truths of Christianity, and each one of them made a touching speech. They spoke with such force. . . . Most of the audience seemed moved."[23]

The Jesuit Martin was frank on the topic of his failures of communication and felt his inadequacy: "Confessions exhaust me exceedingly because of the difficulty I have in understanding them. These people speak with extraordinary quickness, or perhaps it just seems to me so, because I do not yet have a good ear for their language. Tears often come to my eyes when I am at last able to understand what they are saying to me, which they must start over again three or four times."[24] He went on to say, "And these good people do so with marvelous patience, searching for easier words or styles of expression. . . . Nevertheless, when I make numerous mistakes, whether in the style of the language or in pronunciation, which is very difficult, they do not seem to discourage me, saying that they would rather listen to four words from the mouths of the Fathers, even mispronounced and badly arranged, than the grand speeches that their catechists can make."[25]

It is impossible to know whether Martin actually received such assurances that the catechists' speeches did not measure up to the Jesuits' efforts, or whether his flock meant them sincerely, but he clearly hoped they were true. His description of the procession of the Passion he oversaw in Madurai in 1700 suggests his dependence on the catechists for linguistic mediation. When a big crowd of Christians gathered in front of the church, the catechist told the "story of the Passion of our Lord" loudly and at length, while Martin himself made what he described as a "little speech."[26] Elsewhere he admitted that he had to commit his Tamil speeches to memory, which likely took out the spontaneity that would have given the speech force and emotion.[27]

A French officer stationed in India in the 1720s, Chevalier de La Farelle, reflected on the relationship between the Jesuits and the Indian men who taught them local languages: "The reverend fathers of the missions in India must know Tamoul [Tamil], which is the language spoken on the Coromandel Coast, and Telugu, which is the language of the Malabar Coast." He noted a fundamental tension: "What is most curious, and seems to prove the indifference of the Brahamans in regard to the religion they represent, is that it is the Brahamans who teach the Jesuits the languages spoken in India and thus provide them [the Jesuits] with the means to propagate the cult of the only true religion [Christianity]."[28] By making the Brahmans the teachers, in La Farelle's point of view, the Jesuits reinforced the spiritual and intellectual superiority of the local gurus. Even as their language teachers provided the Jesuits with the tools crucial for conversion, the positioning of these same teachers as leaders and superiors of the Jesuits might have undermined their mission. The Jesuits' linguistic difficulties only underscored the instability of their spiritual authority.

Exchanging Language: Commercial Brokers and French Traders

French traders were, like the missionaries, frank about the importance of the linguistic services provided by their intermediaries. While they relied on commercial brokers first and foremost for their extensive networks of trade relationships, they also sought brokers who could serve as linguistic interpreters and were able to speak Portuguese with their French employers and Tamil, Telugu, and Persian with their local connections. Inability to speak French was common among commercial brokers in Pondichéry in the first decades of the eighteenth century and was not considered a liability by French employers. It is important to note that the focus here is on professionally employed intermediaries, who were all men. But important unofficial intermediaries were the locally born women, usually Christian women from a Luso-Indian background, who married or lived with French arrivals and provided entry into local cultural practices and linguistic expertise. The most famous example was Jeanne Dupleix, who on occasion served as a translator for her husband, the mid-eighteenth-century governor Joseph Dupleix, interpreting for him from Tamil to French.[29]

In the text of one of the appeals to overturn Nayiniyappa's 1716 conviction, Nayiniyappa described himself as facilitating "communication between the Frenchman and the Indian." In these exchanges, explained Nayiniyappa, "the French general [i.e., governor] . . . speaks only to [the broker], and he [the broker] alone is known by the Indians." The broker relayed the French authority's orders "as they were given to him, and the Indians accept [these orders] as he conveys them."[30] Nayiniyappa here fashioned his relationship with the French governor as an exclusive one based on communication. He acknowledged his power while suggesting he never abused it by conveying orders differently than directed. Writing to the French authorities seeking his release from prison, of course Nayiniyappa had a vested interest in presenting himself as passing on the information provided by the French exactly as he received it. It seems more likely that he took certain freedoms in reshaping information as it came into his hands, rendering it more comprehensible as it made the leap between social contexts and languages. The crucial point, however, is that Nayiniyappa presented his key task as enabling communication between mutually unintelligible parties.

The French trading company in Pondichéry also employed translators in the Chaudrie court, a jurisdiction where French judges mediated disputes between native actors and where linguistic interpreters played an important part. In the Chaudrie, French traders acted as judges, dispensing justice in accordance with local custom—or, rather, what they could gather to be local custom by relying on local interpreters and clerks. Three members of Pondichéry's Superior Council, all French traders, heard civil cases involving local residents in the Chaudrie. The French judges did not speak Tamil, and many witnesses did not speak Portuguese or French. Nayiniyappa was employed as a Chaudrie interpreter prior to his appointment as Pondichéry's chief broker.[31] As a well-established merchant, he probably took on the work in the Chaudrie in order to seek a more powerful and prestigious position as a broker. The intimate connection he could have forged with French traders as he whispered into their ears in Portuguese would have cemented his position as a man to be trusted. Working in the Chaudrie as an interpreter would also have fortified his place among the town's Tamil population, as a man directly involved in the settlement of disputes. When he left the Chaudrie, Nayiniyappa attempted to maintain his connection to this center of power by arranging for a friend of his to be appointed to the post.[32] Nayiniyappa's sons claimed Governor Hébert bestowed the position as a reward on a man who had testified against their father.[33]

The Chaudrie interpreters appear to have been quite powerful. Bertrand-François Mahé, a high-ranking French official who served in India in the 1720s, ascribed more power to them than to the French judges ostensibly making the decisions. He noted that the interpreters "provide their explanations in such a way that affairs will take the turn they desire, so that often without intending it, the judge is responsible for injustices."[34] This comment, though pejorative, is nevertheless rare in that it acknowledges the power of interpreters to direct events. More often than not, reliance on local interpreters in the collection and creation of political, commercial, or religious knowledge by Europeans was elided.

Linguistic interpreters could also influence the written record of the French colony in the archives of the Superior Council. The majority of texts inscribed in the archives of the French trading company in India underwent a double process of transformation: between modes of transmission—oral to written—and between languages—Portuguese or Tamil to French. When a local resident appeared before the council, he usually spoke in Tamil, an interpreter translated the response aloud into Portuguese for the benefit of the French audience and officials, and a French (but Portuguese-speaking) secretary then wrote down the response in French. A translator read this inscribed version out to the witness in Tamil for verification, thereby repeating the same double circuit of transformation.[35] Hébert introduced an interpreter into Nayiniyappa's interrogations, but normally a Portuguese speaker like Nayiniyappa would not have required a translator in dealings with French officials because the French secretary was fluent in Portuguese. Testimony given in Portuguese would be written in French and read back in Portuguese for verification. The insistence on French in Nayiniyappa's case thus flew in the face of established practice.

Languages less commonly used in the Tamil region also made their way into the French archive. A 1720 case brought before the Superior Council occasioned the attachment of a note in Persian to the dossier after a sworn interpreter of the language verified its content.[36] In another case with global reach involving the English governor of St. George and Madras and merchants in Canton, the council admitted documents in translation from Chinese documents into evidence. The Chinese documents, in fact, were translated and archived in French, English, and Portuguese.[37]

Interpreting the Nayiniyappa Affair

The linguistic aspects of the Nayiniyappa Affair once again make visible the explicit and implicit conflicts woven through the fabric of the young colony. Nayiniyappa and various French and Tamil allies understood incompetent and vicious interpretation to be the central wrongdoing of the investigation against the broker. The appeals claimed that the denial of Portuguese stole from the broker the tools to communicate his own demands and desires, since the use of French made it impossible for him to understand the proceedings against him. The reversal in his fortunes was accompanied and facilitated by reversals in languages and communicative practices. Nayiniyappa again and again presented the denial of language as an act of violence, one that stripped him of his humanity. In one especially vivid section of his appeal he accused his adversaries of "stealing his language, his ears, his eyes, until he didn't speak at all, could understand nothing of what was said to him, and could not see what was written against him."[38] This very physical description calls attention to the somatic nature of interpretation, as a physical experience involving intimacy and understanding that draws on the skills of the body. The theft of his eyes, ears, and tongue calls to mind torture by dismemberment. Rendered mute, deaf, and blind, this state of enforced noncommunication was as much a part of Nayiniyappa's punishment as the public flogging, the confiscation of wealth, or the long imprisonment.

In calling Portuguese "his language," Nayiniyappa claimed the language of business, exchange, and mediation over his native tongue, Tamil. Portuguese had earned him his position in the colony. The affair therefore offers an important corrective to the notion that political struggles about linguistic usage are limited to binary battles between the "authentic" and the "imposed" language. For Nayiniyappa and the men of his cohort, issues of language mastery and belonging in language were spread against a broader canvas, with intimacy in multiple languages being the norm.

The Interpreter: Manuel Geganis and the Denial of Portuguese

Hébert questioned Nayiniyappa on seven different occasions during the course of his 1716 investigation of the alleged crimes of tyranny and sedition. Manuel Geganis served as interpreter for five of those sessions. Manuel's position in the colony as an employee at different times of both the Jesuits and the French trading company, as well as the son of the Jesuits' head catechist, highlights the complex relationship between these two groups. His actions in the course of the investigation shed light on the powerful role interpreters could fill, as well as the densely populated field of Tamil agendas and ambitions that affected the Nayiniyappa Affair. In a departure from the practice of limiting the interpreter's role, the prosecution gave Manuel an active role in making its case, which Nayiniyappa's appeals argued was inappropriate, given Manuel's affiliation with the Jesuits.

Nayiniyappa and his supporters argued that Manuel's position as an intimate of the Jesuits rendered him absolutely unsuitable as an objective interpreter. They emphasized this through repeated reference to him in the appeals as the "son of the Jesuits' catechist." The fact that he had traveled to France, spoke French fluently, was employed by Pondichéry's government as an interpreter, and had close, familial ties to the Jesuit mission through his father, put Manuel Geganis in a special position at the intersection of different streams of knowledge and information in the colony, and Nayiniyappa's appeals emphasized this position.

Manuel gave lengthy testimony on his involvement in the affair in both French and Tamil, in response to questioning by a commission appointed by the king in 1718 to reinvestigate Nayiniyappa's conviction.[39] By his own account, Manuel's official involvement in the affair dates to the very first moments after Nayiniyappa's imprisonment. On February 13, 1716, when Nayiniyappa was first taken to the fort as a prisoner, Manuel was already on the spot—perhaps by mere chance, or perhaps the Jesuits had sent him there, having agitated for Nayiniyappa's arrest. He described how Governor Hébert had summoned him and sent him to tell the Jesuits "that he had put his plan into execution." Finding the Jesuits assembled in their compound, Manuel conveyed Hébert's message. After speaking among themselves for a quarter of an hour, they told Manuel that Governor Hébert "was a great man who had a lot of spirit, and knew what he was doing, and he could therefore do no better than to consult his own opinion in the present affair."[40]

A few days later Hébert summoned Manuel again and gave him three palm leaf manuscripts (*olles* in the French text, *olai* in Tamil), which had been taken from Nayiniyappa's house.[41] Manuel translated them from Tamil into French. Given the fact that he by his own admission could not read or write French, he must have dictated his translations to a French scribe, who would likely have been a Jesuit. Manuel recalled that Hébert's son stated upon receipt of the texts, "These translations are no good."[42] Since Hébert fils could not read the original Tamil, this judgment could not have been a critique of the translation itself. Taking a more pragmatic view of translation, Hébert's son ordered Manuel to take the *olles* to the Jesuit Father Turpin, who was proficient in Tamil, and have him translate the documents again to provide the desired content. According to Manuel's testimony, the Héberts employed Turpin, not Manuel, to translate other Tamil documents germane to the case.[43]

Thus a veritable translation factory was put into place, its workings revealed in the interpreter's testimony. Nayiniyappa's official investigation took place in Fort St. Louis, in broad daylight. Under cover of darkness, in the Malabar neighborhoods, a parallel shadow process was taking place. Manuel explained its workings: "I know that at night, Pedro [the Christian who would replace Nayiniyappa as chief broker] brought Malabars to his house to testify [against Nayiniyappa]. . . . Xaveri Moutou and other scribes wrote these depositions on *olles*, which in the morning were sent to me, along with the witnesses who had made these declarations." The interpreter took the testimonies, inscribed in Tamil, to Father Turpin for French translation. Manuel noted, "I am not sure the translation was accurate, because I never read it, and I don't read French."[44]

Nayiniyappa's appeals painted Manuel as both incompetent and devious, a symptom of a problem simultaneously procedural, linguistic, and moral. According to the appeals, Manuel should not have been there in the first place, he used the wrong language to mediate exchanges, and his entanglement with the Jesuits disqualified him from acting in the proceeding at all. One appeal cited the important French Criminal Ordinance of 1670, which, among many other procedural prescriptions, ordered that any trial that did not used a shared language of the accused, the judge, and the witnesses, if such a language existed, would be declared invalid.[45] Indeed, the records of the Pondichéry Superior Council repeatedly show that non-French litigants provided their testimony directly to the members of the council in Portuguese, their shared language.[46]

Manuel himself lent support to the charge that his role in the investigation was suspicious. In his 1718 testimony, during the inquiry into Nayiniyappa's conviction, he claimed that Governor Hébert had told him that if he ever spoke to anyone of the details of what had transpired in Nayiniyappa's interrogations, he would be punished. As a result, Manuel explained, he had chosen to pay little attention to the witness testimonies to ensure he would not have any sensitive information to divulge.[47] In other words, he claimed to have deliberately sought not to listen to the testimony he himself interpreted. Suggesting the complicated position of the interpreter who may have acted on behalf of an official whose power was now waning, he undercut this description of interpreting without listening by completing his 1718 testimony with the following statement: "Here is everything that I remember, if I am interrogated on other matters, perhaps memory will come back to me."[48]

Manuel Geganis was the central interpreter in the case, with a role that extended far beyond the interrogation room, but he was not the only interpreter. On two of the seven interrogations, Hébert used the services of a French lieutenant in the Pondichéry garrison named Cordier. Cordier, the son of a councillor on Pondichéry's Superior Council, had been born in India, but he was not fluent in Tamil.[49] Questioned in 1718 as part of the same proceedings that provided Manuel's recollections, Cordier testified, "Hébert held a paper in his hand, and told [Cordier] what he must say to Nayiniyappa. Hébert used the Portuguese language, and [Cordier] also spoke Portuguese to Nayiniyappa, who responded in the same language, and [Cordier] then repeated Nayiniyappa's response to Hébert [in French]."[50]

As this depiction of an almost surreal interrogation reveals, Cordier was not so much an interpreter as a buffer: he did little more than repeat Hébert's words, which were already understood by the Portuguese-speaking Nayiniyappa, and then translated into French Nayiniyappa's Portuguese response— merely transmitting through another voice what had already been heard by the Portuguese-speaking Hébert. This evidence therefore bolstered Nayiniyappa's claim that the sole purpose of using an interpreter was to engender willful miscomprehension and abuse the broker by making him mute. Hébert's use of an interpreter served to erase the long history of understanding between the two men.[51]

Governor Hébert did not articulate in any extant document why he chose to deny Nayiniyappa the opportunity to speak to him directly in Portuguese.

Nayiniyappa's sons mentioned in their narrative of the affair only one occasion on which Hébert spoke to Nayiniyappa directly in Portuguese in the course of his incarceration. They claimed that one day, Hébert and his son, who were in debt, came to Nayiniyappa's cell. They made the broker a stark offer, in Portuguese, to restore his freedom for a payment of two thousand pagodas.[52] The joint language that had been conveniently forgotten in an attempt to assert the "Frenchness" of Hébert's regime was suddenly restored, and the path of direct communication tantalizingly—albeit briefly—reopened. If this clandestine visit did take place, the Héberts would have employed Portuguese to avoid having an interpreter witness the offer. An interpreter leaves a trace and, as Manuel's testimony demonstrates, can act as a damaging witness.

The Signature: A Perverted Sign

Signatures played an important role in the Nayiniyappa Affair, most often discussed as signs of questionable and deceptive authority. The confounding use of signatures was an issue not only for Nayiniyappa, who centered many of his appeals on untrustworthy acts of signing, but also for Tamil witnesses and the French judges who had signed his conviction. The discussion of signatures and acts of signing in the affair reveals the semiotic instability of an interpreted world.

Hébert required Nayiniyappa to sign his name in Tamil to each of the council secretary Le Roux's French-language transcripts of his seven interrogations. The practice of putting Tamil signatures to French documents was very much the norm in Pondichéry. Whenever literate Tamil witnesses or defendants were heard in cases brought before the Superior Council (also known as the Sovereign Council), they signed the French documents recording their hearing.[53] The French records scrupulously documented this stage in the proceedings, stating that the interpreter in each case had carefully explained the contents of the text before the witness signed it.[54] Nayiniyappa's appeals and Manuel's testimony alike described Nayiniyappa asking for a full explanation of the documents before he signed them. Manuel admitted Nayiniyappa had asked for a "word by word" explanation but that the only answer he was given was that the documents contained nothing but his own responses.[55]

Manuel testified that Nayiniyappa "denied almost everything we asked him about, and gave very good reasons as his justification. The interrogations complete, the General had sieur Le Roux [the secretary] write what he wanted written, without reading these texts to me; therefore, I could not tell Nanyapa anything that Le Roux had written."[56] The secretary of the council, Joseph

François Le Roux, was a third actor, apart from Manuel and Cordier, whose role affected the linguistic exchanges in the interrogation room. He was present at each of Nayiniyappa's interrogations and at the witness testimonies. He signed every transcription of these encounters. Other company records reveal that Le Roux, a native of Amiens, had become secretary less than six months earlier. In this role he served as Pondichéry's notary. The council had unanimously appointed Le Roux, who had worked for several Parisian notaries and in various offices in France before arriving in India.[57] The post came with generous wages, and his position as a new appointee may have made him eager to please Governor Hébert. Le Roux would leave Pondichéry for Bengal in 1718 and die there in 1719.[58] In a letter written in 1719, Nayiniyappa's ally, the French official La Morandière, claimed that Le Roux had actually fled Pondichéry because witness testimony suggested he had stolen money from Nayiniyappa's business associates. The official accused Le Roux of engaging with Hébert in commerce using illicitly minted money.[59] Le Roux had gone to Bengal to avoid the investigation, he claimed.[60]

According to Manuel, struggles over the signing of these documents recurred throughout the interrogations. "Every time [Nayiniyappa] was questioned, the General told him to sign the documents written by sieur Le Roux, and every time he refused to sign, saying he didn't know what it was they wanted him to sign. He asked that we explain to him what it said, word by word, but we would only tell him that only his own responses were written down, and nothing else. And so he always signed, despite himself. I also signed the papers without knowing what they contained."[61] The official record makes no mention of these interactions; rather, each interrogation record concludes with the statement that the prisoner heard a word-by-word explanation by the interpreter of the contents and that he acknowledged the veracity of the record and signed his name to it.[62] Nayiniyappa's complaint was a procedural one; it stemmed not from the semiotic discrepancy between the French source and the Tamil authorization but from the demand that he sign an unexplained text.[63] Nayiniyappa's signature to the documents thus carried two potential and contradictory meanings: a mark of authentication or evidence of intimidation and coercion.

Why did Nayiniyappa sign the interrogation records if he didn't know their contents? His appeals supply two different explanations of this act. First, he claimed that he was intimidated by the enraged response to his qualms—in one appeal he describes Governor Hébert "roaring in French and slandering and confronting him";[64] in another he describes Hébert, his son and the interpreter Manuel falling "into a furious rage" when he objected.[65] "He was presented with a paper written in the French language; he knew well that it was his own condemnation," described an appeal, but he knew it was futile to resist, "with the Governor so passionate and driven by his ambition."[66] Second, Nayiniyappa explained that he acquiesced because it never occurred to him that Hébert would try to frame him by using his own signature. The idea that "a Catholic and Christian judge" such as Hébert would ask him to sign a false document was inconceivable, the broker wrote.[67] He also described Manuel and Hébert's son reassuring him that he had nothing to fear in signing, although of course Manuel could not himself read the documents. Resigned to his fate, Nayiniyappa had despaired of finding justice on earth when he signed, saying he did so by "lifting his eyes to the heavens asking for justice."[68] The MEP missionary father Jean-Jacques Tessier de Queralay, Nayiniyappa's ally and the Jesuits' rival, also used dramatic language in relation to the reports of this incident and highlighted the manipulation of Nayiniyappa's signature. He cast the Héberts as villains and Nayiniyappa as a victim, calling the broker "a poor innocent whose goods they wanted [who thus] found himself convicted by his own hand without knowing it."[69]

The appeals alleged Hébert and his allies had employed various methods to also persuade the witnesses against Nayiniyappa into signing the papers put before them, including intimidation, threats of vengeance by the powerful French officials, promises that they would benefit by pleasing Hébert, and references to others' compliance. Nayiniyappa's sons claimed that Pedro, their father's rival, told a group of potential witnesses that if they testified they would receive twenty-four pagodas as compensation, but if they refused they would be given twenty-four lashes of the whip.[70]

In their questioning in 1718 about Nayiniyappa's conviction, several witnesses claimed that two years earlier, they had tried to avoid signing the written account of their testimony by claiming that they did not know how to write. The witness Andiapen, for instance, admitted to making such a claim. Andiapen also testified that while the documents pertaining to his deposition made it appear as if he had come to the fort three times—once for inquiry, a second time for *recollement*, and a third time for a confrontation with Nayiniyappa—he was called in only one time.[71] Another man "declared that when Hébert asked him if it wasn't Nanyapa who counseled them to leave the city [in the exodus of 1715], he responded, 'Monsieur, you brought me here and had me sworn in to tell the truth. I am an old man, I do not want to lie, and I do not want to make a false oath.' He also said that he had declared that he didn't know how to write, in order to avoid being made to sign a paper of which he didn't know the content, and many of his friends did the same."[72] Here the witness explicitly linked the proceedings to a threat to his reputation.

Falsification of official documents threatened the very ability to act with purpose and to trust that certain actions—here, the act of putting one's name to a text—would produce certain results, an unbreakable tie between the signed document and the actor who signed it. One of Nayiniyappa's appeals said the caste heads brought in to testify about the employee exodus of 1715 were especially reluctant to perjure themselves with false signatures.[73] Some witnesses claimed, under requestioning two years after their original depositions, that like the accused, they had signed their depositions without knowing their contents. The deposition of a witness named Calichetty centered on the validity of his signature: "First he was asked if he recognized his signature, which was given along with seventeen others at the bottom of Tanapachetty's testimony, declaring the testimony [against Nayiniyappa] to be true. He said it was. Asked if he knew what was written in it, before he signed it, he answered that he didn't know, and that he had asked that it be read to him before he signed it, but he was told that it wasn't necessary and he signed it, because he was afraid."[74] Dozens made the same accusation, saying they had been intimidated and pressured into signing testimonies against Nayiniyappa. "Some of [the witnesses] said they had made some difficulty about signing, because they didn't know what they were signing, but Hébert had told them: 'your friends signed this, you must sign it.'"[75]

Nayiniyappa's sons summarized these questionings, writing that "every single witness stated that his testimony had not been explained or read to him . . . that when someone made some resistance or refused to sign, he was threatened . . . if something was written in their presence, they did not know what it was . . . and when the witnesses or Nanyapa asked that something be read or explained to them, this was refused."[76]

In Indian Ocean practices of attestation, South Asian merchants accepted or denied promissory notes commonly known as hundis according to whether they recognized the validity of the style and form of the note, gathered through personal experience of previous notes.[77] By signing a document they believed to be false, the witnesses would have been jeopardizing their future reliability, and by extension their credit. An incident that suggests that signatures were as much a marker of status and respectability for Frenchmen as for local merchants is described in the diary of the broker Ananda Ranga Pillai. In 1736 he observed a spirited council debate as to the order in which French councillors would append their signatures to documents after the appointment of a new member. One of the councillors learned his signature would henceforth appear below that of the new appointee. Governor Dumas told him, "Your functions will continue undisturbed, and your salary will still be the same. The only change required is in the position of your signature, which you will have to affix after those of the gentlemen already mentioned." The councillor replied, "My means are not so insufficient as to compel me to submit to such an indignity. I regard honor as of greater value. I will, therefore, give up my post," and he stormed out.[78]

In the course of the Nayiniyappa Affair, some signatures were also tampered with in more direct ways. One man admitted that when he was called to testify against Nayiniyappa he was not even in Pondichéry, and others were made to sign in his name.[79] Another signatory said he and his father-in-law had both been called to testify, but his father-in-law hid so as to avoid the summons. The man then signed both his own name and that of his father-in-law under duress.[80] One of Nayiniyappa's associates, Ramanada, claimed he had been made to sign his name to a document that carried the wrong date so as to make it appear that he was present in Pondichéry on a day when he was not. When this was discovered, Ramanada's missionary supporters from the MEP wrote an appeal, describing the falsified document as "false, illusory, abusive."[81]

Most of the witnesses and Nayiniyappa did not deny that they had signed the testimonies. They merely argued the signatures did not signify verification. The issue is one of semiotic integrity: a signature is an index of both presence and intention. It makes the claim "I was here" and the accompanying statement "I agree." While presence was not called into question, since most of the signers agreed that they had physically signed, intention posed more of a problem. When witnesses claimed that they had signed their name only because Hébert threatened them or promised to reward them, their signatures lost their power as marks of verification and markers of proper legal procedure. They accused Hébert and his secretary of semiotic perversion. As Nayiniyappa's sons argued, Hébert and his secretary "abused the signatures of these Malabars."[82] A French supporter of Nayiniyappa echoed the sons' appeal and highlighted the political and religious motivations behind these actions. He described Hébert's crime as "the abuse of Indians' signatures, for the pleasure of the Jesuit Fathers."[83] In a world in which French authorities and the local population had few shared signs—lacking common language, modes of doing business, or rites of religious practice—the manipulation of a signature's meaning only accentuated the semiotic cacophony.

In 1669, Jean-Baptiste Colbert, following the Venetian example, founded the École des Jeunes de langues in Paris, which provided dragomans-in-training with language instruction in Turkish, Arabic, Persian, and Armenian for diplomatic service in the Ottoman lands. Fittingly, the Jesuits—strong advocates and practitioners of linguistic immersion—were entrusted with instruction in the Parisian school.[84] However, this institution did not teach Indian languages. Thus Frenchmen developing imperial interests in India had to pursue other solutions to language barriers, including the local brokers and interpreters who became key players in the Nayiniyappa Affair.

If the affair suggests French ambivalence about this solution, the fact that the directors of the French trading company in Paris would soon decide on a different approach indicates the affair was a harbinger of other approaches to French colonialism in India. Less than a decade after the conclusion of the Nayiniyappa Affair, the directors opined that local interpreters were compromising French interests by failing to take a firm tone with Indian leaders and demand terms that would be most beneficial to the French. In a letter sent from Paris to India in 1727, the directors ordered the company's agents in Pondichéry, as well as in Chandernagore and Mahé, to "choose several young children of French birth, and instruct them in the languages used in the lands where [French] trading posts are located, so that these young men can serve as your interpreters in the future."[85]

The French government in Pondichéry voiced unequivocal support for the idea of tutoring French youth in Indian languages, admitting that "not being able to write or speak to make ourselves understood has caused us great difficulty in many small matters."[86] The colonial council offered a cash prize of one thousand livres to the young resident who became most proficient in an Indian language. But it also warned of many obstacles to ending reliance on local linguistic intermediaries. To start, the local French youth were not eager to undertake the rigors of the study of Indian languages. The council cited only one French boy who was both interested and capable and sufficiently healthy to undertake taxing language studies, and claimed there was no one who could teach him Persian, the language used by the Mughal court. It made no reference to the study of Tamil. Problematic as reliance on Indian interpreters might be, finding a solution proved difficult.[87]

The predicament of interpretation went beyond the issue of interpreters' supposed timidity. Dependence on linguistic intermediaries was disturbing precisely because of its inevitability, and the difficulty was finding a way out of this dependence. Ananda Ranga Pillai revealed the depth of this dependency in one of his diary's entries. Governor Dupleix wanted a missive to be sent in Persian regarding some territorial diplomatic negotiations. But the difficulty in doing so in secret revealed the utter reliance on local intermediaries:

> [The Governor] . . . said that a letter to that effect must be written by
> M. Delarche, and that the Brahman in charge of preparing the Persian
> letters should not know of it. I replied: "The plan is a good one, but

M. Delarche can only speak and read Persian. He cannot write that language." The Governor said: "only a few words have to be written, M. Delarche can manage that," and he then sent for him. He came. The Governor gave him the subject, and asked him to write the letter. M. Delarche said that he could not write Persian, but that he would get the Brahman writer to do what was required, and would strictly warn him not to reveal the secret to anyone.[88]

The problem of interpretation, as the Nayiniyappa Affair so clearly shows, was densely woven into the fabric of colonial life. The reliance on local linguistic go-betweens reflected local social structures and power relations characterized by distributed authority and not so easily overturned. In the course of the Nayiniyappa Affair the polylingual and mediated reality of French governance in Pondichéry was suspended, but the resulting uproar thwarted, at least for a while, those who would remove Nayiniyappa from his post. By refusing to use a shared language, Nayiniyappa's adversaries were refusing to cede authority to their intermediary and tried to maintain control in their hands. While the exoneration of the broker suggests at least partial failure of this effort, the growing use of French by Tamil go-betweens later in the eighteenth century points to the eventual success of this strategy.

Struggles over interpretation and the use of multiple languages revolved around the ability of shared signs—whether textual or oral—to serve as stable markers in exchanges already rich in the possibility for misunderstanding. Nayiniyappa and his cohort of commercial and religious interpreters provided an indispensable linguistic service to traders and missionaries alike, by making disparate sign systems mutually comprehensible. This history explains the outrage Nayiniyappa and his supporters expressed over the denial of shared language in the course of his trial.

Nayiniyappa had amassed significant authority from his position as a go-between. His indignation over the silence and incomprehension imposed on him during his trial stemmed from the striking contrast between his previous life, devoted to mediating and facilitating exchange, and his life after his arrest. As both a Chaudrie interpreter and the company's head commercial broker, he had made his fortune and his reputation because of his ability to communicate. He was accustomed to moving fluently between Tamil and Portuguese, conferring with South Indian rulers on behalf of the French government, firmly negotiating terms of trade with Pondichéry's merchants or laborers, giving loud orders to the members of his household, or speaking to large crowds of the poor receiving his largesse. His life was a noisy, productive symphony of overlapping yet comprehensible speech. How different were the months he spent locked up in a prison cell at Pondichéry's Fort St. Louis. Which would have been worse: the long hours of imposed and solitary silence, when he was not allowed to speak even to his guards, or the incomprehensible babble of French in the interrogation room, where he must have been all too aware that the impenetrable noise was the sound of his fate being sealed?

Chapter 4

Conflict at Court

Over the course of five months in 1716, Nayini-
yappa was held in a cell alone and taken out only to be interrogated by Governor Hébert. It was likely in that very cell that Nayiniyappa died in August 1717
while serving a three-year prison sentence. His death, his sons alleged, was no
accident but the work of Governor Hébert and his son, who "caused the death
of our father in prison by misery, and perhaps by having him assassinated."[1]
Three years after that grim death, the French king not only formally cleared
Nayiniyappa's name but also awarded the restitution of his confiscated wealth
to his surviving family members for their suffering and losses and ordered
Hébert to pay them reparations. How did Nayiniyappa and his allies engineer this reversal, from the solitary confinement to the metropolitan decision
in their favor? The answer lies in a dense legal realm of maneuverings that
unfolded over a wide swath of jurisdictions and geographies. Law, as it was
applied in the Nayiniyappa Affair, was both an attempt to display French sovereignty and a site for the fractures in this sovereignty to be revealed in the
form of colonial factionalism.

This chapter considers the Nayiniyappa Affair as a court case. Nayiniyappa's
trial, it argues, became the occasion for a broad debate about the place
of local intermediaries in colonial rule. It could scarcely be otherwise at a
time when the broker was at the center of discussions about local residents
demanding too many religious freedoms and thereby revealing the limits of

French sovereignty. The judicial agenda enacted the political aims of those who objected to Nayiniyappa's power but also provided tools for his supporters. The trial, then, was not merely a demonstration of French power and sovereignty but as much an opportunity to engage in intra-French and intracommercial rivalries and factionalism.

The legal sphere was yet another stage on which missionaries and the traders-officials of the Compagnie des Indes could vie for influence. In a study of the legal system in seventeenth-century France, David Parker has argued that law provided an arena for local ruling elites to resolve their differences.[2] In Pondichéry, a similar dynamic was in place, with a crucial difference. Given the relatively fluid division of influence and clout among commercial, missionary, and local agents, the legal system was open to manipulation by a surprisingly diverse host of characters. The consistently messy distribution of authority played out in legal terms, much as it did in the familial and linguistic realms described in the previous chapters. Conflicts between Nayiniyappa, the Jesuits, French traders, and Tamil workers and merchants had all taken place on numerous occasions since the broker's rise to the position of chief intermediary. But these conflicts did not rise to the level of an "affair" until Nayiniyappa's arrest and conviction in 1716.

In Nayiniyappa's interrogations, sentencing, and subsequent appeals, all the involved actors made reference to metropolitan legal procedures. This reference to French procedure held different valence for different actors. Nayiniyappa's French detractors sought to use French legal norms to move his local supporters to unfamiliar ground. Legal proceedings, unlike the commercial and linguistic strategies that structured business in the colony, unfolded in a manner in which adherence to French language and metropolitan precedents left local intermediaries like Nayiniyappa at a disadvantage. In this sense, it mattered little that the accusations against Nayiniyappa—tyranny and sedition—were left quite vague in the proceedings against him. In fact, the vagueness of the charges might well have been a legal and political strategy. The very act of putting Nayiniyappa on trial had more weight than the specific charges. Procedure also, however, served the interests of Nayiniyappa and his supporters, since it provided grounds for making claims about the rights due to an accused man. By making arguments about procedure gone wrong, Nayiniyappa and the interest groups that supported him utilized the system that had initially aligned against him. Nayiniyappa's arrest and resulting legal procedure marked the beginning of a new kind of relationship with his French employers. No longer a respected and influential employee, he was an accused man, taken in and out of his prison cell at the will of his accusers. The courtier's demands for proper procedure were a last-ditch effort to impose clarity. The appeals that followed Nayiniyappa's conviction all turned on what had happened in those interrogations and the judicial process that accompanied them.

The Legal Process of the Nayiniyappa Affair

The judicial and legal proceedings of the Nayiniayppa Affair unfolded in four stages, which can be roughly categorized as conviction, appeals, reinvestigation, and demands for reparations.[3] In the first stage, in 1716, Nayiniyappa was arrested, interrogated, convicted of tyranny and sedition, and sentenced to a three-year prison term and payment of a heavy fine, alongside other punishments. Second, the appeal stage saw the submission of detailed and lengthy documents, or *requêtes*. These were not technically speaking legal appeals, since they were not a part of the formal judicial process, but they nevertheless acted as appeals in that they sought to overturn and redress Nayiniyappa's conviction. These lengthy texts were sent to the Superior Council in Pondichéry, to the king in France, and to the Council of the Marine by or on behalf of Nayiniyappa and his allies Tiruvangadan (Nayiniyappa's brother-in-law) and Ramanada, his business associate. Both Tiruvangadan and Ramanada were arrested around the time of Nayiniyappa's arrest, accused of being his accomplices. This appeal stage unfolded between 1716 and 1718. The third stage was the result of these appeals' success and began with the king's order in February of 1718 to reopen the case against Nayiniayppa and undertake a full investigation into the circumstances of his conviction.[4] This stage, which occurred after Nayiniyappa's death, involved deposing most of the original witnesses and collecting depositions from the interpreters involved in his interrogation, as well as statements from the French councillors who had served as judges and signed their name to Nayiniyappa's conviction and sentence. This third reinvestigative stage concluded with the arrest of Governor Hébert, Nayiniyappa's chief adversary, and with the decision by the Pondichéry Superior Council in 1719 to overturn Nayiniyappa's conviction.[5] Finally, the fourth stage involved the filing of claims in Paris by Nayiniyappa's heirs and his allies Tiruvangadan and Ramanada, who all demanded that in addition to the restitution of their confiscated wealth, the disgraced Hébert pay them reparations for the damage he and his son had caused. These demands were met in 1720, when the king's *conseil d'état* ordered that Nayiniyappa's name be formally and publicly cleared and that Hébert pay Nayiniyappa's family amends in the sum of twenty thousand livres.[6] These four stages provided an opportunity for rival factions in French India to air their differences and grievances— especially those among competing trader-administrators who struggled over political positions in Pondichéry and among members of separate Catholic missionary orders, who jostled for influence in the colony's governance. Law was a realm for working out these tense relationships.[7]

The legal debate surrounding the Nayiniyappa Affair posed thorny questions. What rights were due to a colonial, Indian subject like Nayiniyappa under French law? Did the safeguards of the mother country's law apply to men like him? Who in the colony had the sovereign and judicial power to decide his fate? The affair demonstrates how the French in India used law to assert their sovereignty but at the same time reveals all the rifts in this sovereignty as a result of the colony's intensely fractured institutions. The law—and debates over its proper application, procedure, and rights—was therefore also a place for sovereignty to be contested and revealed in its failings. Having law, in other words, did not necessarily mean having power.

Colonial Legal Regimes

Over the last decade or so, scholars have increasingly examined the ways in which legal encounters of various kinds have been central for both the making and unmaking of colonial regimes. Much of this work has found a central interlocutor in Lauren Benton's work on colonial legal regimes and her argument that debates about legal jurisdiction in the colonial contexts are debates about sovereignty. That is, questions about who gets to make legal judgments, who is allowed legal agency, what rules determine how justice should be dispensed, and how those judgments would be enforced were inevitably questions about colonial authority or its absence.[8] As one historian has put it, a history of colonial jurisdiction is a history of power.[9] In French India, legal exchanges were indeed productive sites for debates about colonial sovereignty, as the Nayiniyappa Affair demonstrates, and colonial administrators seized on the law as a means to claim their authority. Such explicit claims making for French authority was especially necessary in India, where the company officials' repeated conflicts with local inhabitants about the limits of religious freedom frequently called French control into question. Yet in the Nayiniyappa Affair it was legal procedure and not jurisdiction that was the most productive and contested aspect debated by all the participants. Nayiniyappa and his supporters questioned the validity and the integrity of the proceedings against him, not the jurisdictional claims made in the course of his case, and in doing so they called into question the authority of the French governor. French factionalism meant that the debate over procedure quickly escalated into a struggle over political authority.

French colonies in the early modern period all dispensed some version of French law to their subjects.[10] Legal issues pertaining to slavery in colonial contexts in the eighteenth century have been the topic of a rich vein of scholarship, especially in the Atlantic world.[11] Nayiniyappa's legal travails, however, differed in important ways from those of slaves, as he retained some of his power, even under arrest, and his position as a legal subject was never called into question. The case is therefore an especially fruitful example of the relationship between metropolitan and colonial law. Significantly, Nayiniyappa was able to successfully appeal his conviction in the metropole. This unusual outcome was the result of his special position in the colony prior to his arrest, as one of its most influential and powerful residents, French or Tamil. Nayiniyappa was not a subordinate subject; in significant ways, prior to his arrest he was the patron and French traders were his clients. He was a rich and well-connected member of a local elite, and his French employers had long depended on him and his connections. The effort to impose a subordinate status on him through his arrest attempted to rewrite the terms of the relationship. But Nayiniyappa's legal claims making drew on his local influence and metropolitan connections to make his views heard and inscribed. He successfully demanded that the procedural integrity of the colonial legal system include him.

The larger point here is not that the system was especially fair but rather that Nayiniyappa's interactions with French law clearly reveal the contested contours of authority in French India. More broadly, the "legal pluralism" that has engaged legal historians' attention did not simply mean the coexistence of so-called customary law and metropolitan law.[12] Nayiniyappa and his peers meaningfully engaged with metropolitan legal systems and their colonial iterations. These engagements did not necessarily affirm the power of the colonial regime. Nayiniyappa's many days at court demonstrate that procedural debates could raise the issue of the legitimacy of French authority over colonial subjects.

Pondichéry's Courts: Creating Colonial Law

Legal diversity was a feature of life in metropolitan France during the Old Regime—a diversity that drew the ire of one famous advocate of legal reform, Voltaire, when he remarked with typical pithiness that "a man traveling in this country changes laws almost as often as he changes horses."[13] Yet even as France itself was a bewildering jumble of legal codes, jurisdictions, and jurisprudence, the colonial context, theoretically at least, presented a relatively unified approach to the law. Pondichéry had two courts of law—the Superior (or Sovereign) Council and the Chaudrie. In this, the colonial arena presented a clearer structure than the jurisdictional jumble in France. Where the French metropole had courts upon courts—"seigneurial courts, church courts, commercial courts, courts for admiralty law and excise tax, courts for royal forests and waterways, courts for salt depots and the constabulary"[14]—Pondichéry's two-tiered system was a model of simplicity.[15]

The court in which Nayiniyappa's fate was decided, the Superior or Sovereign Council, served as French India's highest legal institution.[16] It was also its governing body, making and carrying out the colony's administrative work. This legal-administrative-financial-political institution was created shortly after the French took back control of the colony from the Dutch at the very end of the seventeenth century. *Lettres patentes,* signed in Versailles by King Louis XIV in February of 1701, established the council.[17] It would operate under the decree's guidelines until a series of judicial reforms took place in 1776. It supplanted a similar institution established by royal edict in January 1667 in Surat on the west coast of India, where the Compagnie des Indes had focused its activities prior to its establishment in Pondichéry. Louis XIV's 1701 decree began with a promise, premised on a commitment to the growth of the French project in India and explicitly linking the commercial Compagnie des Indes to the king's juridical responsibility to his subjects: "The Royal Company of the East Indies having considerably enlarged its establishment [in India] . . . we are obliged to provide the means to dispense justice to our subjects."[18]

The decision to create this new judicial body was set against the specific needs of the company in India, but it was also part of a much broader imperial and global effort to weave French law and punishment in a more integrated fashion into the structures of colonial administration. Sovereign councils existed in New France and in the Caribbean colonies, as well as in the metropolitan provinces, most of them created in the seventeenth century and the very beginning of the eighteenth century. The creation of these judicial bodies in the colonies was an orchestrated and global effort, with sovereign or superior councils created in 1663–1664 in Martinique, Guadeloupe, and New France, in St. Domingue in 1685 (then reinstituted in 1701), and in Pondichéry in 1701. Most of them remained in place in one form or another until the revolutionary legal reforms of 1790. While French imperial legal institutions were conceived in a relatively uniform manner, sharing both structural features and codes by which to administer justice, it should not be surprising that the reality was not nearly as cohesive as the plan.

The charter of the Pondichéry council decreed that it would hear both civil and criminal cases and that justice would be available to all, regardless of their "rank, condition or country" (although, as we will see below, a different legal institution, the Chaudrie, heard civil cases involving only Indians). The royal edict of 1701 named the founding members of the council, choosing among Pondichéry's high-ranked traders to sit on it. The fact that the specific staffing of the Sovereign Council was determined in France rather than decided locally is an indication of the importance ascribed to and bestowed on this colonial institution. Of the seven original appointees to Pondichéry's Sovereign Council, two would come to have a central role in the judgment of Nayiniyappa in 1716: Flacourt as one of the judges who convicted him and La Prévostière as Governor Hébert's replacement. The traders who served on the council in Pondichéry were not trained legal professionals. In the first half of the eighteenth century, few colonies had many residents with formal legal training, and other colonial superior councils largely depended on employees of the trading companies and respected members of local French society without legal experience to act as judges, although there were exceptions to this general rule.[19]

The Superior Council was meant to dispense justice according to codes and rules imported from France. French colonies in the eighteenth century relied on one code for civil proceedings, the Coutume de Paris.[20] For criminal cases, they followed the procedures compiled in the Criminal Ordinance of 1670. This ordinance was an explicit Colbert-era attempt at codification and a wholesale reform of the rules of legal criminal proceedings. It was adopted in all of France's colonies, though unevenly applied.[21] As we shall see, Nayiniyappa and his allies understood the ways in which the case against him did not adhere to the rules of the 1670 ordinance, and they used this fact expertly in crafting their appeals against the conviction. Compared with its British competitors in India, France, through its reliance on the Coutume de Paris and the Ordinance of 1670, was able to impose greater legal cohesion on its colonies, at least in theory.[22]

Pondichéry's Sovereign Council was clearly part of the French legal system, one of a network of provincial and colonial institutions, with ties to the royal court in Versailles and Parisian legal courts and expertise. It was also part of a network of courts in maritime Asia, in Gujarat, Basra, Batavia, Bombay and Pegu, a network that, as Gagan Sood has compellingly argued, lay outside the sovereign purview and was utilized by merchants in the Indian Ocean world to resolve their disputes in the most relevant and convenient forum. Sovereign courts such as those run by the Portuguese, the British, and the French were in fact part of this same legal network, drawing as much on accepted legal practices of maritime Asia as on codes imported from Europe.[23] The fact that Pondichéry's council heard cases involving Christians, Muslims, and Hindus and merchants settled in Madras, Canton, and Siam and that it admitted evidence in an array of languages indicates that it indeed served as such a resource for a regional group of actors who were not subjects of the French king but instead drew on the council as an available tool for the resolution of mostly civil disputes.

The second judicial institution in Pondichéry was the Chaudrie, a court that was in place from the late seventeenth century until its dismantling in 1827. In the Chaudrie, French judges were meant to dispense justice according to local modes of dispute resolution. The French traders who heard the mostly civil disputes in this forum relied on local interpreters to hear the cases and then ruled according to what they understood to be local custom.[24] As Jean-Claude Bonnan has noted, the Chaudrie was neither a French import nor an indigenous institution but rather an amalgamation of the two, with the French taking over authority of an already existing institution, one whose exact contours are unknown. Court records from the Chaudrie prior to 1766 have not survived, making it difficult to determine its practices and jurisdiction in the early decades of the eighteenth century.

In the later French empire in North Africa, it was common practice for Muslim courts of law to be folded into the French colonial state.[25] While this was not quite so common in the so-called First Empire of the seventeenth and eighteenth century, Pondichéry's Chaudrie is not the only example of attempts to incorporate indigenous modes of dispute resolution into a formalized, French judicial institution, though it might be the most explicit instance. Even if other colonies did not have the explicit two-tiered system of French and "local" law as in the Sovereign Council and the Chaudrie, French and indigenous forms of justice did meld together in other colonies. Such judicial "middle ground," as Richard White has termed it, was created in the North American Great Lakes region known as the *pays d'en haut*.[26] In New France, historiography that has considered French and Amerindian exchanges has shown how officials in Montreal also tried to incorporate Indian modes of dispute resolution[27] and has highlighted the "normative flexibility" of these legal exchanges in recognition of the agency of the hundreds of Amerindians that appeared before the Québec courts up to 1760.[28] In maritime Asia it was only with the political transformations of the nineteenth century that European practices and conceptions of law made serious inroads; prior to that period, despite European presence, law continued to develop "along what were essentially indigenous lines."[29] The British example is instructive for South Asia, since it was only in the nineteenth century that the panchayat, or village council, was incorporated into the British colonial legal system.[30]

Since the Chaudrie did not hear Nayiniyappa's case, the "native" court played a marginal though not insignificant role in the Nayiniyappa Affair. Nayiniayppa had spent time as an interpreter in the Chaudrie prior to his appointment to the post of chief commercial broker; this role may have influenced the language and arguments he employed in his appeals. Second, part of Nayiniyappa's punishment was fifty lashes of the *chabouc* (a kind of whip), to be publicly given in the grand bazaar. Given that the Chaudrie was located in the bazaar, the decision to whip Nayiniyappa there emphasized that this punishment had the force of law. Most local inhabitants would have had no occasion to ever visit the chambers of the Sovereign Council, where Nayiniyappa's punishment was decided. But the Chaudrie was a jurisdiction to which they were likely to be subject. By whipping Nayiniyappa in the home of the Chaudrie, the council was sharing—after the fact—the jurisdiction over Nayiniayppa with this companion legal venue and making his punishment more exemplary.

Representation in Peril: Nayiniyappa's Interrogations and the Witness Testimonies

The first part of the judicial process against Nayiniyappa, following his arrest, entailed the collection of witness testimonies against him and the interrogation of the broker himself. Both Nayiniyappa and the several dozen witnesses who provided evidence in the case described this process as rife with procedural error and collectively argued that they had not been allowed to adequately inscribe their voices in the judicial archive.

Following Nayiniyappa's arrest in 1716, Governor Hébert interrogated him on seven different occasions, beginning one month after his arrest. There are two records of these interrogations in the archives: transcripts recorded by the council's secretary and the description of these interrogations reproduced in Nayiniyappa's 1717 appeal.[31] Both accounts are of course highly mediated. The actual exchanges between Nayiniyappa and Hébert were polylingual, in Tamil, Portuguese, and French, while the archival record has all been transposed into French. The text presents the exchanges between Hébert and Nayiniyappa in the form of a dialogue between the two men, suggesting they were the sole actors in the drama that unfolded in the council's chambers, although the interpreter, Manuel, and the secretary taking the notes, Le Roux, were also present and active. The appeals in which Nayiniyappa and others recounted these same interrogations are of course mediated by the intention of the narrator—to contest the charges against the broker. While neither version offers an unassailable account of exactly what transpired in the room, together they provide a view of the ways in which legal forms inflected Nayiniyappa's experience at court.

The transcript recounts lengthy questions on Hébert's part and terse responses on Nayiniyappa's. Hébert's questions were almost uniformly replete with people's names, place names, and information about the movements and actions of local people. Nayiniyappa's response was almost always recorded as a terse "He said yes" or "He said no." Occasionally the transcript recounted that the broker said he knew nothing about a topic. This discursive imbalance in the recorded text of the interrogation raises a question that lingers over all court records and many other sources about their ability to reflect the exchanges they describe. The legal historian Brian Owensby, in his investigation into colonial court records in Mexico, has suggested that the lacunae in colonial court records can be as revealing as the existing text.[32] Even if the inscription does not reflect the actual exchanges, the inscribed format is itself revealing: in Nayiniyappa's interrogation, the archival record lets Hébert do all the talking.

Both records—the official transcription of the interrogations and the description of them in Nayiniyappa's appeal—agree that Nayiniyappa repeatedly denied all charge of wrongdoing. The format of the interrogation allowed him to submit information not solicited from him, and the transcript dutifully recorded this information. For example, he volunteered the information that when the town's residents came to consult with him about their threat of abandoning the town in 1715, he had apprised Governor Dulivier of the threat.[33] In sharing this information, unsolicited, Nayiniyappa used the interrogation as an opportunity to present evidence germane to his defense.

The transcript does reveal Nayiniyappa's efforts to take exception to the implicit assumption of guilt within some of Governor Hébert's questions. For example, the transcript of the sixth interrogation includes the question "Interrogated why had he [Nayiniyappa] abused the authority bestowed on him by his office, and carried out many injustices against the people of Pondichéry?" Here a statement was posed as a question but rhetorically functioned as a performative accusation and declaration of guilt. Nayiniyappa's brief response, as recorded, did not seek to answer the question but disputed its very premise: "He said he did not do so."[34]

The appeals describing Nayiniyappa's interrogation included a running commentary on the questions asked of the broker and expanded on his responses. For example, an account of one of his denials of wrongdoing noted in approval that he "could not have responded any better." In another instance, the appeal's authors complained that no witnesses for wrongdoing were produced but then ironically added, "This is how truth and innocence express themselves."[35] This running commentary on the interrogative text reproduced in the appeals stood in stark contrast to the official record of the investigation, in which Hébert's long questions carried the bulk of the narrative drive, with Nayiniyappa allowed only brief denials or affirmations.

"Language for the Mute, Eyes for the Blind"

Nayiniyappa asked for legal counsel in early 1716, soon after his arrest. As in other colonial locales early in the eighteenth century, lawyers were not allowed to practice in Pondichéry.[36] In Saint-Domingue, for example, lawyers were banned until 1737, a ban resulting from a general view of lawyers as being the source of judicial trickery and legal strife.[37] Even in the French metropole, lawyers were allowed to practice only in civil matters. Nayiniyappa was not asking for a lawyer per se but for a counselor, someone who would provide legal advice as the case was unfolding. This person could have helped in drafting written arguments for submission before the council or just consulted with Nayiniyappa in person outside the council's chambers.[38] If anyone was ever in need of legal counsel, wrote Nayiniyappa's sons, it was their father. The reasons for his need, they argued, were numerous: "He was a foreigner [to the French system], he knew nothing of your laws, the accusations were interspersed with a large number of facts that merited discussion, the accusers were for the most part his enemies, and Sieur Hébert was at the same time a judge and an interested party."[39] An adviser, the sons wrote, would have helped Nayiniyappa navigate this difficult situation.

Nayiniyappa described himself as "a man of this land's countryside" and claimed that he was not familiar with the intricacies of French law.[40] He stated that he did not understand "the language or the law."[41] The problem he identified was not simply a linguistic misunderstanding created by the use of Portuguese but a misunderstanding of code, of the legal jargon and conventions to which he was made subject. In an appeal Nayiniyappa sent to the king after his conviction, he described a legal counselor as a man who could provide "language for the mute, eyes for the blind. This [request for counsel] was again refused, with the same barbarity. [Nayiniyappa] did not know the laws, and asked for someone who knew them."[42] He claimed to have been shocked when this request was denied: "He thought that they could not refuse him counsel, who would know the language, who would instruct him in the formalities of the law, and who could help him prove his innocence."[43] The appeal called Hébert's denial of the request "contrary to all justice." As a matter of law, Nayiniyappa's request was well within his rights, since the Criminal Ordinance of 1670 provided this right to external counsel to the accused.[44] Nevertheless, Nayiniyappa claimed, Governor Hébert, his son and the Christian interpreter Manuel, "all flew into a terrible rage" upon hearing this request.[45] Their response to Nayiniyappa's demand for expert legal advice was a violent one: "The general and his son silenced him, cursed him, spit in his face."[46]

Nayiniyappa argued that by being denied legal counsel, he was robbed of the opportunity to understand and participate in the proceedings. As an intermediary he was likely especially cognizant of one's limited ability to represent oneself without an expert go-between. He suggested that a similar denial of comprehension and representation had taken place during the collection of witness testimony against him, and many of the witnesses appear to have agreed with him. Nayiniyappa's appeals repeatedly assailed the veracity of the witnesses, but he railed even more against the procedural irregularities the testimonies occasioned. The large parade of local witnesses served a central role both in Nayiniyappa's conviction and in his appeals.

Before Nayiniyappa himself was ever questioned, Governor Hébert took witness depositions from twenty-five Indian witnesses, with Manuel acting as interpreter.[47] Given that Nayiniyappa did not admit wrongdoing, these testimonies, attesting to his tyrannical behavior and abuse of the locals under his authority, as well as accusations of financial wrongdoing and his involvement in organizing the local workers' mass exodus of 1715, were crucial to his conviction. Following the witness testimony, according to French legal procedure, the witnesses were brought again before Hébert. Their testimony was read back to them through the services of an interpreter, and they swore to the truth of the testimony, in a process known as *recollement*.[48]

Witnesses who had testified against Nayiniyappa were requestioned two years later, following the Crown's 1718 order to open an investigation into Nayiniyappa's conviction. Many of them claimed that they had signed their depositions without knowing their contents. Nayiniyappa's sons wrote in their appeal that "every single witness stated that his testimony had not been explained or read to him . . . that when someone made some resistance or refused to sign, he was threatened . . . if something was written in their presence, they did not know what it was . . . and when the witnesses or Nanyapa asked that something be read or explained to them, this was refused."[49] Nayiniyappa used the very fact that the group of witnesses against him was large and diverse to make the case that their testimonies could not be trusted. The men who testified against him, he argued, were "insignificant and poor men" and didn't know the facts of the case. He argued that the division of local society into castes meant they didn't even know him. They knew only their own castes and the caste chiefs who gave them their orders.[50] This argument seems far-fetched—all accounts, including Nayiniyappa's own, make it clear that the broker was an important personage in the colony's daily life, and local shopkeepers like the men in question would have known him by reputation if not personally.

The French criminal legal code also required these witnesses to confront Nayiniyappa. This process aimed to allow the accused a chance to defend himself vis-à-vis each accusation, and the witnesses were made to claim ownership of the charge made. This procedure was routinely performed in cases heard before the Sovereign Council and regularly granted to Tamil as well as French defendants. The 1717 appeal's account of one of interrogations records that when the French governor asked Nayiniyappa if he had paid the "mutinous residents" in the worker rebellion that took place in 1715, the broker "loudly denied it, and demanded that witnesses to this fact be brought before him. No witnesses."[51] The only time witnesses were brought before Nayiniyappa, according to his appeals, was during his seventh and last interrogation. But even then they were not allowed to speak to him directly, as the law called for—instead, the appeal alleged, they "spoke very quietly with the judge," thereby keeping secret what should have been shared.[52]

The Judges: Debating Rights and Justice

Conflicts over judgment of the affair reveal that debates over rights and justice were key to the negotiation of authority between French colonists, missionaries, and local go-betweens like Nayiniyappa. Much like Nayiniyappa and the witnesses, the French judges who convicted him later pointed to irregularities in the judicial process and claimed to be victims of irregular procedure.

The judges who decided Nayiniyappa's case were members of the colony's Sovereign Council and therefore were Pondichéry's most senior judicial and administrative officials. They were all later excluded from serving on the 1718 commission that examined Nayiniyappa's conviction.[53] In addition to Hébert, four other councillors served as judges in the Nayiniyappa Affair: Flacourt, Lorme, Legou, and La Morandière, the man responsible for producing Nayiniyappa's later appeal to the king (his role is discussed below). Hébert's son also attended the deliberations, but, with his low rank, he could not technically serve on the council. When these men were questioned in inquests in December 1718 and January 1719, in the course of the reinvestigation of the affair, all four stated that they had favored a much milder punishment for Nayiniyappa than the one carried out.

One of the judges said that when the time came to decide Nayiniyappa's punishment, Hébert told them that the broker was an evil man and took out of his pocket a piece of paper on which the suggested sentence was writ-ten: hanging, strangulation, enslavement of his children, and confiscation of all his goods.[54] When all the other judges objected to this harsh sentence, Hébert pulled out another preinscribed piece of paper, saying, "Gentlemen, since this sentence doesn't suit you, here is another one." This paper detailed a milder sentence of imprisonment, whipping, the payment of amends, and banishment of Nayiniyappa's children from the colony, which all but one of the judges accepted.[55] This sentence would ultimately be carried out. Mul-tiple accounts concur that one judge, Lorme, loudly objected, and his own testimony stated that he acquiesced only after saying, "You gentlemen are apparently of this opinion, but it is not my own."[56] La Prévostière, who acted as the king's attorney (procureur général) in the case, suggested a fine be the only penalty, and all four judges later said they would also have favored a fine as the sole punishment.[57] Hébert's preparation of two alternative sentences suggests he anticipated resistance from the other judges and perhaps used the extreme punishment to make them more inclined to agree to the second one. It remained to the judges to set the fine. Hébert, according to one judge's account, proposed a massive fine of 8,888 gold pagodas without providing any accounts to justify the number.[58]

Before Hébert and the other judges settled on Nayiniyappa's punishment, the Jesuits in town also tried to impact Nayiniyappa's sentencing. The strug-gle between Hébert and his fellow judges and the involvement of the mission-aries in the question of the severity of Nayiniyappa's sentence suggests how violence was measured, debated, and negotiated in the context of colonial officialdom. A petition submitted to the council by the Jesuit missionaries in Pondichéry, Madurai, and the Carnatic mission and penned by the Jesuit supe-rior Father Bouchet eight days before the procureur général made his sentenc-ing suggestion supported and perhaps motivated the severe punishment.[59] The Jesuits argued that Nayiniyappa had caused great harm to their mission and acted as the "Restorer and Protector" of idolatry in the colony.[60] His crimes, in the Jesuits' eyes, were long-standing. They accused Nayiniyappa of previously "conserving the abominable pagoda of Lingam," referring here to the Vedapuri Ishwaran Temple in Pondichéry, which the Jesuits had repeat-edly attempted to shutter or tear down in the first decades of the century. In addition, the Jesuits argued that Nayiniyappa had undermined their efforts to convert Indians and over many years had "rendered useless the work of the missionaries in the backcountry."[61] The letter framed Nayiniyappa's punish-ment as a preemptive and protective measure, not simply a matter of retri-bution: "There is not a single person in Pondichéry who doesn't think that Nainiapa wants to take vengeance on the missionaries, whom he considers the authors of his misfortunes, and he will make every effort to harm the [Christian] religion if he is granted his liberty," Bouchet argued. He also asked that the council keep secret the Jesuits' request to hold Nayiniyappa in prison.[62] Here the Jesuits revealed that they feared Nayiniyappa's wrath and that of his allies, even as he was imprisoned. Without quite admitting their own role in his persecution, they suggested the broker might believe they had aided his enemies. This fear was further acknowledged by their next request: that Nayiniyappa and other gentiles (non-Christians) in town never be told that the Jesuits had made this petition to keep him imprisoned.

Punishing Nayiniyappa became a means of protecting the Jesuits' own safety and position in Pondichéry and beyond. Historians of the colonial world have argued that violence against colonial subjects, such as the punishment that the council inflicted on Nayiniyappa, was an integral part of the rule of law rather than an aberration opposed to it.[63] The Jesuits' petition never to release Nayiniyappa from his prison reveals that the amount of violence meted out was in direct proportion to the importance and position of colonial actors. That is, the powerful required a larger measure of violence so as to balance the ledger of authority.

Precedent would have backed the more moderate punishment all the other judges except Hébert and the king's attorney had in mind. The most serious accusation against Nayiniyappa was sedition, premised on the notion that he had brought about the mass exodus of Indian inhabitants in 1715. Yet when the merchant Nalachetty was convicted in 1704 of having "seduced the inhabitants of this city to go live elsewhere," he paid amends of only twelve pagodas and received a warning that if it happened again, he would be punished more severely.[64] While the greater investment of trust the company had put in Nayiniyappa might have supported a slightly harsher punishment, the difference was extreme. Nayiniyappa's similar alleged crime brought upon him punishment in many orders of magnitude greater: the prison term, public whipping, huge fine, and perpetual banishment from the town.

The severity of this punishment testified to the threat the broker posed. After all, he could simply have been dismissed, even made to leave Pondichéry. Instead, he was stripped of all his wealth and was flogged at the most public locale in the city, the main bazaar. As his brutal public punishment demonstrates, Nayiniyappa's very success as a broker made him a viable threat and thus necessitated his complete destruction. The public aspect of the punishment was a crucial feature of it, at least according to the account provided by Nayiniyappa's sons. When Hébert and his son threatened Nayiniyappa in the course of his interrogation, it was this feature of his humiliation that they highlighted, by taunting him thus: "Where are your supporters now, your patrons who will save you from the whipping we will give you tomorrow, after we bring you in shackles in front of everyone, to the middle of the market?"[65] Of course we cannot know if this exchange took place as the sons reported it, but it was their father's public annihilation that the sons protested. The fact that the whipping took place in the Tamil section of town also meant that the audience witnessing Nayiniyappa's punishment would have been composed of both his peers and his former subordinates, thereby making his humiliation and mortification all the more complete.

In the course of deciding his punishment, the judges had Nayiniyappa brought before them. Hébert briefly questioned the prisoner "on three or four matters," as one of the appeals stated.[66] Before the judges, Nayiniyappa again denied any wrongdoing. On this occasion, the same day on which final judgment was rendered, La Morandière remembered that Nayiniyappa turned away from Hébert to face the silent judges directly, saying, "'Messieurs, I have never stolen from the company, nor done it any harm." The judge recalled that Hébert fils responded, using the familiar second person *tu*: "You are a thief, we know you well."[67]

The judge Flacourt admitted that he signed the severe judgment only because "seeing the others sign, he signed out of fear of causing problems for himself with Hébert."[68] La Morandière and Lorme similarly claimed that they went with the majority in part because they feared retribution. Yet the official text of Nayiniyappa's sentencing revealed none of the judges' debates about the severity of the punishment. Only the subsequent inquest revealed these had occurred.[69] Although the transcript of the interrogations provides no confession by Nayiniyappa, the sentencing document claims that he confessed under questioning.[70]

Like several Tamil witnesses, French members of the Superior Council claimed that Hébert and his allies had intimidated, manipulated, and coerced them, even though these were some of the most powerful and influential men in the colony. One of Nayiniyappa's appeals refers to these claims when it condemns Hébert as a "perverse and bad judge."[71] Hébert's means of compelling the compliance of each of the judges was to address each of them separately, asking for their opinion in a low voice.[72] Two judges said he actually whispered in their ears.[73] While this does not directly explain why they did not speak more loudly in response, it makes clear that Hébert had the power to manipulate the judges, even as they claimed to be united against him. Whisper and conquer. Even in a room shared by French-speaking men, comprehension could be muddied, and a whisper served the same goal as an unfamiliar language. Not knowing that they in fact were in agreement with one another, or so they at least claimed after the fact, the judges were more easily intimidated into complying with Hébert's wishes.

The 1720 appeal by Nayiniyappa's sons emphasized Hébert's manipulation in addition to many other procedural violations, stating that the governor "fooled all the judges, by persuading them that the sentence they had signed was passed by a majority."[74] Further, Hébert had "abused the credulity of the judges . . . and made them sign a judgment contrary to their opinion," thereby positioning them as victims as much as Nayiniyappa.[75] The appeal absolved the judges and Nayiniyappa alike and positioned Hébert as the true culprit.

In fact, most of the other judges and the *procureur général* had preexisting conflicts with Hébert, explaining perhaps why they so quickly turned against him once an inquiry into the Nayiniyappa Affair began. In 1711 Hébert had ordered the removal of Flacourt from his position as chief of the French outpost in Bengal. On the very same day he described La Prévostière, who was *procureur général* during the affair, as one who "reveals the secrets of the Company and has risen up against his superior, by spreading various calumnies about him in all the homes in Pondichéry."[76] Hébert would later claim that La Prévostière had maligned him during the affair because of this enmity and claimed, "Everyone in Pondichéry knows that [La Prévostière] is my sworn enemy."[77]

Factionalism at Court: Nayiniyappa's French Advocates and Adversaries

The decision to convict Nayiniyappa gave rise to a struggle over this conviction between various factions in the colony's commercial and religious institutions. As the battle lines were drawn for and against him, the affair became the ground for missionaries and traders with incommensurable interests to articulate their view about the direction in which the colony should head. This conflict was expressed either in the appeals that agitated for Nayiniyappa's exoneration on the one hand or in letters that reiterated his guilt on the other.

Company Traders as Legal Advocates

While Nayiniyappa was not allowed to consult with anyone during his interrogation, multiple Frenchmen assisted him in the writing and distribution of his appeals after his conviction. None were trained legal professionals, but they were powerful traders employed by the company. Nayiniyappa's first appeal, dated 1716 and translated into French from Portuguese, gave only a few details of the interrogations. Father Tessier, the MEP missionary in Pondichéry, may have assisted Nayiniyappa in the translation from Portuguese. The missionary's letter dated August 1716 complained about Nayiniyappa's treatment by the Héberts and noted that "M. de Sault [a Parisian agent who assisted in the distribution of Nayiniyappa's appeal] has all the necessary documents in hand"; it suggests at least that Tessier actively supported the broker.[78]

It was Nayiniyappa's subsequent appeals that most benefited from the help of French company employees. His most important French ally was a French trader named Nicolas François Le Noutre de La Morandière. He was one of the judges who convicted Nayiniyappa and subsequently was a coauthor of several of the appeals submitted in the affair, by both Nayiniyappa and his partners Tiruvangadan and Ramanada. La Morandière's position surely gave him a privileged view into the proceedings that had led to the conviction and therefore helped him collaborate on the text of the appeals. La Morandière did not initially acknowledge the collaboration, but in a letter Hébert sent to the directors in Paris on January 14, 1719, he blamed La Morandière for his involvement, and La Morandière himself acknowledged it in a letter written just ten days later to the directors.[79]

La Morandière wrote that he had immersed himself in the task of submitting appeals and requests on behalf of Indians who had been harmed by Governor Hébert. "For almost five months," he wrote, "I had to devote myself to the Indians' affairs, always busy with writing requests for people who had been crushed by M. Hébert and were asking for recompense from [the Compagnie des Indes]."[80] He explained that he was driven to act on behalf of the oppressed Indians because of the Héberts' "tyrannical oppressions" and "insatiable avarice" and the extent to which their wrongdoing was harmful to the rule of the French company. Writing the appeals, he added, was a way to shed light on the true culprit—Hébert—thereby protecting the interests of the company, which would otherwise be held responsible. As a result of his efforts as the author of these appeals, he argued, "the Indians received justice and remain here content, calm is reestablished in the city, and all is returned to the same order which always reigned under previous governments."[81] La Morandière's description of a previous calm and order was clearly revisionist—Pondichéry had been in a state of one kind of political turmoil or another since the French returned to it in 1699. Yet in his account, the dispensation of justice to local inhabitants in the Nayiniyappa Affair was a means to return to a lost utopia of accepted French rule, even if such utopia was always a mirage.

La Morandière had served as company bookkeeper at the rank of *sous-marchand*, but just on the cusp of the Nayiniyappa affair, the Superior Council accepted his request for a promotion to the rank of merchant and appointed him a councillor. It was in this role that he would serve as a judge in Nayiniyappa's case—signing on to a verdict he would later renounce. But this promotion was short-lived. In the margin of the very same decree that recounted the swearing in of La Morandière to the council, the following undated comment appeared, describing the reversal of the appointment: "Since the reception [into the council] of the said La Morandière, his conduct has appeared so opposed to the interests of the company . . . and we have received several complaints. We have removed the said La Morandière from the position of merchant and councillor, and in addition have barred him from taking on any other role."[82] Hébert likely penned the comment, as he signed the decree. The removal it describes took place on September 15, 1716, while Nayiniyappa was in the process of appealing his conviction. The conduct "so opposed to the interests of the company" was almost certainly La Morandière's support of Nayiniyappa.

In two letters sent to Paris, penned in January 1719, La Morandière's described the principles that guided him in writing complaints on behalf of Nayiniyappa and his family and associates, revealing in the process his sophisticated understanding of the law.[83] He understood his role in the appeals as providing proper legal representation previously denied. He stated that he "conformed to the styles of advocates who composed requests in France to present before the king," mindful of the consequences and the importance of the truth. He also critiqued earlier versions of the appeals, arguing that they had "been composed based on a badly done translation of manifestos in Portuguese that the Indians had sent to France."[84] In an appeal sent by the sons, with La Morandière's help, in 1718, they described the earlier texts submitted by Nayiniyappa as sorely lacking because of the circumstances of their composition. Those appeals had been "composed while he was ill, and in haste in his prison cell."[85]

Far from renouncing his role in rendering the judgment against Nayiniyappa, La Morandière highlighted his involvement in the affair and his qualifications as someone who knew the events the appeal described in greater depth than any other advocate might. Taking on the role of improving the overly simple appeals first filed against Hébert, explained La Morandière, was a matter of both justice and duty.[86] He wrote that his rewriting of the appeals entailed a significant transformation of the texts, since the first appeal Nayiniyappa submitted in 1716 to the Compagnie des Indes and the king "did not express more than a tenth of the things" relevant to his case.[87]

La Morandière described how he had revised the initial appeal presented by Tiruvangadan, Nayiniyappa's business associate and relative, who was also arrested. Tiruvangadan's first appeal, written without La Morandière's help, simply mentioned that Hébert the younger owed Tiruvangadan 1,022 pagodas, the local gold coin. "But my [text] added a fact," explained La Morandière, "which this Malabar and almost all of Pondichéry did not know." This added fact was the claim that Hébert père had approached the Jesuit Father Turpin and secretly conspired with him to arrest Tiruvangadan for being a bad Christian who had assisted in a "procession of a demon and adoration of idols." This was done, explained La Morandière, to cover up the fact that Hébert the younger owed Tiruvangadan money and disregarded the fact that the Indian was not, and never had been, a Christian.[88] La Morandière found a record of these secret exchanges between the Jesuit and Governor Hébert by going through the records of the council's proceedings, exploiting his privileged access to company records. The Indian claimants would never have had knowledge of these alleged machinations to blacken Tiruvangadan's reputation, since the contrived charge against him was never actually brought forward.[89]

La Morandière also claimed to have strengthened the legal appeal of Ramanada, Nayiniyappa's business associate who was arrested alongside him. Ramanada's first appeal, explained La Morandière, had ascribed all the blame for his arrest to the Jesuits. It argued that the Fathers of the Society were angry because Ramanada served as an informant on local religious practice to the Jesuits rival, the MEP missionary Father Tessier. The information provided by Ramanada was in turn used in the course of the ongoing Malabar Rites controversy, a struggle between Jesuits in the East and the church hierarchy in Rome, regarding the Jesuit practice of accommodating local cultural practices among their converts. The Jesuits' local missionary rivals, the Capuchins and the representative of the MEP, opposed the use of the Malabar Rites, claiming that such accommodation diluted Christianity and made for bad converts. In the context of the Nayiniyappa Affair, the Malabar Rites controversy underlay much of the hostility between the Jesuits and other missionary groups in the Tamil region.[90]

But it was a mistake, suggested La Morandière, to situate Ramanada's arrest only in the context of his involvement in the Malabar Rites controversy, as an informant for the MEP missionary. Instead, La Morandière's text offered a fuller account of the agendas driving Ramanada's persecution. He argued that Hébert exhibited a "veritable passion" against Ramanada, which originated with Ramanada and Nayiniyappa's involvement in bringing an end to a scheme to raise taxes that would have been extremely profitable to Hébert. This fact, wrote La Morandière, reflected badly on Hébert. Since he was seeking vengeance, his actions against the Indians were a "real crime."[91] La

Morandière's change to the appeal, which added all this background information, transformed it from a matter of religious squabbling between two Catholic missionary groups to an issue of political and commercial malfeasance.

While Nayiniyappa, Tiruvangadan, and Ramanada had ongoing professional and commercial relations with the French, they could not match La Morandière's insider status and his access to the official and sometimes secret record of the colonial government's doings. Because of this access, his legal appeals were more densely evidentiary than anything they could have presented themselves. For example, the 1717 appeal he coauthored incorporated the record of the seven interrogations of Nayiniyappa and used it to make the case that the interrogators had coerced and intimidated Nayiniyappa.

Acting as an advocate for the Indians involved in the Nayiniyappa Affair put La Morandière in a very awkward position, as he himself acknowledged, since he had to "lift his pen against many men about whom it was not my place to complain."[92] While he could count Hébert an enemy, complaining about him implicated the directors in Paris, who had appointed Hébert, and this was politically dangerous. The trader noted "that the requests of an advocate are not orders [arrêts], and these requests are not always granted to the parties for whom he pleads." He wrote that it was difficult but necessary to his sense of justice to write "against people whom one venerates, and whom it is a pleasure to serve"—that is, the directors.[93]

La Morandière's advocacy was wide-ranging and was likely driven in some measure by his conflicts with Governor Hébert and a desire to see a change in the colony's leadership. In addition to his appeals on behalf of Nayiniyappa, Tiruvangadan, and Ramanada, he was responsible for crafting some on behalf of a scribe imprisoned for refusing to provide false testimony against Nayiniyappa, a merchant wrongly treated by the council, and a local Christian who had been mistreated by the Jesuits, all of whom he claimed were victims unfairly swept up in the Nayiniyappa Affair.[94]

La Morandière was not the only Frenchman who took an active role in advocating for the Indians. Shortly after Nayiniyappa's conviction in May of 1716, the French trader Cuperly also wrote impassioned letters to France on Nayiniyappa's behalf.[95] Cuperly was a member of Pondichéry's French elite, as the nephew through marriage of the colony's venerated first governor, François Martin. Like many of Nayiniyappa's advocates, Cuperly centered his complaints around procedural issues, claiming Hébert had taken on too many different positions in the course of the affair. Referring to Manuel's connections with the Jesuits—"the son of the Jesuits' catechist, Naniyapa's cruelest enemy"—he claimed that the translator had interpreted according to his intentions and not according to justice.[96] He likewise argued that Hébert had suborned the witnesses, who were exacting retribution for past wrongs, and he decried the council's failure to allow Nayiniyappa to face his accusers. Ironically he described the prosecution as "this beautiful procedure."[97] The final French trader who might have participated in the preparation of the appeals was Hébert's rival, Dulivier, the man who preceded him as governor and was displaced by Hébert's return to India. Hébert accused him of agitating on the convicted Indians' behalf.[98] Indeed, Dulivier sent the Marine Council a lengthy complaint about Hébert's misdeeds and mistreatment of Nayiniyappa, Tiruvangadan, and Ramanada.[99]

Missionaries and the Law

Missionaries in Pondichéry also used the legal arena to act out their rivalries and conflicts, both with the French colonial state and with one another. After all, as Dale Van Kley has noted of the Old Regime, "religious matters are only metaphysically distinguishable from constitutional and jurisdictional ones during this entire period."[100] Several French missionaries in India joined the appeal effort in the Nayiniyappa Affair. Even as the Jesuits were writing petitions asking that Nayiniyappa be severely punished, the head of the Missions étrangères mission in Pondichéry was writing letters to France vigorously defending him. Nayiniyappa's fate became a new battleground in the ongoing strife and power struggle between the Jesuits and the other missionaries in town. Father Tessier, who headed the MEP outpost in Pondichéry, wrote to his superiors in Paris the summer after Nayiniyappa's conviction. In his first letter, he described Hébert and his son as being "the instruments of the Jesuits' vengeance."[101] He argued that the persecution of Nayiniyappa was to be abhorred not only because of the price paid by the man itself but because a reputation for injustice harmed the colony as a whole: "Pondichéry has truly come to be viewed with horror by all the nations, and no one wants to come here," he warned. Any appeal to the Héberts for justice would be pointless, he wrote, since "nothing restrains them, neither justice, nor conscience, nor honor, nor religion."[102]

The judicial record shows that missionaries regularly and actively participated in the colony's legal arena. Not only did they make regular appearances before Pondichéry's court, they also made an effort to shape and direct legal proceedings. In some cases this reflected an interest in local law: Father Bouchet, who was the Jesuit superior in Pondichéry at the time of the Nayiniyappa Affair, had himself authored a text on local practices of dispute resolution in 1714.[103] In the course of the Nayiniyappa Affair, the Jesuits attempted to shape legal proceeding more directly, although they tried to conceal their interference. That they played a role in the collection of witness testimonies (as chapter 2 explained) and in the sentencing of Nayiniyappa—a process in which they had no official capacity whatsoever—demonstrates the extent to which they were embedded in the processes of colonial rule and judicial action.

The French missionaries in India held a complicated position with respect to judicial authority. French missionaries in Pondichéry fell under the ecclesiastic authority of the bishop of Mylapore, who was appointed by and acted under the auspices of the Portuguese *Padroado* in India.[104] Yet the French Jesuits arrived in the East as emissaries of the French king and therefore acted by his authority, not that of the *Padroado*, and the Pondichéry Superior Council had judicial authority over them in secular matters. Both Capuchin missionaries and the MEP *procurateur* also fell under the authority of the French king in his role as the head of the Gallican Church. Pope Gregory XV had also tried to exert authority over missionaries abroad when in 1622 he created the Sacred Congregation for the Propagation of the Faith (Propaganda Fide), which sought to centralize the oversight of missionary work. French missionaries in South India thus occupied a special position and had to maneuver between rival lay and religious institutions invested in their mission. Disagreements among missionaries about strategies of conversion in the colonial mission field only rendered this politically fraught negotiation more complex.

While during the Nayiniyappa Affair the Jesuits took on a prosecutorial role, a much more common involvement for missionaries of all orders in French India occurred when they appeared before the Superior Council as claimants or defendants. Missionaries came before the Superior Council for various reasons, usually involving property or financial disputes of the kind brought before the council by many of the colony's residents. Occasionally missionaries' appearances in the judicial records were more clearly a result of their religious position and were evidence of rupture or discord, as in the repeated discussion of the struggle over the Malabar Rites controversy, which largely played out in the religious arena with papal bulls and missionary missives but occasionally came before the secular court of Pondichéry.[105] The involvement of the council in this struggle between the Capuchins and the Jesuits about the incorporation of local cultural practices into the lives of Christian converts also suggests the intermingling of the political, religious, and legal domains in the colony.

This intermingling had lately brought the council into conflict with the Vatican. As part of the Vatican's attempts to settle the Malabar and Chinese Rites Controversy, a papal legate, Thomas Maillard de Tournon, patriarch of Antioch, was sent to the East. Pondichéry was his first port of call. The council warned that before making any pronouncements that might be "prejudicial to the laws of His Majesty or his subjects," Tournon must present them to the council of Pondichéry and the *procureur général* for authorization and modification "for the benefit of the public and the maintenance of the state's laws and practices."[106] Tournon's failure to comply with this order when he published in 1704 a declaration against the practice of accommodation led the council to declare that apostolic visitors seeking entry to French India and the Indian Ocean island colonies must have the express permission of the French king. They also renewed their demand to review any decisions and pronouncements such papal visitors might make.[107] Such conflicts between papal authority and the French Crown had, of course, a long metropolitan history, culminating in the creation of the Gallican Church headed by the French king in 1682. The council's already tenuous hold on authority in the colonial context only sharpened these struggles. Given the Compagnie des Indes's repeated difficulties in asserting its sovereignty over non-Christian subjects, who threatened to pick up and leave whenever their religious liberties were compromised, the council perceived the dicta to abandon the Malabar rites and the disregard of council directives as a threat to the colony's viability.

On occasion, the Catholic missionaries themselves brought their doctrinal conflicts into the chambers of the Superior Council for resolution—or at least an airing out. In February 1712, four years before Nayiniyappa's arrest, the Jesuit superior Father Bouchet approached the council with a grievance about declarations that Capuchins and their supporters in India had made. His grievance hinged on the issue of legal jurisdiction. A Capuchin missionary had accused one of the Jesuits of an infraction against the papal ban on the Malabar Rites. The Capuchin brought the complaint before a religious tribunal headed by the bishop of San Thomé. The Capuchin had bolstered his case with the testimony of multiple Indians "before the secular judges of this city"—that is, the Superior Council.[108] The borders between religious and secular jurisdiction were porous.

Father Bouchet claimed that the Indian's testimony against the Jesuits was false. He demanded the court bring before the court one of the false witnesses: "Ramanaden, Malabar of this city and agent of the premier courtier of the Royal Company."[109] This was the very same Ramanada who was Nayiniyappa's close business associate and later was arrested alongside Nayiniyappa. Bouchet blamed Nayiniyappa for Ramanada's damaging testimony against the Jesuits. He claimed that "the ascendance in this town of this first courtier of the company, who through his office is the head of the Malabars," made him all too powerful. Bouchet argued that accusing the Jesuits of wrongdoing harmed the neophyte Christians in the colony more broadly and that the council must protect them from such injustice.[110] The council decreed that Bouchet and the other Jesuits should present all the documents and accusations they wished to press against Ramanada and his associates—again, a reference to Nayiniyappa.[111] Several years before Nayiniyappa was arrested, then, he and the Jesuits were already in conflict before the colony's court.

Another incident just prior to Nayiniyappa's arrest likewise demonstrated the missionaries' consciousness of the council's authority over their reputation. When the Superior Council convened on November 4, 1715, it discussed a request by the Capuchin missionaries in the town for certificates of good behavior—documents attesting to the fact that they had "never caused nor created any scandal during the time that they had served the chapel of this fort and as missionaries under the auspices of the company."[112] The Capuchins, in explaining the need for this certificate, cited various "calumnies" brought in France against them. While they did not specifically name the Jesuits, the ongoing enmity between the two orders in French India meant they were most likely the unnamed defamers. The council considered the request and acquiesced by providing a document declaring that the Capuchins had "never caused any scandal or provided a bad example" and that on the contrary, they had always led exemplary and pious lives.[113]

The Jesuits also had some experience appearing as defendants before the Pondichéry court prior to the Nayiniyappa Affair. In 1707, the *procureur général* filed suit against the Jesuits, in a land dispute between the company and the missionaries.[114] A lengthy exchange between the superior of the Jesuits, Father Tachard, and the *procureur général* ensued, with decrees and responses flying back and forth.[115] The council ordered that trees the Jesuits had planted—a mark of property ownership—be razed to the ground.[116] Clearly, this was an acrimonious legal encounter. On occasion the Jesuits also appeared before the council in a powerful position, as in the 1720 discussion of the loans the missionaries had extended to the perpetually cash-strapped company.[117] Overall, the judicial records of the first few decades of the eighteenth century reveal that missionaries both drew on the council for legal support and were at times willing subjects of its jurisdiction. During the Nayiniyappa Affair, the Jesuits' explicit intervention in matters of law was an attempt to insert themselves into the highest reaches of the colony's governance.

Following a lengthy and detailed investigation, in the course of which officials in both India and France considered and debated Nayiniyappa's multiple appeals, the council overturned his conviction in Pondichéry on January 20, 1719.[118] Nayiniyappa had by that point been dead for two years. The presiding *procureur général*, Pierre Dumas, signed the decision, which referenced multiple inquiries and inquests into the original interrogations and conviction. Dumas stated, "I conclude that the case made against Nayiniyappa by sieur Hébert is declared void, as is the judgment that was the outcome of this case." The decision called for the restitution of all profits from the sale of Nayiniyappa's goods to his heirs, the exact details of which were to be determined in France by the king's council.[119]

News that Nayiniyappa's name had been cleared spread quickly in the Tamil region. A letter written shortly thereafter by Nayiniyappa's advocate La Morandière to the directors in Paris described a town in a celebratory mood:

> The government had scarcely been in the hands of M. La Prévostière when a large number of Indians who had left for Moorish lands in order to put themselves out of reach of the violence of M. Hébert, returned to Pondichéry. They already knew of the order it had pleased his Majesty to give in favor of Nainappa, Tiruvangadan, and Ramanada, and they assumed, with reason, that his Majesty's justice would similarly be offered to them as to the three Indians who had the happy experience of bringing their complaints before his Majesty's tribunal.[120]

Indeed, the governor who replaced Hébert, La Prévostière, warmly received the returning residents. French officials even entertained the idea of some jubilant fanfare—a ceremony, a shooting of the cannons, perhaps making the king's order known to the sound of trumpets—but Governor La Prévostière judged that such celebrations would alienate Frenchmen who had served alongside Hébert, many of whom were still filling important roles in the colony.[121] In the end, after all the battles, the hundreds of pages of testimonies, appeals and deliberations, and much unlike the very public punishment Nayiniyappa had endured, his exoneration was a quiet affair.

The Nayiniyappa Affair unfurled almost entirely in one legal forum, French India's highest court, and was then appealed through the proper metropolitan channels. The broker and his allies immersed themselves in the legal system, with its metropolitan contours, and in so doing successfully adapted, adopted, and co-opted that very system. The forums were not multiple, but the legal strategies were quite varied: appeals in India and in France, formal appeals by the convicted men (Nayiniyappa, Tiruvangadan, and Ramanada), informal letters of support by both traders and missionaries, and evidentiary documents sent across the seas. Yet as Nayiniyappa and his allies engaged the legal system, in their success was enfolded an implicit critique of French colonial implementation of the legal system.

If Nayiniyappa's interrogation and conviction reflected the legal nature of imperial authority, his and his supporters' ultimately successful appeals demonstrate that the colonial state was porous, open to manipulation, and had multiple and sometimes contradictory nodes of decision making. Colonial legal institutions were, to a great extent, recently congealed resources and practices rather than established institutions. Both French and Tamil actors performed power and authority through arguments about proper procedure. Claims of ignorance and lack of knowledge, as much as those of knowledge and experience, could form the basis for these performances, as both Nayiniyappa and his judges demonstrated. At a time of instability in a young colony, where friction about which kinds of order, authority, and morality were going to prevail, various actors made claims for proper procedure in an attempt to determine what such order would actually entail. Both sides won, and both sides lost, with the tools and procedures of the judicial arena. Ultimately, though, the decision was made not in terms of the law. The verdict was overturned because the law allowed the economic and political interests at play to be expressed.

An account of the legal aspects of the Nayiniyappa Affair reveals that colonial subjects demanded legal cohesion from their position in the colonies, thereby revealing the tensions of imperial rule. Law in French India provided indigenous and European actors alike an opportunity to participate in a global endeavor on which local agendas bestowed meaning. Colonial subjects like Nayiniyappa could simultaneously expose the lack of cohesion in the French legal system and make a claim for equality under the same law. The affair's evolution exemplifies the heterogeneity and friction of the moment of legal encounter in overseas France.

The Nayiniyappa Affair reminds us that even though judicial institutions were an arm of the colonial state, we should not assume that the decisions made in these institutions always and inevitably favored the agenda of that state, since indigenous actors were able "to utilize the judiciary to achieve their own ends," as Niels Brimnes has argued.[122] The legal aspects of the Nayiniyappa Affair also show the extent to which missionaries in Pondichéry were involved at every level of decision making in the colony, even in arenas, like the judicial one, in which they ostensibly had no role. The Jesuits, who pushed for Nayiniyappa's arrest and subsequent punishment, and the MEP missionaries who advocated for his rehabilitation all moved with ease in the legal realm.

In his account of France of the Old Regime, Alexis de Tocqueville noted, "The practice of the law courts had entered in many ways into the pattern of French life. Thus the courts were largely responsible for the notion that every matter of public or private interest was subject to debate and every decision could be appealed from; as also for the opinion that such affairs should be conducted in public and certain formalities observed."[123] The Nayiniyappa Affair shows the extent to which France's colonies were equally entangled in a legal regime that, while capable of being used for personal or institutional gain and manipulated by individual actors through intimidation and persuasion, was also open to appeal.

PART THREE

The Afterlives of the Affair

CHAPTER 5

Between Paris and Pondichéry

Nayiniyappa was already dead when his eldest son, Guruvappa, made his way from India to Paris in an attempt to reclaim his father's reputation and riches. Guruvappa was tremendously successful in the metropolitan capital: he was baptized as a Christian in the chapel of the royal family, powerful royals served as his godparents (or so at least ran the family lore), he became a knight of a French noble order, and his family's fortune was restored. When he returned to India, he took his father's place as Pondichéry's chief commercial broker and *chef des malabars*, displacing his father's rival, Kanakarâya Pedro Mudali. But Guruvappa's triumphant trip to Paris is but one example of an intermediary on the move among many in Pondichéry at the time of the Nayiniyappa Affair.

In Pondichéry, Tamil men employed by French traders and missionaries as professional go-betweens traveled in India, across the Indian Ocean, and between India and France. This chapter examines both the mobility of local intermediaries and French reliance on this mobility. It advances two related arguments, the first concerning go-betweens' mobility and the second concerning French responses to this mobility. First, the concomitant presence of mobility and stability in the lives of colonial intermediaries helps explain the extensive role these men filled in Pondichéry's development in the first decades of the eighteenth century. The journeys undertaken by several of Pondichéry's commercial and religious intermediaries reveal that these

Indian employees had the contacts, experience, and ability to act as avatars for their French employers in far-flung locations. They used their portable connections and skills while also deploying travel to improve their own social position. That is, somewhat paradoxically, their stability and relative enmeshment in long-standing social structures enabled them to move with relative freedom between ports, markets, and associations. In the lives of intermediaries, mobility and stability were mutually constitutive. Being known—as a neighbor, relative, creditor, coreligionist—opened up pathways of travel, making go-betweens accepted visitors. At the same time, the benefits accrued from traveling on behalf of French employers bolstered the position of go-betweens in their communities of origin. Movement not only was a physical practice in space but could also contribute to movement of a different kind, up the social scale.

The Nayiniyappa Affair again supplies a prism, here shedding light on the mobility of intermediaries in the context of empire. This is demonstrated by the travels of two intermediaries, both intimately connected with the affair, from Pondichéry to Paris. The first is Guruvappa, who became a professional intermediary as a result of his travels; the second is Manuel Geganis, son of the Jesuits' catechist (religious intermediary) and the central interpreter in Nayiniyappa's investigation. Their travels illuminate the broad geographical breadth of the Nayiniappa Affair as a local scandal with global dimensions. Long-established roots in the Tamil region made both men's travels possible. While Nayiniyappa had been stripped of his riches and died in prison, the family's position within a broad network of well-off merchants most likely enabled and funded Guruvappa's travel, and connections with the MEP missionaries in Pondichéry secured him an introduction in Paris. He returned to India with a French name, clothes, and confession but still with the habits of a local (more on that below) and was quickly reincorporated into the local landscape. Much the same holds true for Manuel, who traveled to Paris because he was part of a local clan that was well connected with the Jesuits, and his ties of kinship served as the basis for his travels. Once he was back in India, his journey to the metropole enabled him to serve a crucial role in the Nayiniyappa Affair as its chief interpreter.

The second argument advanced here stems from an examination of French approaches and reactions to intermediaries' capacity for mobility. The tense divisions between French commercial and missionary projects played out in yet another field. French traders traveled from port to port across the Indian Ocean, buying and selling as they went, and ventured inland to fill their ships' holds with goods before returning to France to sell them. As Europeans, they lacked reputation, credit, and history in the trading associations of the Indian

Ocean. Without local commercial brokers they could not act effectively in new markets. Missionaries also needed to travel from the moderately Christianized coast to the "pagan" hinterland, where souls were not quite waiting to be harvested. They viewed this as a spiritual journey as well as a physical one, traversing an arduous physical path just as they asked that their converts undertake an epistemological shift from one set of practices and beliefs to another. They relied on catechists, or religious interpreters, to negotiate this unknown physical and spiritual terrain.

Traders and missionaries both employed Indian intermediaries to act on their behalf, going where they were not known or welcome, and so moved their agendas while staying in place. But traders and Jesuit missionaries reacted very differently to the constraints and dependence they both faced. French traders and officials of the Compagnie des Indes showed considerably less resentment over this dependence than did the Jesuits. French traders were, by and large, willing to accept their dependence on intermediaries, which aligned with their general preference for sustaining the trading networks along which merchandise profitably flowed. French Jesuits, on the other hand, while they were reliant on their catechists to act on their behalf in towns and villages where European missionaries were not welcome, were often resentful of this dependence. The forcefulness with which the Jesuits interfered with company business when they encouraged Governor Hébert to arrest Nayiniyappa suggests this resentment; they also had ongoing conflicts with their own catechists.

Journeys and itineraries by intermediaries cemented and complicated the connections and relationships between the various outposts of empire, rendering meaningful the initial voyage that created a colony. Mobility and stability, coming together in the personal histories of Pondichéry's intermediaries, allowed go-betweens to participate in the creation of a relationship between India and France. In the course of such voyages they wove together the French empire, creating a world where Paris and Pondichéry productively jostled one against the other.

A colony begins with a journey, made by settlers. Colonial histories have often focused on the mobility of colonial settlers while paying less attention to the travels of other agents in the colony.[1] In this, historians have followed the lead of European colonial actors, who presented themselves to their supporters at home as emphatically mobile, although their position in the colonies as suspicious strangers severely circumscribed this mobility. Traders and missionaries in French India shared the predicament of this duality, and they consequently looked to local intermediaries for aid. Go-betweens addressed this problem without entirely resolving it.

Over the past several decades, scholars of both premodern India and Old Regime France have overturned perceptions of these societies as static realms, with a peasantry strictly bonded to a geographically restricted existence. The opportunities of early modern Europeans and South Asians alike to travel outside their natal communities have garnered increasing attention.[2] One study has suggested that the category of "circulation" might adequately capture the vibrant exchange of goods, people, and ideas in the Indian Ocean.[3] The crucial link between mobility and imperial settings and horizons has been trenchantly highlighted, yet with an emphasis on the "high" imperialism of the nineteenth century.[4]

At the same time that men and women in France were enjoying increasing opportunities for a mobile existence, the French actors who might have seemed to embody the epitome of mobility—those who traveled across the seas in pursuit of commercial and religious agendas—were in fact coming to terms with the limits of and strictures on their own mobility. As the next section will demonstrate, colonial administrators and missionaries had a well-articulated vision of French projects as cosmopolitan and of transregional and global reach. But this vision was undermined by Frenchmen's limited ability to make room for themselves in these locales.

As Stephen Greenblatt has pointed out, the cultural mobility of ideas, practices, and metaphors relies on the literal, physical aspect of mobility—bodies moving in space.[5] The contradiction between French ambition and limited French physical mobility led colonists pursuing both commercial and religious agendas to rely heavily on the physical transportability of the go-betweens who could travel on their behalf. But ultimately the contradiction that French employers faced, between mobile ambition and hampered movement, made the mobility of their intermediaries a fraught issue.

Pondichéry and Its Settings

Connections across the region and the Indian Ocean more broadly were central for Pondichéry's development. The colony was the administrative, commercial, and judicial center not only of the French holdings in India but also of the French Indian Ocean. A key component of French imperial strategy in the Indian Ocean was the founding of French colonies in Île Bourbon (present-day Réunion, first claimed by the French in 1642) and Île de France (present-day Mauritius, a French colony beginning in 1715).[6] An unidentified French writer noted early in the eighteenth century, "Commerce in the Indies, by its nature as well as the current state of affairs, is connected to the operations of government, and the administration of our colonies and our factories in the eastern seas is connected to the commerce of the Indies. In order to guarantee this commerce we must have a fulcrum in this region." The writer argued that French administrators must consider Île de France in the context of the Indian Ocean. "As long as we possess this important island, the door of the Indies will be open to us; if we lose this island, the door of the Indies will close forever."[7] Pondichéry's success or failure was irrevocably tied up with the state of other French interests in this maritime region.

The French desire for continuous presence and influence across the Indian Ocean region was often thwarted. Where French officials imagined a spectrum of similarity, made coherent and cohesive by virtue of French governance, the reality of Indian Ocean dissimilarities provided an unwelcome reminder of the fragility of this imperial imaginary. Displaying their ignorance of the complexities of local affiliations, the Parisian directors requested in 1719 that "a dozen young Christian Malabar girls, capable of spinning cotton" be sent to the company's colony in Île Bourbon. The Pondichéry council had to explain that complying with the company's request would undoubtedly lead to violence and dire consequences.[8]

Opportunities for French expansion, commercial or religious, were not limited to locales where Frenchmen had already achieved some semblance of sovereignty, such as the Indian Ocean island colonies or the French *comptoirs* in India. French officials viewed the British-ruled city of Madras, Pondichéry's largest neighbor, as an important hunting ground for such opportunities. Linguistic and historiographical specialization has led scholars to divide the study of Portuguese, Dutch, British, and French projects in India into separate realms of analysis and in turn to keep those separate from Indian regional history. In the case of Pondichéry and Madras, most scholars have studied the cities separately or imagined them as pawns in the global struggle between France and England. A regional context reveals that the history of Madras and Pondichéry's relationship depended as much on the two cities' proximity as on their strategic value in a global tussle. Pondichéry and Madras were woven together in ways that circumvented the divisions imposed by European rivalries, a fact both European and Indian agents recognized and made use of early in the eighteenth century.

Parisian directors and trader-officials in Pondichéry alike sought to recruit Madras's wealthy and well-credited merchant class. The Pondichéry council declared that "there is only one solution" to the problem of supplying merchandise to French ships, "which is to employ every possible means to convince the merchants of Madras, powerful and accredited, to come and settle in Pondichéry."[9] Local employees had familial and commercial connections in both cities, and Nayiniyappa and his extended family allowed the council to tap into this resource. Nayiniyappa himself had relocated from Madras to Pondichéry as a young man, and once established there, at the urging of Governor Hébert, convinced his brother-in-law Tiruvangadan, a wealthy merchant in the city, to join him in Pondichéry.[10] Tiruvangadan and Nayiniyappa then lured a network of their associates to the French colony.

A memoir written by Tiruvangandan's descendant late in the eighteenth century recounted how these new arrivals from Madras used their connections to populate the French colony with their acquaintances. "[Tiruvangadan and Nayiniyappa] wrote to their correspondents in the towns and villages of this province, who sent merchants, weavers, cloth painters and workers of all kinds of métiers and professions, and thus the colony took on a certain luster," recounted the memoir. "They began to produce and paint fabrics here, and commerce opened up, by both sea and land." Prior to these efforts, the writer claimed, Pondichéry was little more than a village, peopled only by petty shopkeepers and farmers, lacking a proper commercial class.[11] The connections of men like Nayiniyappa across the region, rather than conditions created by the French, were most crucial for the creation of such a class.

Tiruvangadan's network of associates in Madras was precisely what made him an attractive recruit for the French. Prior to the explosion of the Nayiniyappa Affair, colonial officials explicitly asked him to arrange for the shipment of merchandise from various ports by deploying his friends to do so. Tiruvangadan mentioned that brokers relied on the ties of friendship more than once in a document he submitted in the course of the Nayiniyappa Affair when he recounted his connections with the French company. As he noted, "In order to succeed [in the job given to him by the company] I invested my capital and that of my friends."[12] French newcomers had much more difficulty forging such friendships.

In 1716, Governor Hébert claimed that Tiruvangadan was in possession of funds embezzled by Nayiniyappa and arrested him. Tiruvangadan wrote an appeal that began by laying claim to his well-established position in Madras as the anchor of his respectability: "I, being a merchant of this town of Madraspatan, land of the English, where I lived with my business dealings, my reputation and the credit of my person."[13] Later, when he was banished from Pondichéry, he returned to Madras and there composed an appeal to the French Crown, using a French-speaking notary in Madras. He returned to Pondichéry after Nayiniyappa's exoneration, and according to the family memoir written by his grandson, the five richest merchants in Madras and their families accompanied him. These merchants brought with them something more important than capital: sought-after Indian Ocean connections, crucial to Pondichéry's ambitions of becoming an important trading center.

As soon as these merchants were settled in the colony, they began fitting out ships and sending them all around the Indian Ocean—to Manila, Aden, and Mocha. Thus, Tiruvangandan's grandson wrote, "Due to the intervention of my grandfather and the merchants he brought with him, commerce opened up and was linked to all ports."[14]

Tiruvangandan's actions proved immediately beneficial to the company's global commercial interests. In April of 1720, when the Christian Pedro was still chief broker, the Pondichéry Sovereign Council recorded that "Tirouvengadam, a malabar merchant and resident of this town" (not certainly but very likely Nayiniyappa's brother-in-law), had brokered a relationship with Portuguese merchants in Macao, who were interested in regularly sending ships to Pondichéry—a very desirable proposition for the French, who were constantly trying to lure credited and established Indian Ocean merchants to their port. The Macao merchants demanded lower taxes as their privilege, and the council readily acquiesced.[15]

The ties between Madras and Pondichéry could also be cemented back in Europe in unexpected configurations. The diary of Nayiniyappa's nephew Ananda Ranga Pillai mentions that on one occasion when the French and English governors of the neighboring Indian colonies found themselves in Europe at the same time, they became housemates. He heard from the captain of a ship recently arrived from Europe that "Mr. Pitt [the governor of Madras] was living in France in the same house with M. Lenoir [the governor of Pondichéry], and that they were inseparable companions."[16] Thus it was that being neighbors in India made unlikely bedfellows in France of the governors of rival colonies.

Intermediaries, Information, and Regional Connections

When Ananda Ranga Pillai was chief broker to the French, he received daily reports from the *corps des marchands des malabars* and the caste chiefs on what had occurred in each of their districts the previous day. The reports and their frequency indicate the importance of connections outside Pondichéry.[17] By serving as a clearinghouse for regional information, Ananda Ranga Pillai could create commercial opportunities, drawing on wider resources than those available in the French colony. Even before he was promoted to chief broker, when the French wanted to begin producing blue cotton in Pondichéry rather than importing it from the important trading port of Porto Novo (Parangipettai) sixty kilometers away, Pillai made this possible. He orchestrated a series of complex political negotiations and some strategic gift giving that resulted in the relocation of skilled weavers from Porto Novo to Pondichéry.[18] In compensation for his efforts, the Superior Council of Pondichéry rewarded him the privilege of supplying blue cloth for ships headed for Europe, Île de France, and other places.[19] Beyond the financial reward, this mark of distinction further strengthened the broker's importance and influence in the region. It likely was a crucial step in securing him the position of chief broker in 1746.

The story of Nayiniyappa's sons' banishment from the colony after their father's death and subsequent return to Pondichéry also illustrates how intermediaries' acceptance in the local landscape could have more than mere commercial benefits. Nayiniyappa was well into his sixties at the time of his arrest. Nevertheless, the sons claimed that his death less than a year into his three-year sentence occurred under suspicious circumstances. Nayiniyappa, wrote his sons, "suffered incredible pain and misery" after his whipping and during the months of his imprisonment.[20] On the night of August 6 he suffered a loss of blood, and the following night he died. "It was made known to us," the sons claimed, "that on the Thursday night before his death, Hébert fils and some soldiers came to our father's prison cell, and one of them hit our father several times with the hilt of his sword. But we have no certain proof of this. One of the surgeons of the company visited our father that Friday, and filed a report that he found him seriously ill, but not at all in danger of death, nevertheless he lost the ability to speak, and died."[21] Nayiniyappa's sons were not the only ones who claimed that the broker's death was suspicious. An anonymous history of the Compagnie des Indes, one critical of Hébert, described Nayiniyappa's death in these terms: "[Nayiniyappa] died in prison after some time, a death that surprised everyone."[22]

Three days after their father's death, Nayiniyappa's sons relocated to a village away from Pondichéry and French rule. But merely leaving Pondichéry, they complained in one of their appeals, was not enough to protect them from Hébert's wrath: "Three *pions* were sent from Pondichéry to assassinate us," they claimed.[23] Sensible of their position in the region, the Indian ruler of the province to which the sons had relocated commanded the village chiefs to guard them day and night and assure their safety.[24] One day, when a servant from Pondichéry arrived in the village, he was immediately identified as a stranger and therefore as a threat. Under interrogation, the man could supply no satisfactory explanation for his presence in the village. In fact, the networks of regional knowledge exposed him as a fraud: he claimed to be on his way to visit friends at a neighboring village but was not able to supply their names. Finally, the man admitted he had come to see Nayiniyappa's sons. But when the sons arrived, they did not recognize him. The sons claimed that at this point the man admitted that Pedro, the new head broker, had recruited him and others to kill them in return for cash, jewelry, and lifetime employment in the service of the French company.[25]

There is no way of knowing whether this alleged assassination attempt actually occurred. But its telling suggests the special benefits of being known and the drawbacks of being unknown. Nayiniyappa's sons expected their story to be considered plausible when they claimed local leaders had protected them because of their family's stature in the area. They likewise knew that the claim that a stranger coming after them took a risk in doing so would have the ring of truth. The Frenchmen who heard their story would know better than anybody the risks of being a stranger and that some people would be recognized, protected, and accepted where they were not.

Guruvappa's Travels: A Tamil Broker in Paris

It was one of Nayiniyappa's French supporters who first suggested that a representative from the family travel to France to present in person the case for the restitution of Nayiniyappa's fortune. The Pondichéry governor had reversed the verdict against the broker in 1719, but the earliest mention of the plan to travel to Paris appeared even earlier than that. Denyon, a former engineer who was responsible for the building of Pondichéry's fort, proposed this course of action. Back in Paris, Denyon, along with a man named de Sault (a relative of Hébert's rival, Governor Dulivier), served as the Paris liaison for the appeals filed by the Indians before the French king. In a letter he wrote in 1718 to Tiruvangadan, Denyon argued that any effort he himself could undertake in Paris would have only limited success: "I believe that affairs that are important and of delicate consequences could not be decided in your favor and others before the departure of the ships for India; you would do well to engage Rama [Ramanada] to go to England to come here [France] and throw himself at the feet of the king."[26]

It was Guruvappa who soon acted on Denyon's advice. In a notarial document filed in Pondichéry in 1719, he anticipated that this journey and his stay in France would prove expensive. He petitioned the council to order Governor Hébert and his son to pay his expenses, claiming that it was their evil machinations that had necessitated his trip.[27] Leaving Pondichéry for Madras, Guruvappa embarked on a British ship that set sail for London, and from there made his way to Paris.[28] He arrived there not as a stranger, for his French allies in Pondichéry had set the stage for him. Father Tessier, the MEP missionary in Pondichéry, had written to the directors of the MEP seminary in February of 1719, exhorting them to warmly welcome Guruvappa in their expansive rue de Bac headquarters. "I beg you, messieurs, to give this Malabar all the help you can offer him, in acknowledgment of the great services his deceased father provided to our missions here," wrote Tessier, and he explained the reasons for Guruvappa's travel to France.[29] It appears that the MEP directors granted Tessier's request: when Guruvappa's widow herself wrote to the directors in Paris after her husband's death, she reminded them of the warm welcome they had given him.[30]

Tessier required two things from his Parisian brethren: first, that they help Guruvappa in putting forward his claim for financial restitution before French officialdom, and second, that they make every effort to convert Guruvappa to Christianity. "The greatest service you could give to Nainiapa's son would be to try to make him into a good Christian, and instruct him in his duties. I pray the Lord he will grant you this grace," he wrote.[31] Presumably Tessier had attempted to bring about this conversion himself in India. He clearly hoped that a period of immersion in a Christian land might complete the work. This, indeed, proved to be the case.

A search of the registers of the St. Eustache parish in Paris, where Guruvappa became a Christian, did not yield a copy of his baptismal record. Nevertheless, there are numerous reports, both from Guruvappa's own family and from French observers, that this conversion took place on Sunday October 8, 1720. The directors of the MEP seminary baptized Guruvappa in the chapel of the Palais Royal. A nineteenth-century account claimed that the regent, Philippe d'Orléans, served as the godfather, and the godmother was the regent's sister, Elisabeth Charlotte.[32] Guruvappa was given a new name, one that traveled with him back to India: a 1724 registrar record from Pondichéry refers to him as "sieur Charles Philippe Louis Gourouapa."[33]

In Paris, a royal decree made in favor of Guruvappa restored his father's fortune and officially cleared Nayiniyappa's name of any implication of wrongdoing. The declaration, signed by the king in September 1720, decreed that Hébert's judgments against Nayiniyappa, Tiruvangadan, and Ramanada were overturned, the sums seized from them were to be returned, and the men's reputations would be rehabilitated. Hébert was ordered to pay them damages.[34] The fact that Guruvappa was present in Paris when this decision was made proved crucial, since he was able to press forward his efforts to actually collect the damages from Hébert and to be paid in gold or silver instead of with bank notes.[35]

Guruvappa stayed in Paris for a little while longer after the decision was made. His conversion was but the first of his Parisian transformations. The second, performed by *lettres patentes* of February 28, 1721, made him a chevalier, a knight of the French order of Saint Michel. The order, founded in 1469, was initially a most prestigious honor, but its status had changed by the eighteenth century. Bankers, artists, members of the bourgeoisie who had performed some important service, and most pertinently, visiting foreigners regularly received this honor. Guruvappa would have cut a striking and unfamiliar figure—a young Indian knight—and a nineteenth-century French account refers to him as a man well known in regency Paris.[36]

Back in Pondichéry, Guruvappa must have regaled his family with stories of his adventures in Paris, and the Pillai family memoir, written late in the eighteenth century, fondly recalled how Guruvappa was "covered in honor" during his stay in France.[37] When Ananda Ranga Pillai received a report of France provided by a Frenchman, he noted that this man's "descriptions tallied with what we had heard before from other European gentlemen, and from Chevalier Guruva Pillai."[38] Guruvappa's travels, and the stories he told upon his return home, clearly remained a family benchmark of authority for all things French.

There are other indications that Guruvappa's travels to France made a lasting impression on his relatives. In 1757, when Ananda Ranga Pillai was involved in a dispute with a senior official of the company in India, Georges Duval de Leyreit, he wrote to complain to the current *générale de la nation*, the official's superior. After detailing a litany of complaints, Ananda Ranga Pillai concluded by saying that if the matter could not be resolved promptly in India, he wanted permission to travel to France as soon as possible and plead his case there.[39] He mentioned Nayiniyappa's arrest, saying, "His son, Gourouvapapoullé, went to France to throw himself at the feet of Monseigneur the Duc d'Orléans, Regent of the Kingdom." The exoneration of Nayiniyappa and the honor bestowed on the knighted Guruvappa, continued Ananda Ranga Pillai, were matters of global renown: "All of France and all of India are familiar with this example of justice rendered unto an Indian."[40]

Crossing the ocean back to India, successful in his mission of restoring his father's fortune, the Chevalier Charles Louis Philippe Guruvappa was appointed Pondichéry's chief broker. Yet Guruvappa's status now posed a categorical conundrum: Indian or French? Pagan or Christian? Intermediary or noble? The archive reflects that these questions confounded Frenchmen in the colony for the remaining two years of Guruvappa's brief life (he died of dropsy in 1724). The fact of his ennoblement would have been a delicate matter, since it is likely that the only other knight in the colony was the governor—now Guruvappa's employer.[41]

Guruvappa's confessional status was also confusing to French observers. According to the agreement made between the Jesuits and the Capuchins in Pondichéry, the Jesuits ministered to the Malabar Christian population, while the Capuchins were in charge of the parish for Europeans. Guruvappa was, without a doubt, a Malabar convert. Yet he was also a knight of the order of St. Michel and as such was designated a member of the Capuchin parish.[42] Further, Nayiniyappa's persecution by the Jesuits presumably would have made his son loath to submit to their religious authority, and his new liminal status as a French knight made this possible. Guruvappa no longer fit neatly into preexisting categories that attempted to draw clear distinctions between colonists and Indians.

How enduring was Guruvappa's conversion to Christianity? His widow described herself as a practicing Christian in 1726; an observer described his descendants in the nineteenth century as faithful Christians.[43] Guruvappa was buried as a Christian, according to the record of the Pondichéry état-civil, tended by the Capuchin missionaries, which reads, "Today, August 13 1724, I buried in . . . our cemetery of Saint-Lazare . . . the chevalier Gourapa, who died between midnight and eight in the morning," having celebrated the rites of Easter.[44] The Capuchin Père Esprit de Tours signed his certificate of death.[45]

But some signs indicate that Guruvappa may have emulated his Hindu father's adoption of the Catholic rosaries as a suitable gift for the poor while maintaining his local religious practice. His comportment discomfited French missionaries. "Upon his return to Pondichéry, Gourouappa persisted in the exterior profession of Christianity," wrote a later missionary historian, "but in his conduct, he unfortunately gave unequivocal signs of insincere faith."[46] An MEP missionary stated that Guruvappa "hardly exercised his [Christian] religion," yet nevertheless he "lived in the European manner" (il vivait à l'européenne).[47] Guruvappa's trip to Paris perhaps did not bring about any radical change in his religious practice, but it did clearly make a lasting impression on his habitus.

Guruvappa posed a semiotic problem after his trip to France: he projected a confusing series of signs. With his Christian name, European clothes, and stories of his triumphant trip to the center of French power, he should have been a shining example of the benefits of Christian conversion. Yet the message he gave potential converts was mixed at best. Much like Nayiniyappa's distribution of rosaries, Guruvappa's postconversion behavior is an example of the shaky dichotomy the missionaries tried to enforce between real and fake conversion. Instead of serving as a model Christian, Guruvappa added Christianity to his arsenal of religious practices, comfortably accommodating both the old and the new.

Guruvappa's journey to Paris, his success there, and his subsequent elevation to the post of Pondichéry's chief broker illustrate both the opportunities
of intermediaries to travel among the outposts of empire and the benefits
that could be accrued by such travel. With the support of French and British
accomplices, Guruvappa managed to make his way to France, while his rival
Governor Hébert was trapped in Pondichéry, his letters trailing Guruvappa in
both speed and efficacy. Once in France, Guruvappa maintained his "exotic"
appeal while simultaneously embracing norms that would have made him
better accepted there. Returning to the colony, he kept the habits—in both
senses of the word—that suited him and shed those that did not. He returned
to Pondichéry a force to be reckoned with, displacing the current chief broker, Pedro.

Significantly, in 1724 when the Catholic Pedro himself was reappointed
to the post of chief broker after Guruvappa's unexpected death, the council referenced his mobility. They highlighted Pedro's maritime experience:
"S. Gourouapa having died last September of dropsy, we named as courtier in his place Pedro, who already was [courtier in the past]," reported the
Pondichéry council. "He is wise and we were pleased with his conduct in the
voyage he made to Manila on the *Soucourama* in the capacity of captain and
supercargo."[48] Pedro's sea voyage would have endowed him with desired
commercial skills, but it also would have enabled him to forge personal connections in the important port of Manila.[49] Thus even Pedro, whose claim
to authority largely rested on the support of the Jesuits in Pondichéry, still
needed to demonstrate that he was able to reach beyond the confines of the
colony.

The highest-ranking brokers—such as Nayiniyappa, Guruvappa, Pedro,
and Ananda Ranga Pillai—all traveled in the region and beyond, thereby
acquiring the connections and experience that rendered them effective
brokers. But go-betweens at more humble stations were similarly mobile.
A man named Arlanden, who served in Pondichéry as the valet and broker
of a French trader called Judde, serves as a telling example of how brokers
were both able and required to move about as part of their duties. Judde and
Arlanden were both implicated in a slave-trafficking case, which was brought
before the Pondichéry council in 1743.[50] In the course of investigations, which
resulted in the release of most of the captives, it was revealed that Arlanden
had traveled extensively throughout the Tamil region, abducting and ensnar-
ing potential slaves through a network of local associates. The place origins
of the enslaved men and women held by Judde revealed Arlanden's itinerary,
for he captured slaves for his French employer in Tranquebar, Karikal, and
especially Arcot.

Commercial brokers had to establish both local and regional lines of credit and reputation so as to draw on a wide array of commodities and ports. But travel—and its mutually constitutive counterpart, situatedness—was also a central practice for the other kind of go-between examined here, the catechists.

Manuel's Travels: Catechists at the Frontiers of Catholicism

Guruvappa's travels to France were unusual but not unique.[51] Like Guruvappa, the interpreter Manuel was a professional go-between whose father was also a go-between. Before he served as the chief interpreter in the investigations against Nayiniyappa, Manuel traveled to France with one of the Jesuits. While the archives never refer to him as a catechist, his father, Moutiappa, was the head catechist to the Jesuits in Pondichéry, and this was often a hereditary position, in Pondichéry and elsewhere in South Asia. Second, a Jesuit manuscript that relates the founding of a mission in the Tamil region mentions that two catechists were sent to pave the way for the Jesuits' arrival; in an unusual departure from most Jesuit writings, the catechists are mentioned by name, and one of them is referred to as Gigane—possibly Manuel Geganis.[52]

Two documents related to the Nayiniyappa Affair reference Manuel's travel to France. One of the appeals put forward by Nayiniyappa's sons mentions that "the interpreter was a servant of the Jesuits, son of their catechist, and was once a valet to one of the Fathers in France, returned to India with Hébert in 1715."[53] Another appeal, presented by Ramanada, Nayiniyappa's business associate, contains a note in the margins that offers more intriguing detail: "The son of the catechist is a Christian Malabar, whom Father Petit took to France as his valet in 1705, and whom he presented in that kingdom as a man of quality in the Indies; he returned with M. Hébert in 1715. Since he spent almost ten years among the French, it is not surprising that this valet, who has aptitude and who is entirely devoted to the Society [of Jesus], speaks French as well as he does, having been taught [by the Jesuits]."[54]

Why did Father Petit take Manuel with him to France and keep him by his side for a decade? Surely, servants could be found in France, but were there services that only Manuel could provide, or a special connection between the two men?[55] Ramanada's reference to Manuel's being presented as a "man of quality in the Indies" offers a possible explanation: a converted Indian, one of supposed high social rank and fluent in French to boot, would have been an important fund-raising tool for Jesuits. Such a man could have served as a living, breathing indication of their success in India. By presenting Manuel as a man of quality, the Jesuits might have been attempting to disguise the reality of the intersection of class and confession in India, a reality in which Christian converts were much more likely to be poor and of the lower castes.

Having spent a decade in France bestowed special status on Manuel, who was one of the few residents in the colony who could speak both French and Tamil fluently. Being intimately familiar with the daily details of life in France would have been another uncommon attribute and one that would explain how Manuel came to fill a position of prominence in what were at times rival institutions: the French trading company and the Jesuit mission. His unusual position as an intimate of the Jesuits and an employee of the company allowed vicarious entry into the interrogation room to both the Jesuits and the local Christian community of which he was a member.

While Manuel was unusual in having spent so much time in France, all catechists traveled in the course of their duties.[56] Since only a handful of missionaries were responsible for a vast expanse of land surrounding Pondichéry, reliance on catechists was complete. According to Father Martin, the Jesuit missionaries each employed "eight, ten and sometimes a dozen Catechists, all wise men and perfectly instructed in the mysteries of our sainted religion. These Catechists precede the Fathers by several days, and predispose the people to accept the sacraments. This greatly facilitates the ministrations of the missionaries."[57] He described the Jesuit superior Jean-Venant Bouchet departing each destination after a few days, while the catechists would linger for a good deal longer.

The missionaries who attempted to lure Indians into the fold of Christianity faced a problem: they had no spiritual reputation. They were nothing more than foreigners, and the salvation they promised was as questionable as the credit of their commercial counterparts. Jesuits were endlessly concerned with their low status in India, bestowed on them as Europeans, or *Paranguis*. The difficulties that the Jesuits encountered as Paranguis would have been familiar. The global Jesuit project was in fact premised on overcoming the hardships of being a foreigner, with the ultimate mark of success and God's favor being martyrdom at the hands of those who refused to accept Jesuits into their world. The fact that Jesuits did not limit themselves to missions protected by European colonial powers (for example, their ambitious mission in China) made violent attacks or indifferent dismissal all the more likely.

Although the Jesuits often paid tribute to the benefits their mission reaped from the catechists' position in their communities of origin, the letters they wrote suggest they resented their dependence on catechists more than their commercial counterparts resented their local brokers like Nayiniyappa.[58] Discussing the difficulties newly converted Christians faced, the Jesuit father

Martin wrote that the catechists were sometimes those who provided the worst examples: "The catechists are often the first to scandalize the people with the bad example they provide, or obstruct the missionaries in the exercise of their ministry, due to their stubbornness and opinionated nature; and yet the missionaries dare not punish the catechists, for fear of bringing a cruel persecution on the whole mission."[59] This passage described a power struggle without a clear winner. Martin found the catechists headstrong and independent but had no way to control them. Their regional connections made them potentially dangerous foes.

In a letter of December 10, 1718, the Jesuit father Le Gac created a revealing juxtaposition between two stories concerning catechists. The first story presented a commendable catechist and the other, an errant one. The first described a catechist who came to a village in order to instruct a group that expressed interest in Christianity. Upon his arrival in the village, where he was unknown, he was arrested as a spy.[60] He was then presented before the village head, and the catechist told him that the Sanyassi (meaning the missionaries, described here with the Hindu term for ascetic) for whom he worked enjoyed the protection of the governor. The catechist was nevertheless put in prison, but throughout the night he fearlessly read aloud Christian texts.[61] Two important Indian men from a neighboring village, who knew the catechist, came and vouched for his innocence and virtue and obtained his release.[62] Le Gac approved of this catechist's piety and fortitude.

The second story, presented a few pages later in the letter, concerned a catechist who was summoned by a Hindu man with an interest in Christianity to instruct him in his village. But the catechist made various excuses and delayed his arrival for a long period. Once he made the journey, he remained in place a mere three days before returning to the mission. The catechist was worried for his own safety, for it was known that in this village strangers were often subject to severe punishments.[63] Le Gac denounced the catechist who refused to travel, blaming him for his timidity.[64]

Taken together, the two stories demonstrate that the Jesuits demanded fearlessness from the catechists and a disregard for their safety. A catechist who brought persecution on himself was presented in heroic terms, while one who demonstrated warranted caution, for cruel treatment was often the lot of imprisoned catechists, was denigrated as a coward. The first story also reflected the missionaries' powerlessness to protect the catechists; an intimate network in which they were unable to participate, connections forged of neighborhood and family ties, achieved their man's release. The refusal of the second catechist to travel to the village also illustrated the difficulty the missionaries encountered in their relations with the catechists and in the mission field in general. The catechist did not want to put himself in a situation where he would be penalized for being a stranger in an unknown village. But for the Jesuits, the experience and danger of being a stranger were inescapable anywhere in India. The missionary's anger at the timid catechist might have been sharpened by his realization that he had given up the privilege of belonging by coming to India.

Father Tachard admitted that his knowledge of Indian religious practice originated with reports given to him by the missionary Father Bouchet (the future Jesuit superior and adversary of Nayiniyappa). Father Bouchet, in turn, relied heavily on local catechists, employing as many as a dozen at on time. Father Tachard conceded that residence in India and even travel throughout India had done little to improve his knowledge of the place: "Even though I lived for several years in Pondichéry on the Coromandel coast, in Balassor in Orissa and Ougouli [Hugli] in the kingdom of Bengal and in Surat, where religion and mores are almost the same, and I had several discussions with infidels about their religion," he admitted that he did not consider himself an expert on the topic. "I can honestly declare that I have gained very little solid and certain enlightenment. Because the gentiles [Hindus] who live along the coasts, where Europeans live, hide from us and disavow as much as they can their fables and superstitions."[65]

Jesuit attitudes toward the travels of catechists oscillated between two poles: reliance and resentment. Scarcity of missionaries, the vastness of the mission field, and the unlikelihood that Jesuits would be welcome and respected visitors all made it a mission imperative that catechists travel on behalf of missionaries. Yet the ability of catechists to insinuate themselves into communities of potential converts meant that they took an outsized role in the life and direction of the mission, becoming stand-ins for the missionaries and thereby rendering the missionaries dispensable. For catechists, the opportunity to travel away from Pondichéry, an enclave of tenuous European authority, offered a chance to exercise these powers. In Pondichéry, it must have been clearer that the Jesuits were in charge and the catechists were their employees. But what of a place like a new mission in the hinterland, where the Jesuits admitted they had to hide in order to further their own cause? There the distribution of authority between Jesuits and catechists was even less clear-cut than in the colony.

The creation of new Jesuit missions proved to be more successful if catechists rather than missionaries established them. A manuscript account by Father Bouchet recounted the history of the founding of the Tarcolam mission, showing how such projects could simultaneously depend on the mobility of catechists and be a local, community-led effort.[66] The mission was the initiative of a young Indian man, Ajarapen, who converted to Christianity and then convinced the French Jesuit Father Mauduit to start a mission in his hometown of Tarcolam. Ajarapen's story itself revolves around the oscillating forces of mobility and stability, as Father Bouchet wrote: "Eight or nine years ago a young boy born in the town of Tarcolam left his parents and traveled to several places in these parts. . . . During his voyages to the coasts he was baptized and resolved himself to return to his land to see if his relatives, who were all idolaters, were still alive."[67] The coast here figured as a transformative and liminal space: a young boy goes to the water's edge, immerses himself in the new practices borne over the seas, and then carries droplets of the coast back with him to his place of birth. Yet this watery transformation adhered more easily to the bodies of converts and, later, catechists—not missionaries, who were not effective carriers for this immersive change.

Although Ajarapen was not explicitly labeled a catechist in the text, he was described as working as an assistant to Father Mauduit, presumably in Pondichéry, where Mauduit was stationed. When Father Bouchet, the Jesuit superior, arrived in the village, it was only after Ajarapen had prepared the ground for a visit by Father Mauduit and several catechists had already been sent to the village.[68] Ajarapen's work was especially successful: when he told his family stories about his guru, a relative offered to donate a plot of land on which the Jesuit mission could be built. When village opinion coalesced against the decision to build a mission, the village elders emphasized the fact that the missionaries were strangers (gens inconnus) rather than raising any religious objections.[69] Father Bouchet believed the potential donor was reconsidering his gift because it had been revealed the missionaries were Paranguis, and this was their undoing: "Experience has already taught me several times that our missionaries were always well received before there was any suspicion that they were Europeans, but as soon as they were recognized [as Europeans], they were shamefully chased away, or they were treated with scorn," lamented the Jesuit. Bouchet believed it was Indian traders who had themselves spent time on the coast who recognized the missionaries as Europeans.[70] Knowledge acquired at the coast again proved pivotal. The Jesuits here remind us that contact was not merely an occurrence of so-called colonial contact zones; it also seeped deep inland.

Word traveled quickly, not only from the coast inland but also between neighboring villages. This was what most concerned Jesuits about their possible failure in Tarcolam: it would severely compromise their chances in the entire region and sully their reputation beyond repair. Ajarpen's support had given them a chance at Tarcolam, but word of mouth would also be their downfall if everyone knew they were Europeans. As Bouchet admitted,

"If we left here with infamy [attached to us], we would not easily find an occasion to return; word would spread to the surrounding tribes."[71] Ultimately the Jesuits were given the land for their mission at Tarcolam as a result of Ajarapen's efforts.[72]

French actors encountered significant difficulties when they tried to move through the Indian landscape and relied on the mobility available to intermediaries. Go-betweens deployed their mobility to enhance their status as professional go-betweens in the French colony, such that mobility both depended on and enhanced their stability in the region. Traders and missionaries alike experienced this dependence on mobile local employees. But as in the realms of kinship and language, mobility was another arena in which French agents of commerce and religion approached similar issues differently. Traders, such as the Frenchman Georges Roques in Surat, might have grumbled about their reliance on commercial brokers: "Whatever reputation or credit you might possess, nobody will deal with you unless you have a private broker. This is the custom of the country. You have to follow it. . . . Hence, let us choose one and then close our eyes!"[73] But like Roques, traders generally accepted this as the cost of doing business. Missionaries on the other hand, and specifically the ambitious Jesuits, attempted to shift the social reality that made catechists crucial to their efforts and were therefore much more ambivalent about their dependence on catechists to move in their stead.

The prism of the Nayiniyappa Affair spotlights the issue of colonial mobility. Nayiniyappa's position as a node for information that traveled through the town and across the region made him both a valuable asset to the company and a threat to traders and missionaries alike. After Nayiniyappa's death, the unfolding of the affair occurred over space as well as time. His eldest son traveled from India to Europe, successfully reversing the more common itinerary that originated in the metropole and concluded in the colony. Once in France, Guruvappa made ample use of a French and global network of supporters that facilitated his movement up the social ladder, capping his trip with a French knighthood. But as his actions upon his return to India demonstrate, this is no simple story of assimilation. Guruvappa adopted some of the habits he picked up in France and discarded others, with no harm to his position in the colony.

From the other side of the Nayiniyappa Affair, Manuel's travels to France exhibit the special nimbleness intermediaries like Manuel and Guruvappa could exhibit, drawing on linguistic and cultural expertise to traverse the internal French boundaries that separated the missionary and commercial projects. Taken together, the movements of these two men between India and France, alongside the travels of other commercial and religious intermediaries across the Indian Ocean region and within India, demonstrate that the travels performed by intermediaries enabled them to acquire and sustain the special skills and abilities French *colons* and missionaries valued so highly.

French traders and missionaries in India both undertook projects that required them to be mobile if commerce and conversion were to succeed. But there was a significant gap between this articulated vision of imperial mobility and the realities of their limited ability to move through colonial space. Lacking reputation, credit, local ties, or moral authority, they often found it difficult to venture beyond Pondichéry or to transform Pondichéry into the busy and Christian hub they envisioned. Professional intermediaries filled this gap between ambition and reality, traveling on behalf of their employers, inserting Pondichéry into preexisting Indian Ocean networks, and using the connections and skills accrued in the course of travel to bolster their position as stable figures of authority in the colonial landscape. Pondichéry's intermediaries enjoyed uncommon opportunities to journey between outposts of empire, and in the course of this crisscrossing they constituted the empire as a connected entity, a well-traversed map of overlaid European and Indian itineraries.

CHAPTER 6

Archiving the Affair

In the course of the Nayiniyappa Affair, one of the charges leveled at Governor Hébert concerned the destruction of Nayiniyappa's personal archive. "Never was there a Malabar," wrote Nayiniyappa's sons in one of their appeals, "who had his affairs in better order."[1] When Nayiniyappa was first arrested in 1716, Hébert seized all his papers. This extensive personal archive and other documents, all written in Tamil on palm leaves (Tamil: *olai*, or *olles* in the French rendition), were kept in Pondichéry's fort on the town's waterfront. The dampness in the air, claimed the sons, spoiled the palm leaves, rendering them illegible. Nayiniyappa's sons vividly described the transformation from the legibility that bestows credibility and authority to the useless illegibility of the ruined archive: "Today [these documents] are in a horrible state, all eaten up, desiccated, broken, resembling litter more than account books."[2]

There does not exist, in France or in India, a formally constituted and indexed archival collection devoted to the Nayiniyappa Affair. But the principal actors most affected by the affair actively tried to create and preserve such an archive. The two central characters—Nayiniyappa and Governor Hébert—both explicitly described the destruction of their archival efforts as part of the punishment inflicted upon them as the affair unfolded. Nayiniyappa was the hero and victim in the archive he created; Hébert was the hero and victim in his own archive. Their respective accounts suggest much was lost. Yet their narrative efforts were so ambitious, coherent, and passionate that the broadly distributed archive that remains provides a more general story of Pondichéry in the early eighteenth century. The yearly judicial and administrative records of the Compagnie des Indes, as well as the archives of the Missions étrangères des Paris, reveal that the Nayiniyappa Affair was a defining event of the period 1715–1724 for people on two continents. The affair is the throbbing center of what Ann Stoler has termed "the pulse of the archive."[3]

This chapter examines the making and unmaking of the archives of the Nayiniyappa Affair and, more generally, the archiving practices of three central groups in the colony: Tamil intermediaries, French traders, and Catholic missionaries. The colonial officials, missionaries, and native intermediaries who created the documents that make up the archives of French India, and more specifically the Nayiniyappa Affair, were keenly, desperately aware that official documents were crucial in determining political struggles and future reputations. Depositions, appeals and counterappeals, commercial records, missionary missives, and even personal diaries—these were the weapons with which the Nayiniyappa Affair was fought. As the affair wound to a close, its participants were eager to preserve and shape the archive that attested to its importance.

By "archive" I mean a collection of texts or artifacts that are collected and carefully curated so as to enable making claims about the past. Historians and anthropologists alike have called for taking paperwork seriously.[4] Some have suggested that there has been an "archival turn," the reflexive examination of archives and their conditions of knowledge.[5] This chapter will reveal that the collating of documents into archives was crucial to making claims about the injustice of the Nayiniyappa Affair for all the participants.[6] Both Nayiniyappa and his allies, as well as their rivals, claimed that archives were the bedrock of both truth and reputation. While we tend to think of the creation and curation of archives as acts both institutional and metropolitan, individuals in the colony, including both Governor Hébert and Nayiniyappa, undertook intentional and often-successful historicizing efforts in the colony.

The two kinds of documents most discussed in the course of the Nayiniyappa Affair were commercial records and diaries. Both function in the archive as collections of documents of business transactions and daily events, respectively. Historians focusing on archive creation have for the most part examined documentary collections created by organizations rather than the small-scale archiving efforts of individuals. Yet archive creation and sustained concern about the possibilities for crafting historical narrative are not the sole purview of large and bureaucratic organizations. Small-scale, nonprofessional archiving efforts have radical potential, since these unofficial archival repositories diverge from hegemonic organizing logics.[7] In Pondichéry, local intermediaries, company traders, and Catholic missionaries all undertook explicit efforts at archiving, and in the process tried to craft competing narratives of their histories in South Asia.[8]

Traders and Their Archives

As with any governmental organization, the Compagnie des Indes's offices in both Paris and Pondichéry were the site of a relentless document-producing bureaucratic operation. The Superior Council produced most of the documents recording Pondichéry's commercial, administrative, and judicial doings.[9] The trader-administrators in India maintained yearly logs of reports sent to Paris, which contained exhaustive and meticulous descriptions of changes in personnel, new building projects, and discussions of the political situation surrounding Pondichéry. In Ananda Ranga Pillai's diary, he often commented on the constant effort in the council's chambers to prepare missives to be sent back to France. In an oft-repeated observation, he once noted, "The work of signing the letters for France, and putting them into envelopes was going on apace."[10] Writing and governmental functions, here as elsewhere, were complementary processes. This, as Miles Ogborn has written, was a "world made on paper as well as on land and sea."[11]

The reports from India to France generally followed a prescribed format, moving back and forth between the global and the particular: commerce with Europe, commerce in India and its surroundings, matters pertaining to Pondichéry, matters pertaining to the other French *comptoirs* in India, reports on troops, reports on company employees, fortifications and building projects, and accounts relating to the French colonies in the Indian Ocean, Île de France, and Île Bourbon.[12]

The archive also includes the directives of the Parisian directors about management of the colony. Ships traveled between France and India according to a schedule determined by the monsoons, which meant the Superior Council in Pondichéry could write and send its reports between September and January, and the directors in Paris could respond between October and February. The trip between India and France took six to eight months, and stops along the way might mean letters would arrive a year or more after the time of writing.[13] This delayed communication afforded the administrators in India a large measure of independence: on multiple occasions they wrote the

Parisian directors to say that their orders had arrived too late and decisions contrary to their wishes had been carried out.[14] Geographical space, not only language barriers, could make miscomprehension possible.[15]

In their response to Nayiniyappa's arrest and punishment, the directors argued that they needed access to the documentary archive compiled in India if they were to make informed decisions. For example, when the association of traders from St. Malo complained in 1717 about Hébert's performance and the treatment of Nayiniyappa, the directors wrote that "the company responded to [this complaint], but in a manner very different than it could have done if it had been better instructed and if it had had here a copy of the charges and interrogations of the whole trial."[16] They demanded that the council ship the entire documentary record to France by the first ship departing Pondichéry, "other than the one which will carry M. Hébert" and threatened that their judgment of misconduct could have dire consequences for the errant party.[17] The inclusion by the directors of the specification that the full archive should not be on the same ship as Hébert suggests they were suspicious of Hébert. This suspicion was of a piece with the directors' decision to recall Hébert back to France. Most likely they did not expect the archive would be wholly reliable. The directors also noted that when the merchants of St. Malo sent their request calling for Nayiniyappa's release and Hébert's dismissal, the Malouins supported their complaint with "various letters and certificates."[18]

Written exchanges between the directors in Paris and members of the Pondichéry Superior Council in India at times evinced significant tension, often revolving around the problems of communicating at a distance and uneven access to information. In 1726 the directors requested more information about rights of taxation given to Nayiniyappa's daughter-in-law, known in the French archive as the widow Guruvappa. They scolded their subordinates in India about their inadequate communication practices, writing, "The company is not adequately informed by your letter."[19] The councillors' reply the next year was peevish: "We have had the honor of writing you everything we know about this matter in our letter of January 23, 1723 and by that of October 15, 1725."[20]

Information about Nayiniyappa and his fate arrived in Paris from multiple directions. In addition to official correspondence with the French employees in Pondichéry, various actors with knowledge of the affair registered their dissatisfaction with the directors of the Compagnie des Indes. A veritable documentary parade arrived in Paris, penned by Frenchmen in Pondichéry, including the trader Cuperly and the Missions étrangères de Paris missionary Tessier, who all agreed, according to the company directors, that "the procedure was the most irregular ever undertaken in a foreign language."[21]

The company's ability to make money and govern Pondichéry depended on administrative, commercial, and judicial archives. Such commercial archives also held meaning for their creators, as mercantile papers allowed privileged formats for a mercantile society to articulate its understanding of its own ambitions, agendas, and values.[22] As a historian of a mercantile archive connecting seventeenth-century Amsterdam and New Netherlands has observed, such archiving efforts reflect a world in which "understandings of reality and self-realization were largely worked out in account books, business correspondence, official reports, notarized papers, and records of local judicial proceedings."[23] The collection, archiving, and rereading of mercantile papers could be a form of self-fashioning.[24]

Missionaries and Administrative Archives

Missionaries in Pondichéry took an active role in the creation of the colony's official record. The Jesuit Father Turpin, who translated the testimonies of witnesses against Nayiniyappa, was perhaps the most explicit example of such involvement, but missionaries served as translators and creators of official records at other times too. Catholic missionaries in the East were involved in a massive project of producing knowledge of various kinds—linguistic, religious, ethnographic, and scientific. Efforts at producing documents attesting to this knowledge were at the heart of missionary work, mostly as letters written by missionaries and sent back to Europe but also in the large body of published scholarly work penned by missionaries.[25] The Jesuit missionaries in India, following the dicta of the founder of the society, Ignatius of Loyola, wrote frequent, detailed letters about their doings. They sent their letters to their brethren and contacts in Europe, as well as to other Jesuits working in the East. These missives were meant to be circulated and soon found a broad European audience outside the order.

In addition to their letters and scholarly work, the Jesuits and other missionaries also participated in the making of administrative archives in French India. An incident following the meeting of the Superior Council to discuss the local unrest regarding religious freedoms in 1715—the same unrest that Hébert would later accuse Nayiniyappa of fomenting—suggests both groups' dedication to documentation. After the councillors discussed how they should respond to the locals' threat of abandoning the colony over religious restrictions, they presented the write-up of the discussion before the missionaries whom they had consulted. The three Jesuits involved, led by the superior

Father Bouchet, refused to sign this account, saying that it did not adequately reflect the statements they had made before the council. Essentially they argued that the translation of their statements, from the oral to the written, was inadequate. The Jesuits submitted their own account, which the council incorporated into its records. As at other points, the archive here was explicitly multivocal, reflecting opposing missionary and commercial agendas and voices.

The Capuchin missionaries also fought with the colony's administration about matters concerning the dissemination of official decrees. On January 12, 1716, a Sunday, the Capuchin missionary Father Esprit read aloud and published a text in the Malabar language (Tamil), which he said had arrived from Rome, concerning the Malabar Rites, the Jesuit practice of allowing their converts to keep adhering to certain non-Catholic practices. Two days later, the council gathered, and the *procureur général* noted that "he didn't know on which authority this publication had been made, nor the contents of this document" and demanded that the Capuchins provide the council with the original text within twenty-four hours.[26] The council ordered that "all [religious] Superiors of communities and all other persons, no matter who they may be, may not in the future read, publish and distribute any memos, bulls, mandates or any other writing of any nature" without first receiving the approval of the council. The same declaration prohibited all the king's subjects from keeping such writings in their houses without first receiving the council's stamp of approval— thereby staking a claim for controlling even archives privately constructed and maintained.[27]

Once more, the approaches of the trader-administrators of the Compagnie des Indes and Catholic missionaries followed markedly different routes. The missionaries' approach to communication, as in other realms, was much more ambitious than that undertaken by the traders. The missionaries wanted to crack the code of Indian social and spiritual structures, and the result was a massive project of learning and data collection. The knowledge archive they produced relied on their own linguistic immersion; they intended it for wide distribution as a means to equip other missionaries who would follow them. These archives were meant to be outward facing and open. The missionaries' fund-raising texts took a different approach, highlighting the conversion of thousands, the acceptance of missionaries by local rulers in their courts, and children swarming the fathers in remote villages. It also glorified the martyrdom of dead missionaries slain by unwelcoming locals. The collection of documents produced by the Compagnie des Indes was an inward-facing ledger book, and it often detailed more failures than successes. As an internal document, pitched to solicit more funds from the directors in Paris, it provided a litany of failed company efforts, insufficient funds, an intractable local population, and unsatisfying employees.

Go-Betweens and Their Archives: The Diaries of Tamil Intermediaries

A diary is "an archive that situates self in history."[28] The most ambitious archival effort by a Tamil intermediary in Pondichéry is Ananda Ranga Pillai's twelve-volume diary. The chief commercial go-between for the French company in the period 1747 to 1761 and Nayiniyappa's nephew, Ananda Ranga Pillai started keeping a journal in 1736, when he was only twenty-seven, and kept up the practice to his dying day.

The diary began with an explicit, reflexive statement on the task he was undertaking, appended to the text before the very first entry of September 6, 1736: "I proceed to chronicle what I hear with my ears; what I see with my eyes; the arrivals and departures of the ships; and whatsoever wonderful or novel takes place."[29] This preamble promised to rely on first-person and tangible evidence, focus on Pondichéry as a commercial hub, and relay marvelous events. The actual diary, with its gossipy critiques of rivals and detailed descriptions of commercial transactions, does not quite live up to that promise.

Ananda Ranga Pillai conceived of the diary as a complement to his work as a professional broker. When the French company sent his brother to Madras as its agent, Ananda Ranga Pillai advised him to start keeping his own daily diary and provided him with materials for doing so.[30] He treated his own diary as an alternative archive to that of the company, at times translating company documents into Tamil just as the Company translated Tamil documents into French for their own registers. For example, the diary includes a Tamil translation of a letter from one French director to his Pondichéry-based cousin that does not omit reports on the well-being of the man's wife and children.[31] Ananda Ranga Pillai also used the diary as a depository for decisions that had little to do with his own commercial interests but evinced a more general concern with the history of Pondichéry. An entry in his diary in 1738 discusses the enmity between Jesuits and Capuchins in the town and traces the conflict to a papal bull of 1712. While not a Christian, Ananda Ranga Pillai was well versed in this intra-Catholic religious conflict. The diary also includes his transcription of the entirety of a decree about public offenders published by the French governor, and the text of a decree about coins allowed for use in town.[32] His copy of a 1741 council decree regarding caste disputes in Pondichéry reproduced the signatures of the members of the council, in the order in which they appeared in the original document.[33] Such transcriptions are best understood as archive making par excellence.

Most of the principals of the Nayiniyappa Affair had already died by the time Ananda Ranga Pillai started writing his diary in the 1730s, including Guruvappa, his cousin, and his father, Tiruvangadan. Yet in the diary, he continued to engage with the aftermath of the affair. The central conflict animating the first decade of the diary's existence is the competition between the diarist and his rival, the chief commercial broker Pedro Modeliar, who served after Guruvappa's death. The diary refers to him by his Tamil name, Kanakarâya Mudali. Dozens of entries mention Pedro/Kanakarâya's commercial and personal successes and failures. Throughout, the diarist organized many events he described through a single question: Who emerged on top, he or Kanakarâya?

The diary recounted this exchange about the inherited rivalry. A French trader, M. Dulaurens, asked, "What has given rise to so much animosity between Kanakarâya Mudali and you?" The response, also recorded: "You may remember all the mischievous acts of which he, out of sheer jealousy, was the author during the time of M. Hébert. In spite of my unremitting efforts to act in accordance with his wishes, he still cherishes in his heart the old ill-feeling."[34] The diary here acted as both testament and repository of ill will tracing back a generation, the animosity cherished and kept alive like a precious inheritance.

Even as Ananda Ranga Pillai lay dying, while the British were laying siege to Pondichéry in 1761, his thoughts turned to his documentary output and its meaning. He apparently asked an associate to complete the account, as the last three entries in the decades-long effort record his illness in another's hand.[35] The very final entry concluded with a description of the sick man dictating a letter berating an uncooperative associate. The scribe wrote, "[Ananda Ranga Pillai] told me to write such a peremptory letter and have it dispatched. I wrote one and brought it to him for his signature. He got up and sat, ordered the two doors to be opened, and putting on his glasses, signed it, adding, 'This must be considered my last letter.'"[36]

This commitment to the creation of personal archives moved down the generations, beyond Nayiniyappa, his son Guruvappa, and Ananda Ranga Pillai. The man who likely wrote the final entries in Ananda Ranga Pillai's diary, a relative, kept his own daily journal for nearly a decade, also while serving as a commercial broker.[37] Other members of this clan of intermediaries continued these efforts. All told, Tamil diarists of Nayiniyappa's lineage who were involved with the Compagnie des Indes in Pondichéry created in their diaries a record of French India that extended past the days of the French Revolution.[38]

Late in the eighteenth century a member of the Pillai family also authored a little-known French-language text attesting to the family's influence and power.[39] He was Tiruvangadan's grandson and Ananda Ranga Pillai's nephew and also named Tiruvangadan. The document bears no date but likely was written after March 1791—the date the author was named courtier and *chef des malabars* in the colony, the title by which he refers to himself in the text.[40] The history describes the "services he and his ancestors provided to the establishment of Pondichéry."[41] This manuscript history was left in Pondichéry's archives when the majority of French records were moved from India to France following India's independence.

This Tiruvangadan Pillai's late eighteenth-century historical account is revisionist in significant ways. It tried to position the arrival of the author's grandfather, Tiruvangadan, as the beginning of prosperity for the French holding. "This city was only a small village at the time, properly speaking a wood full of palms and bad trees, lacking any kind of workers and peopled only by petty merchants, most of whom were shopkeepers," Tiruvangadan wrote of the period when his grandfather Tiruvangadan was a young man in Madras.[42] He credited Nayiniyappa—his own great-uncle—and his grandfather Tiruvangadan with charting a new course for the colony; they did so by writing to their broadly distributed regional network of acquaintances, business partners, and skilled artisans, inviting them to the colony, and so improving it.[43]

The memoir described Guruvappa's successful trip to Paris, saying, "All of France knew about the harsh decision made by the *conseil d'état* about Governor Hébert's [mistreatment of Nayiniyappa]."[44] It named the French governors that succeeded one another through subsequent decades, framing French governance in relation to its reliance on the services provided by local brokers. The memoir also described battles between regional rivals and agreements made with local leaders from the point of view of the company's successive generations of chief commercial brokers. In short, it provides an alternative archival account to the one provided by sources produced by French officials or missionaries.

The Destruction of Nayiniyappa's Archive

Even after Nayiniyappa was exonerated, his heirs did not drop the matter of the destruction of his archive and brought it up again and again. "Hébert had our *olles*, registers, and correspondence destroyed, so that the theft of our father's goods could not be discovered," they complained.[45] On another occasion they named Hébert, his son, and the governor's secretary as all complicit in this act: "The Héberts and Le Roux their secretary, after pillaging our home, destroyed the *olles*, registers, and accounts books of our father, such that no information can be extracted from them."[46] In a separate letter the sons explicitly called the destruction of this archive an attack against multiple generations: "The Héberts, so as not to allow Nayiniyappa and his descendants a remedy against their injustice, took all his *olles* and registers and put them in a place so humid that they perished entirely, and it is impossible to know anything from them." In their own account, the destruction of the archive was one of the worst crimes perpetrated against their family. "This is one of the chief complaints that the supplicants have presented before the commissioners named by the council for a revision of the trial, and which will without doubt be proven true by the report of these same commissioners."[47] The French advocate La Morandière concurred that the Héberts had destroyed Nayiniyappa's palm leaf documents as an intentional and malicious act, meant to hide exactly how much of Nayiniyappa's goods the Héberts had managed to confiscate.[48]

Governor Hébert had seized the ledgers from Nayiniyappa's home on the grounds that they proved financial malfeasance on the broker's part. The ledgers, he argued, justified both the confiscation of Nayiniyappa's goods and the demand that the broker should reimburse the company with thousands of pagodas, as his sentence decreed. At the same time as he described the documents as a central piece of evidence against the broker, the sons charged, Hébert claimed they were unnecessary for actual examination. According to Nayiniyappa's sons, when the judges in the case were interrogated about their involvement in the trial, they said they had asked Hébert how they should decide what damages Nayiniyappa should be sentenced to pay the company. Hébert answered that he had determined the amount on the basis of the translations he had made of the palm leaf and account books. When the judges asked to see these account books, "Hébert fils said, 'They are at the Registrar's office, that is enough.' And Hébert said, 'Let us move on, or we will never finish.'"[49]

There is no way to determine whether the fragile *olles* disintegrated in the humid heat by design or the simple incompetence of Frenchmen used to paper. The loss had, to be sure, a pragmatic impact. The ledgers documenting Nayiniyappa's business dealings, the accounts owed and transactions paid, would have made it far easier for his family to collect on debts and continue doing business. Indeed, as late as 1725 French authorities referenced the seizure of Nayiniyappa's papers as a complicating factor when trying to sort out some local business dealings.[50] But the outrage over the destruction of an archive was also more fraught and multivalent. The obliteration of the archive tragically mirrored the annihilation of the man; like his archive, Nayiniyappa himself was thrown into a holding cell in the waterfront fort. Removed from his home and stripped of his ability to tell convincing tales through the denial of Portuguese in his interrogations, he was ruined in much the same way his documents were ruined—both were rendered mute and illegible. The archive here served as a potent symbol of both the past-oriented careful accumulation of accounts and connections and the future-oriented loss of opportunities. By bemoaning the destruction of their family documents, Nayiniyappa's sons were also voicing regret for losing the archive as a foundation on which to base their own telling of events and as source material for bolstering their claims to power. For them, the archive served not as a "monument" of the state and its power of ordering things and narratives but as a ruin and a relic of their family's position.[51]

The Destruction of Tiruvangadan's Archives

Nayiniyappa's associate and relative Tiruvangadan also complained of tampering with his personal business papers.[52] Tiruvangadan had been recruited to relocate from Madras to Pondichéry in 1715 as part of an ongoing French effort to lure well-established local merchants to the colony. Before he arrived in town, Nayiniyappa approached him and asked him to purchase a promissory note in the sum of 1,022 pagodas, which Governor Hébert's son had given to a man in Madras, one M. Lapotre. The money would be a short-term loan, as the governor's son promised he would repay the money as soon as Tiruvangadan arrived in Pondichéry. Tiruvangadan's appeal claimed that once he was in the French colony, the governor and his son greeted him warmly and promised him that he would shortly be repaid for the promissory note.[53] Thirteen days later he was arrested without being told the reason why, and as he wrote in his appeal, "All my accounts, promissory notes, and all my personal effects" were taken.[54] Hébert told Tiruvangadan that Nayiniyappa had been taken prisoner, and Tiruvangadan was accused of hiding Nayiniyappa's money—money the company was now claiming had been embezzled. Tiruvangadan answered that his own record books as well as Nayiniyappa's would reveal that the chief broker actually owed him money and not the other way around.[55] But the record books of both men had been seized in the process of their arrest, making such claims hard to prove.

Tiruvangadan was sent back to prison. After three months, he recounted, the Christian broker who replaced Nayiniyappa, Pedro, visited him in his cell.

"He asked me where the promissory note was which I had bought back from M. Lapotre, saying that M. Hébert [fils] had sent him to find this out so that he could repay me. I responded that I had it among my other papers in a little armoire."[56] The council's secretary then showed up at the imprisoned Tiruvangadan's house with a locksmith and ordered him to break the locked armoire, at which point Tiruvangadan's sister provided a key. The secretary removed the promissory note—the same one that Tiruvangadan had bought in Madras and for which the Héberts owed him 1,022 pagodas.[57] The next day French officials removed the remaining papers. Hébert summoned Tiruvangadan's clerks from Madras with additional account books.

The council had a number of documents, including the promissory note, translated into French.[58] While this was going on, the councillors prevented Tiruvangadan from communicating with his clerks to prevent them from making changes based on his directions. Tiruvangadan wrote in his appeal about the events that followed under Hébert's orders: "The next day I was taken to a house, and there were the catechist's son [Manuel] and ten or twelve clerks, who had with them Nainapa's accounts. These clerks or scribes and the catechist's son examined these accounts carefully, balancing everything over four or five days and asking me for clarification."[59] The clerks concluded that Tiruvangadan had spoken accurately: Nayiniyappa owed him a small sum, and he held none of Nayiniyappa's money.

Tiruvangadan argued that Hébert had arrested him because he hoped to avoid paying for the promissory note by proving that Tiruvangadan had purchased the note with Nayiniyappa's money. This would have made the note the property of the company, according to the charges against the chief broker. Hébert fils himself conducted the interrogation about the origins of the funds used to buy his promissory note. Tiruvangadan suggested that the general's son clearly implied that providing the desired answers would lead to his release. "Hebert fils asked, 'Have you nothing more to say?' I answered, 'What more can I say?' And having heard that he turned his back on me and said, 'You do not want to leave this prison,' and had the corporal put me back in the cell."[60]

After several months in prison, Tiruvangadan was released and banished from Pondichéry. At that point, his confiscated papers were returned to him—except for the promissory note bearing Hébert fils's name.[61] Tiruvangadan sent his sister to ask for the note and wrote Governor Hébert demanding its return.[62] A letter from Pedro informed him that the governor had read his letter and decided that his punishment for wrongdoing committed in Pondichéry was a fine of 1,022 pagodas—conveniently, the exact sum that Hébert's son owed to Tiruvangadan.[63] Tiruvangadan wrote again to the governor, only to again receive responses from Pedro the chief broker.[64] Pedro's third response to Tiruvangadan concluded, "This is all that M. le Général told me to write you."[65] Tiruvangadan's appeal, sent to Paris in demand for recompense for his losses, included the three letters Tiruvangadan wrote to Governor Hébert and the three letters from Pedro he received in response as tangible evidence of Hébert's vexing silence. Much as he had insisted on using French instead of Portuguese in Nayiniyappa's interrogations, here the governor refused to have direct communication with an individual he had frequently dealt with directly in the past.

To instill the letters with greater evidentiary force, Tiruvangadan had their veracity attested to by a French notary in Madras.[66] The notary explained that Tiruvangadan's own letters had been translated from Portuguese into French. He shed more light on the process of producing these texts by naming the man who had translated the letters into Portuguese from the original Malabar (Tamil) in which Tiruvangadan had composed them.[67] Both Tiruvangadan and the Tamil-Portuguese translator appeared in person before the French notary to vouch for the documents. A large crowd of supporters attended this attestation, including two French Capuchin missionaries, in another example of the involvement of missionaries in the minutiae of the Nayiniyappa Affair.[68]

Tiruvangadan made extensive efforts to spread the message about the wrong done to him, producing multiple versions of his complaints and sending them to the king, to the directors of the company, and to M. de Nyons, a man formerly employed in Pondichéry who had returned to France. The Indian merchant hoped this French ally would make sure his letters reached as wide an audience as possible in the metropole.[69] Given that several of the appeals of Nayiniyappa, Tiruvangadan, and their associate Ramanada were crafted while the men were still held in prison, both the production and distribution of these documents posed special challenges.[70] Yet the company directors ultimately awarded restitution to Tiruvangadan along with Nayiniyappa's heirs, ordering that Hébert pay him ten thousand pagodas in damages. However, Tiruvangadan died in 1726 before the restitution was paid out, and it benefited only his heirs.[71] Guruvappa experienced the same unfortunate circumstance.

The Destruction of Governor Hébert's Archives

A man at the height of his power was thrown into prison, his personal belongings confiscated, his allies turned into enemies. Nayiniyappa suffered this fate—but so did Governor Hébert, twice: first, when he was removed from his position as governor of Pondichéry in 1713, and again when he was arrested in 1718, as a result of Nayiniyappa's posthumous exoneration. Governor Hébert and Nayiniyappa, over the evolution of the Nayiniyappa Affair, more than once found themselves unlikely twins on a fateful seesaw that put one on top as the other was down. So it was also in the matter of personal archives.

Like Nayiniyappa and his allies, Hébert actively tried to create a documentary archive that would cast him—and not Nayiniyappa—in the role of both hero and victim. Historians have largely turned a deaf ear to the clamoring of Hébert's paper trail, giving Nayiniyappa and his supporters greater credence. Yet both men conceptualized a personal collection of documents as the bedrock for their true stories. Both carefully created and curated bodies of texts, only to see destruction, seizure, or denial of documents render their efforts ineffectual. Like Nayiniyappa's sons' statements after their father's death, Hébert's statements reveal that the dismantling of archives and personal writing was a particular and painful punishment.

Hébert's first fall from grace had happened three years before Nayiniyappa's arrest. Dulivier, following orders from secretary of the Marine, Comte de Pontchartrain, and the general directors, replaced him as governor in October 1713.[72] Hébert had failed to make significant money for the company, and when Dulivier took over the position, he found a measly fourteen pagodas in the company's coffers.[73] Hébert's conflicts with the Jesuits, whose powerful allies in the French court would have been in a position to affect hiring decisions in the colony, probably also influenced his ejection from the governor's seat. Hébert found himself in what must have seemed an unbelievable reversal. His experience uncannily prefigures and mirrors that of Nayiniyappa three years later. Like the broker, Hébert found himself defending himself before the very same institutional structures in which had had filled an important position. Hébert's first removal from office in 1713 may have been even more unlikely than Nayiniyappa's own surprising fall from power, given that the Superior Council questioned Hébert for malfeasance a mere few days after he had been their president.

Dulivier demanded that Hébert provide his accounts to the council, in accordance with orders he brought from Paris. Six days later, on October 13, 1713, the council opened an investigation. It noted Hébert's refusal to obey the order to provide his accounts and issued a summons.[74] No tangible outcome resulted. The company offered Hébert the much less important position of governor of Île Bourbon. He refused and returned to France to seek a better position.[75] It was testament to Hébert's political acumen that he returned to the colony in 1715, this time with an appointment as Governor Dulivier's superior, with the newly created title of "General of the Nation."

The second time Hébert fell from grace, he would not have such a quick recovery. On July 14, 1718, he and his son were signing their names to a standard deliberation of the council.[76] The very next deliberation in the record, dated August 19, 1718, notes the arrival of a ship from France, carrying orders from the king to remove Hébert from his position as governor and president of the council and replace him with La Prévostière as interim governor.[77] The following day the new governor read before the council a letter from the company's general directors regarding Hébert's removal. It demanded the seizure of all Hébert's papers, furniture, personal effects, account registers, and books—and not only those kept by Hébert himself but anything belonging to him that might be held in other hands.[78]

Perhaps worried that Hébert would make scarce either his papers or himself, the councillors immediately dispatched two of their members to Hébert's house with the seals of the company as tangible proof of their authority over their former superior.[79] In December of 1718 the council's records noted that Hébert had refused to comply with the seizure of his goods and that the company had accommodated him in this matter.[80] At this time, the council members wrote, they had received new information regarding embezzlement by Hébert and his son, including a claim that Hébert owed the company the enormous sum of one hundred thousand livres.[81] In the meantime, claimed the council, in order to protect the interests of the company and of the multiple people who had brought complaints against the Héberts, father and son must be held at the fort until the departure of the next ship to prevent an escape or a spiriting away of their fortune.[82]

That Hébert and his son found themselves as prisoners at the fort—the very same fort in which Nayiniyappa was held and where he died—must have carried special resonance for both the former governor and the men who had been his subordinates. The *procureur général* suggested that the Héberts be sent to France as prisoners under the authority of the ship's captain until they could be transferred to the king's officers immediately upon disembarkation in France.[83] When the council signed this order on December 15, 1718, Hébert completed his transformation from prosecutor to prisoner.

Hébert described his arrest: "On the 15th of December, as I was returning from mass, I was taken from my house, dragged through the streets of Pondichéry, and taken by a troop of soldiers as if I were a scoundrel and a villain, and confined in a small prison alongside my son."[84] As in Nayiniyappa's case, all his requests for an explanation for why he was being subjected to such "cruel and harsh treatment" were denied.[85] His son also complained that his requests for clarification were ignored. This complaint mirrors Tiru-vangadan's complaints regarding his three unanswered letters to Governor Hébert. Hébert protested that he had sent two letters to Governor La Pré-vostière but received no response.[86] The seizure of the personal papers would also draw Hébert's ire: he complained that they had been taken from him precisely at the time that he most needed them in order to present a case in his own defense.[87]

Once Nayiniyappa's conviction was overturned in 1719, company records positioned Hébert firmly in the role of culprit. An account penned by La Morandière, the councillor and judge who became an advocate for Nayini-yappa and author of his later appeals, suggested he actively tried to redirect blame in Hébert's direction. La Morandière revealed in one of his letters that when local Indians wanted to complain about their mistreatment, they complained against Pedro, the Christian broker who replaced Nayiniyappa. But La Morandière redirected these complaints from Pedro to the Héberts, because—so he argued—everything that happened in town was done at the instigation of Hébert, and Pedro was only his tool.[88] He reassured the direc-tors: "You have not at all been implicated, Messieurs, in these disturbing affairs."[89] This depiction of Pedro as an agency-free tool is highly question-able, given his active campaign of collecting evidence against his rival, Nay-iniyappa. The implication that attacks against Hébert served the additional role of shielding the directors of the company in Paris from blame provides a motive beyond La Morandière's ongoing animosity for Hébert. Thus these statements bolster Hébert's claims of being targeted by his enemies.

Three days after the Pondichéry council overturned Nayiniyappa's con-viction and cleared the broker's name, Hébert wrote a response, presenting his own version of events. It was titled "A protest by me, the undersigned, for-merly *général de la nation française* in the East Indies, and presently director of the company, made against the violence and injustice committed against me by Sieur de La Prévostière."[90] In it, Hébert described his removal from office the prior year in the most dramatic terms. The previous August, he began, a ship had arrived from St. Malo, carrying orders that he was to give up the government of Pondichéry. The company then demanded the seizure of his papers, echoing the efforts to seize his papers in 1713 when he was first dis-missed from his post.[91] Hébert wrote that he could not agree to such a shame-ful thing, and he put down his objections in writing, and there matters rested for a while. He claimed he had "the best reasons in the world" to object to the examination of his affairs by La Prévostière, since he had twice dismissed La Prévostière from the company's service, and "we had for quite some time lived in a state of open enmity."[92] He had decided "to let things run their natural course. I quickly realized that I was the dupe of my own good heart."[93] Hébert referenced Nayiniyappa's sons and allies when he wrote, "The Blacks whom I had chased away from town as public pests returned triumphant, protected by the governor and the government."[94] He accused the Indians' advocate La Morandière of exacerbating the upheaval, saying that his enemy "encouraged the Blacks to present the most insolent complaints against me, of whom he himself was the author."[95]

Once Hébert realized "but too late, that I was in the hands of my cruelest enemies," he understood it mattered little what arguments he made or what information he provided, since nothing would deter his adversaries from the plan to crush him.[96] The similarity to Nayiniyappa's claims is startling. As Nayiniyappa argued that Hébert refused to hear him out and made him voiceless, so did Hébert complain in a similar vein. "I waited with patience, entirely resigned to the will of God, for the conclusion of such cruel persecution," he wrote.[97] In much the same terms Nayiniyappa described signing the paper bearing his conviction "while lifting his eyes to the heavens asking for justice."[98]

Hébert recognized the parallel nature between Nayiniyappa's predicament and his own subsequent woes when he thus raged against it: "[La Prévostière] covered my white hair with the worst infamy, he equated a French name with that of the most odious [of men], the most unworthy who has ever been known in all of India. Me, a white man and a Frenchman, with a negro regarded in this country as a slave; me, a director of the company and consequently one of the masters of this place, with a miserable servant; me, a general of the nation, with a worthless black villain, an idolater."[99] However much he fumed at being compared to Nayiniyappa, and highlighted in racial and racist terms the differences between them, Hébert found himself making the very same claims the broker and his allies had made when they tried to overturn his conviction. For both men, the act of selecting a body of documents to prove their probity and innocence stood at the center of their respective calls for justice, and accusations about the destruction of these personal archives were a recurring motif.

As the investigation shifted its shape over the course of 1718–1720 and focused on Hébert as perpetrator instead of prosecutor, the disgraced governor made claims very similar to Nayiniyappa's about the importance of his stash of documents, as when he complained about the council's attempt to seize his papers. Hébert adamantly refused to hand over his papers, claiming that the request was both damaging and shaming.[100] Worse still, he claimed, the seized papers were not properly inventoried.[101] Thus the harm inflicted on his personal archive would be a permanent one. He acknowledged his former subalterns had examined the information he provided in his defense, but, he wrote, "all my arguments were ignored, all my requests were dismissed as frivolous."[102] He realized none of the information he supplied would make the slightest difference, nothing would stop his adversaries from "oppressing" him.[103] Nayiniyappa's sons used highly similar language in their appeals. In an instance of uncanny doubling and sonic reverberation, Hébert was repeating the words of the sons, who wrote that the Jesuits had been "oppressing" their father.[104]

La Morandière presented another view of the seizure of Hébert's personal archive. In addition to being a judge who had condemned Nayiniyappa, a longtime enemy of Hébert, and an eventual defender of the broker, La Morandière had been the company's bookkeeper. He claimed that Hébert had falsified the company's account books. La Morandière also accused Hébert's son of hiding the company's receipt book, thereby making it impossible to determine how much money the company had on hand.[105] He claimed, of his inquiries into the Héberts' disreputable bookkeeping practices, "All these inquiries, which I undertook in the course of my role as your [the directors'] bookkeeper, brought upon me the wrath of Hébert and his son. . . . They raged to a point I cannot express, and promised that as soon as they arrived in France they would have me shamed and removed from your service."[106] The bookkeeper La Morandière's role in crafting the appeals by Nayiniyappa and his associates helps explain their emphasis on record keeping as a central means for effective claims making in the Nayiniyappa Affair.

Of all the papers that had been taken from him, Hébert was especially indignant about the seizure of one document. "Among my papers was a journal that I had kept, day by day," wrote Hébert, in a moment of easy-to-identify-with writerly vulnerability. "This [journal] was a secret thing, it might as well have been my confession. . . . No one had ever seen this journal, not even my son, and it should never have been revealed. Everyone knows that such things are sacred."[107] In this journal, Hébert explained, he had written with absolute honesty of his unfavorable opinions about his colleague La Prévostière and other members of the council, never guessing they might read it. Hébert wrote of the incendiary contents—unfortunately not preserved, "You will easily judge the effect that passages in my journal had on the people concerned."[108] The publication of his diary's content, Hébert suggested, was a deliberate attempt to alienate people who might have otherwise supported him. When the council convened to discuss Hébert's culpability in the Nayiniyappa Affair, three of the commissioners recused themselves under different pretexts—Hébert likely felt they might have been allies if they had not read his diary.[109]

On the day of his departure from India, ignobly removed from the town he had so recently ruled, Hébert made sure to deposit a copy of a written appeal in the Pondichéry *greffe* (court clerk's office), ensuring that a paper trail proclaiming his innocence would remain in the colonial archive even after he was gone.[110] He made multiple copies of this document, sending another version of it to Paris from Brittany, where he was held upon arrival in France.

Throughout his ordeal, Hébert would emphasize the seizure of his papers in Pondichéry. His writings pose a formulation of private archives as complex and multifaceted creations: some documents must be made public, yet their veracity is denied; others must remain private or be desecrated. In either case, the writing is the measure of the man.

Distributed Authority, Distributed Archives

Most of the documents that made up the archives of the Compagnie des Indes in Pondichéry were shipped from India to France in 1954.[111] The company collections pertaining to India were then moved from the National Archives in Paris to Aix-en-Provence, to the newly constituted Archives d'outre-mer—an archive that was itself part of an explicit French effort to reckon with the colonial past. Documents, this reminds us, end up in archives through the intentions and machinations of people and institutions, and the archive is shaped and made legible through political agendas.[112]

The distribution of the remnants and traces of the Nayiniyappa Affair in archives in Aix-en-Provence, Nantes, Paris, and Pondichéry suggests the global contours of the affair itself. This chapter has suggested that far-flung archives serve as both semiotic referent and embodiment of the global ambition of the French imperial project. The actors most intimately involved in the affair understood their personal documentary collections to be the bedrock of their authority and reputation.

In addition to the official and unofficial records produced by company officials, missionaries, and the brokers they employed, the archive of French India consists of daily records created in global settings, as ships crisscrossed the ocean between France and India. Evidence of Nayiniyappa's position in the colony prior to his fall can therefore be found archived in unexpected places. The journal with which this book began, written aboard a fleet of three merchant ships that traveled between Brest and Pondichéry in the period 1712–1714, is such a place. The fleet of the *Mercure, Vénus,* and *Jason* had come to Pondichéry to fill the ships' holds with Indian goods, mostly cloth woven by local artisans.[113] The majority of the journal was written at sea and thus devoted to matters of wind and navigation. But when the merchant sailors arrived in Pondichéry in 1714, they were impressed by the massive wedding celebration hosted by Nayiniyappa in honor of his son.[114] It is poignant to think of this demonstration of power and family taking place so shortly before Nayiniyappa's lonely death in his prison cell. But it is also noteworthy that this trace of Nayiniyappa's family affair should appear in the record of a ship's journal currently held in a departmental archive in Nantes, penned by one M. Robert, a man who had surely never before heard of Nayiniyappa or his importance for the French project. Yet there Nayiniyappa is in the journal, "a *facteur* of the Company, a Black gentile."[115] The ship's scribe described the wedding ceremony as being carried out "in the manner of the gentiles, and with all possible magnificence," and the writer breathlessly reported that the wedding cost more than eight thousand pagodas.[116] When the town's Christians—French and Tamil alike—married, Pondichéry's civil records recorded the fact in a brief entry. The record of a journey from Brest thus provides the only source for the elaborate details of a marriage that appears to have taken over the streets of Pondichéry, both "White Town" and "Black Town," for days on end, with the cannons in the fort booming in celebration.[117] Both the global distribution of the archiving of this event and the munificence it described—striking enough that a visitor newly arrived to the colony would devote several pages of a ship's journal to detail the wedding celebrated by the colony's broker—reveal Nayiniyappa as a man occupying significant space in the colony's early days and its historical record.

The Nayiniyappa Affair demonstrates that while archives are an instrument of power, access to the act of archiving is broadly available, at least to actors with the literacy and social authority to produce records that have probative value.[118] The affair made visible the existence of a shared vision in the colony of archives as a prerequisite for action, knowledge, and reputation. Just as the Nayiniyappa Affair had global reach and concerned issues of shared and unexpectedly distributed authority, so its archives are also globally constituted and in turn widely distributed. The distribution of the archives is emblematic of the distribution of authority.

Epilogue

After Nayiniyappa's son Guruvappa died in 1724, French officials in Pondichéry considered doing away entirely with the post of chief commercial broker. The French governor at the time, Joseph Beauvollier de Courchant, worried about appointing another powerful local to the job: "Chevalier Guruvappa having died, and Tiruvangadan [Nayiniyappa's brother-in-law] being the kind of man to take on too much authority if we were to make him courtier, we announced to the Blacks that from now on there will be no modeliar [chief broker]."[1]

But Beauvollier de Courchant encountered opposition from other high-ranking French officials in Pondichéry, who insisted that they simply could not operate without an Indian courtier. The governor himself also came to the realization that he could not govern the colony without the help of a Tamil courtier. He needed a broker, he wrote in a letter to Paris, to warn him in advance of all the rumblings and doings in the town.[2] He ultimately selected Pedro, the native Christian who had filled the post after Nayiniyappa's arrest in 1716 and before Guruvappa's ascension in 1722. As he wrote, "We could not choose anyone but Pedro, beloved by the Blacks, and who would never take to himself more authority than that which we had given him."[3]

The governor's justification for ruling out Tiruvangadan—that he was "the kind of man to take on too much authority"—and approving Pedro as the kind of man who would do no such thing pointed to the central problem the French encountered when employing professional intermediaries. A broker could not succeed without authority. But how much authority was too much? What actions or powers would tip the balance, changing an intermediary from a trusted helpmeet to a threat? No clear answer could be given. Even the most valued intermediaries raised the specter of danger, as Nayiniyappa's downfall reveals. But the aftermath of the Nayiniyappa scandal reshaped Pondichéry in the 1720s, as the reluctance to appoint an intermediary intimates. French officials had reason for their reluctance to make another Indian—especially one who had a knack for procuring power—a central actor in the colony.

More than half a century after Nayiniyappa's arrest, the issues that animated the Nayiniyappa Affair and its details still informed and motivated French colonial policy. In 1776, exactly sixty years after Nayiniyappa's arrest, a letter signed by Louis XV provided instructions for the newly appointed governor of Pondichéry, Guillaume de Bellecombe. At the time, French officials in the colony were fighting about the appointment of a new chief commercial broker, with different factions in the colony making the case for different local men. The king's orders from Versailles settled the matter by decreeing that one of Nayiniyappa's descendants be appointed to the post. "His ancestors have always filled the position since 1715 [the actual date was 1708], and one of them came to France and was decorated with the Order of St. Michel for the important services he provided to the nation."[4] The new appointee, the royal order hopefully continued, would surely prove to be as devoted to the French as his illustrious ancestors were. The Nayiniyappa Affair was unfinished business, as colonial and metropolitan French officials continued to struggle over the best way to implement their rule in India while relying on local intermediaries.

Distributed and delegated authority, I have argued, was the hallmark of the early decades of French presence in India. The simultaneous codependence and antagonism between the French projects of commerce and conversion engendered a crisis of authority in Pondichéry. As a result of the inherently partial, fractured, fragmented potential of early projects of expansion, colonial authority was widely and unexpectedly dispersed. That is, colonial power and agency were, partly because of their mediated nature, distributed power and agency. This allowed Tamil intermediaries employed by the French—commercial brokers and religious interpreters—to rise to positions of prominence and power, much to the discomfort of their French employers. In Pondichéry's early days, sovereignty was bifurcated because of the clash of religious and commercial agendas. The reliance on local intermediaries was in part a result of this bifurcation; as missionaries and traders were in an ongoing and voluble state of conflict about the kind of rule they wished to implement in India, both groups needed to rely on local go-betweens to help them advance the agenda to which they subscribed. The reliance on go-betweens also entailed efforts to limit and circumscribe this very dependence.

Even as historians have shown that French absolutism was more propaganda than reality in Europe, they have failed to examine the limits of French claims to power in the colonial context.[5] The tensions between commerce and conversion in Pondichéry were the site-specific example of a broader feature of early modern European empires, in which attempts to imagine or present a unified vision of authority, one that enacted the agenda of the metropolitan state, encountered the friction of practice. In Pondichéry and in the offices of the company in Paris, officials wanted to strengthen their authority in the town—but this authority was not the same ideological construct as hegemonic sovereignty, familiar from later colonial examples. In religious, commercial, linguistic, and legal realms, French rule in India did not, as a general rule, demand a monogamous relation to the authority of the Compagnie des Indes. For native residents of Pondichéry, political identity and allegiance could be multiple, such that there was no need to consider themselves unambiguously and exclusively subjects of the French king. French deployment of political, religious, and legal authority was a delicate balancing act.

At the time of Nayiniyappa's arrest, France's entangled imperial efforts were straining at the seams, ridden with contradictory ideologies and methods of pursuing success. Trader-officials' and missionaries' visions of French rule in India were not always compatible with one another, and interactions with local professional intermediaries allowed and at times required the articulation of incommensurate agendas. By revealing the repeated conflicts among and between agents of the French state, the Compagnie des Indes, and religious authorities, this book has shown how early imperial formations could never fully achieve hegemonic authority, fracturing instead into factions and foes. These conflicts were articulated through and with colonial intermediaries.

The intersection of interests of traders, missionaries, and go-betweens prior to and following Nayiniyappa's arrest demonstrates not only the constant and ongoing conflicts between colonizers and colonized—a widely analyzed phenomenon—but also the less commented-upon tensions and factionalism between various branches of the French overseas project. The Nayiniyappa Affair therefore highlights the fact that in French India, the lines between colonizer and colonized, patron and client, could not be quite so sharply drawn. Nayiniyappa's position as *chef des malabars* and chief commercial broker to the Compagnie des Indes allows a privileged view into the roles colonial intermediaries in Pondichéry filled. As a professional intermediary par excellence, Nayiniyappa reflects the ways in which the intermediary position was Janus-faced, simultaneously facing home and away, toward past and future, the familiar and the new. Different colonial agents held varying expectations of Nayiniyappa and intermediaries like him, and the global and sustained interest that the Nayiniyappa Affair generated was the result of French ambivalence in both commercial and religious quarters about dependence on such intermediaries.

The Nayiniyappa Affair was a pivotal event for French India in that contemporaries understood it as both momentous and transformative.[6] Nayiniyappa's arrest disrupted the established order and called into question the practice of distributed authority. As an event, the affair was both revelatory of social structures and transformative of these same structures. In the context of colonial South Asia in the eighteenth century, in which European rule was a shaky proposition at best, scandals and trials provided privileged opportunities for hashing out the meaning and shape of sovereignty in both its Indian and its European guises.[7] The Nayiniyappa controversy provided the involved actors an opportunity to consider and argue for different visions of France and its empire.

By the end of the affair, the colony was becoming a place in which colonial power exerted itself in more familiar forms—with a greater reliance on French language and French (or at least Christian) personnel. In the mid-eighteenth century, and especially under the ambitious French governor Dupleix, the nature of the French presence in India changed. This period saw much more aggressive, military attempts to bring about French territorial expansion in the subcontinent.[8] But in the first half of the eighteenth century, the French in India were clients as much as patrons. This was true in relation to Indian rulers, from regional courts and principalities all the way up to the Mughals. But this was also the case in their relationships with their local intermediaries, relations that were always symbiotic and reciprocal, in which the balance of influence and reliance occasionally shifted, such that the French could be patrons one day, clients the next. Working relations between French administrators and the moneyed commercial brokers in Pondichéry did not always allow for clear hierarchical distinctions, and affiliation with the French company and even with French missionaries did not necessarily entail subordination. French trader-administrators, cognizant of their profound dependence on local markets and patterns of familial obligation and patronage, largely refrained from attempts to restructure or displace these patterns, as would become common in later colonial projects. The French did seek to circumscribe the power and centrality of Tamil players in the governance of the colony in the second half of the eighteenth century. But the transformation was never complete. When the Christian chief broker Pedro died in 1746, the French authorities replaced him with Ananda Ranga Pillai, Nayiniyappa's relative, who was not a Christian. The lure of the services a well-connected local man could provide proved stronger than the preference for a Christian.

In constructing an account of the colony from the details of the Nayiniyappa Affair, I have told an imperial history in a local register. The affair might seem too minor a prism. These are, after all, the trials and tribulations of one man. Arlette Farge and Jacques Revel have suggested that historians studying events that might appear at first glance too minor or atypical should play with scale, simultaneously paying close attention to the minutiae of the archive that "resist generalization and typology and are perhaps ultimately incomprehensible," as well as to the systemic and structural frameworks in which such events take place and from which they both derive meaning and imbue with new signification.[9] The temporally concise framework of the Nayiniyappa Affair contains an elaborate, expansive, and complicated webbing of affinities, commitments, animosities, rivalries, and ideologies of French traders, missionaries, and their Tamil intermediaries. By describing the various assemblages and clusters and the seemingly contradictory and disparate explanations for the conviction of Nayiniyappa and his exoneration, I have sought to provide a view of the whole. The history of empire revealed through the affair shows that accounts of the largest of large-scale processes, such as global networks of commerce and conversion, can still make room for the human-sized experiences of loyalty, fear, vengeance, and love.

In the summer of 2008, a direct descendant of Ananda Ranga Pillai, and therefore an indirect descendant of Nayiniyappa himself, gave me a tour of his property.[10] Exactly three hundred years after Nayiniyappa was first appointed to a position of prominence in Pondichéry, the carefully guarded yet darkened mansion serves as a potent reminder of the family's former power and the memorializing of that power by subsequent generations. A businessman, Ananda Ranga Ravichandran lives with his family at the center of Pondichéry's "Tamil Town," adjacent to the city's central market, where Nayiniyappa was flogged. His house is a simple, well-maintained structure, no different from the others on the street. But a door leading from the kitchen opens into a small backyard, and this opens a portal into a family's glorious past. There was an ancestral home, the now-dilapidated but still striking mansion that Ananda Ranga Pillai built for his family in the 1730s (figure 4). Approaching the

FIGURE 4.   The sign, in Tamil, identifies the building as "Ananda Ranga Pillai's mansion," viewed here from the central market of Puducherry, as the town is now called. Photograph by author.

house from the parallel street, I could readily see vestiges of the house's former glory, though the clutter of the market street muted the effect.

When the British razed Pondichéry in 1761 as Ananda Ranga Ravichandran's famous ancestor lay dying, few of the colony's mansions survived. The situation of Ananda Ranga Pillai's house, farther from the coast's so-called White Town, saved it. The mansion's architecture is a clear mix of Tamil and French styles, with heavily carved wooden pillars in the Tamil style surrounding the ground floor's main space and white columns supporting the second floor veranda, in the French manner. When I asked to take a picture of a golden statue of Ananda Ranga Pillai, Ravichandran proudly stood next to it, his body as close as possible to the pedestal, head tilted toward his illustrious ancestor (figure 5).

Behind the statue, on a back wall next to photographs of Ravichandran's parents, hangs an eighteenth-century portrait of Ananda Ranga Pillai, painted by an unknown artist. A lavishly illustrated volume about the history of the *Compagnie des Indes* includes a reproduction of the portrait, which is partially discernible in figure 5.[11] The caption in the volume notes the source merely as a "private collection," obscuring the spatial and familial specificity of the portrait's survival from the eighteenth century.

FIGURE 5. A statue of Ananda Ranga Pillai, chief broker to the Compagnie des Indes in the mid-eighteenth century and Nayiniyappa's nephew. Standing next to him is his descendant Ananda Ranga Ravichandran. Photograph by author.

Although the mansion stands empty most of the time, it serves as a memorial of the influence members of Nayiniyappa's family once wielded in the colony. Pondichéry's French Institute once held a conference devoted to the diaries of Ananda Ranga Pillai in it, and the local government recently recognized it as a heritage site. Ravichandran said he was hoping to receive funds for the mansion's restoration so that he could convert it into a boutique hotel. Pondichéry's robust tourism industry nostalgically evokes an imagined French colonial past, one carefully scrubbed of the violence and inequities of colonial reality.[12]

As I walked through the mansion, with its imposing golden statue presiding over empty rooms, it was easy to imagine it as a repository of sorts, an archive of material sources for a biography of colonial power, its unexpected forms, and ultimately its decline. In maintaining the mansion and keeping the memory of Ananda Ranga Pillai alive for Pondichéry's present and future, the family was making a claim for its own historical significance. Just a short walk away, the "Rue Nainiappa Poullé" attests to that significance. The cracked street sign is made of blue tin, of the same kind used for Parisian street signs (figure 6). With its Tamil name rendered Francophone, its Parisian-inspired tin weathered by the local heat, the sign is a tangible remnant of the distributed authority that created the Nayiniyappa Affair.

FIGURE 6.   In Puducherry today, one can walk along Rue Nainiappa Poullé. Photograph by author.

Notes

The following abbreviations are used in the notes:

ADLA   Archives départementales de Loire Atlantique, Nantes, France
ADN   Archives de Nantes, Nantes, France
AMEP   Archives, Missions étrangères de Paris, France
AN   Archives nationales de France, Paris, France
ANOM   Archives nationales d'outre-mer, Aix-en-Provence, France
BC   Bibliothèque franciscaine des Capucins, Paris
BNF   Bibliothèque nationales française
COL   Fonds des colonies
DPPC   Dépôt des papiers publics des colonies
FM   Fonds ministériels
GR   Greffes
INDE   Fonds territoreaux, Établissements français de l'Inde
MAR   Fonds de la Marine
MF   Manuscrits français
NAF   Nouvelles acquisitions françaises
NAIP   National Archives of India, Puducherry Record Centre, India
Vanves Archives Jésuites, Vanves, France

Introduction

1. "Journal de bord de navires le Mercure, le Jason et la Vénus, formant une escadre envoyeé aux Indes orientales sous le commadement de M. Guimont du Coudray, pour aller faire la course puis la traite, commencé en 1712 et fini en 1714," ADLA, série C, 875.

2. The writer of the journal, one M. Robert, unfamiliar with Indian names, wrote the name phonetically as "Aniaba" but references him as the company's chief agent, the role filled by Nayiniyappa in this period. The description of his influence and the phonetic similarity of the name's rendering make clear that the man in question was Nayiniyappa.

3. The ship's journal is not paginated, but the entries describing the marriage celebrations are for May 30, 1714; May 31, 1714; and June 1, 1714. "Journal de bord de navires le Mercure, le Jason et la Vénus."

4. This description of Guruvappa's baptism is taken from a memoir written in the latter half of the eighteenth century by one of his relatives. NAIP, eighteenth-century documents, folder 20.

5. Guruvappa is referred to by this name in a record of a 1724 commercial transaction in Pondichéry, held in ANOM, FM, DPPC, GR/675.

6. For an examination of partial and contingent sovereignty of company rule in a Dutch context in the Indian Ocean, see Kerry Ward, *Networks of Empire: Forced Migration in the Dutch East India Company* (Cambridge: Cambridge University Press, 2012).

7. Both Indian and Hindu are anachronistic categories that do not appear in the French sources of this period. The French sources refer to practitioners of local religions, who today would be glossed as Hindu, as "gentiles," "pagans," or "idolaters." I use "Hindu" occasionally when not quoting French actors to dispense with the pejorative stance implicit in these designations. "Indian" is just as anachronistic. The sources most often use "malabar," and occasionally "blacks" (*noirs*) to refer to Pondichéry's residents with origins in the Tamil region. I also use "Tamil," which does appear in French sources (*tamoul*) albeit rarely.

8. K. S. Mathew, "Missionaries from the Atlantic Regions and the Social Changes in French Pondicherry from the Seventeenth to Nineteenth Centuries," in *Les relations entre la France et l'Inde de 1673 à nos jours*, ed. Jacques Weber (Paris: Les Indes savantes, 2002), 349–69. On MEP, see Adrien Launay, *Histoire générale de la société des missions étrangères* (Paris: Téqui, 1894).

9. Seema Alavi, *The Eighteenth Century in India* (Oxford: Oxford University Press, 2008); P. J. Marshall, *The Eighteenth Century in Indian History: Evolution or Revolution?* (New Delhi: Oxford University Press, 2005). On decentering colonialism in narratives of eighteenth-century India, see Jon E. Wilson, "Early Colonial India beyond Empire," *Historical Journal* 50, no. 4 (December 2007): 951–70.

10. Robert Englebert and Guillaume Teasdale, eds., *French and Indians in the Heart of North America, 1630–1815* (East Lansing: Michigan State University Press, 2013), 1.

11. Reviews of the growing scholarship on French empire are in Sophie Dulucq and Colette Zytnicki, "Penser le passé colonial français, entre perspectives historiographiques et résurgence des mémoires," *Vingtième Siècle. Revue d'histoire*, no. 86 (April 2005): 59–69; Alice L. Conklin and Julia Clancy-Smith, "Writing Colonial Histories: Introduction," *French Historical Studies* 27, no. 3 (Summer 2004): 497–505; Christopher Hodson and Brett Rushforth, "Absolutely Atlantic: Colonialism and the Early Modern French State in Recent Historiography," *History Compass* 8, no. 1 (January 2010): 101–17.

12. Even historians of French India characterize "failure" as its dominant feature. Catherine Manning, *Fortunes à Faire: The French in Asian Trade, 1719–48* (Aldershot, UK: Variorum, 1996), xiii; Philippe Haudrère, Gérard Le Bouëdec, and Louis Mézin, *Les compagnies des Indes* (Rennes, FR: Ouest France, 2001), 70–71; Michael Smithies, *A Resounding Failure: Martin and the French in Siam, 1672–1693* (Chiang Mai, Thai.: Silkworm Books, 1998); Paul Käppelin, *La Compagnie des Indes Orientales et François Martin: Etude sur l'histoire du commerce et des établissements français dans l'Inde sous Louis XIV (1664–1719)* (Paris, 1908), 1; Aniruddha Ray, *The Merchant and the State: The French in India, 1666–1739* (Delhi: Munshiram Manoharlal Publishers, 2004). For a work that aims to implicitly critique the trope of failure, arguing for a strong post-1763 French trade in South India, see Arvind Sinha, *The Politics of Trade: Anglo-French Commerce on the Coromandel Coast 1763–1793* (Delhi: Manohar Publishers, 2002).

13. On slavery, see, in New France, Brett Rushforth, *Bonds of Alliance: Indigenous and Atlantic Slaveries in New France* (Chapel Hill: University of North Carolina Press, 2012); in Mauritius, Megan Vaughan, *Creating the Creole Island: Slavery in Eighteenth-Century Mauritius* (Durham, NC: Duke University Press, 2005). On race and métissage in New France and Louisiana, Gilles Havard, *Empire et métissages: Indiens et Français dans le Pays d'en Haut, 1660–1715* (Paris: Les éditions du Septentrion, 2003); Sophie White, *Wild Frenchmen and Frenchified Indians: Material Culture and Race in Colonial Louisiana* (Philadelphia: University of Pennsylvania Press, 2012). On trade and privateering, Shannon Lee Dawdy, *Building the Devil's Empire: French Colonial New Orleans* (Chicago: University of Chicago Press, 2009).

14. Cécile Vidal, ed., *Français? La nation en débat entre colonies et métropole, XVIe–XIXe siècle* (Paris: Éd. de l'École des hautes études en sciences sociales, 2014).

15. Central for this scholarship is Richard White's identification of the "middle ground," a place where mediation is relied upon. Richard White, *The Middle Ground: Indians, Empires, and Republics in the Great Lakes Region, 1650–1815* (Cambridge: Cambridge University Press, 1991). Recent considerations of White's argument are Kathleen DuVal, *The Native Ground: Indians and Colonists in the Heart of the Continent* (Philadelphia: University of Pennsylvania Press, 2007); Pekka Hamalainen, *The Comanche Empire* (New Haven: Yale University Press, 2009); Michael Witgen, *An Infinity of Nations: How the Native New World Shaped Early North America* (Philadelphia: University of Pennsylvania Press, 2013); Michael McDonnell, *Masters of Empire: Great Lakes Indians and the Making of America* (New York: Hill and Wang, 2015); Robert M. Morrissey, *Empire by Collaboration: Indians, Colonists, and Governments in Colonial Illinois Country* (Philadelphia: University of Pennsylvania Press, 2015).

16. For examples from the early modern period, see Alida C. Metcalf, *Go-Betweens and the Colonization of Brazil, 1500–1600* (Austin: University of Texas Press, 2005); Brian Owensby, *Empire of Law and Indian Justice in Colonial Mexico* (Stanford, CA: Stanford University Press, 2008); Yanna Yannakakis, *The Art of Being In-Between: Native Intermediaries, Indian Identity, and Local Rule in Colonial Oaxaca* (Durham, NC: Duke University Press, 2008); Noel Malcolm, *Agents of Empire: Knights, Corsairs, Jesuits and Spies in the Sixteenth-Century Mediterranean World* (Oxford: Oxford University Press, 2015). In the Indian Ocean world more specifically, see Kenneth McPherson, "A Secret People of South Asia: The Origins, Evolution and Role of the Luso-Indian Goan Community from the Sixteenth to Twentieth Centuries," *Itinerario* 11, no. 2 (July 1987): 72–86; Mark Horton and John Middleton, *The Swahili: The Social Landscape of a Mercantile Society* (Oxford: Blackwell, 2000); Sanjay Subrahmanyam, *Three Ways to Be Alien: Travails and Encounters in the Early Modern World* (Lebanon, NH: Brandeis University Press, 2011).

17. Some recent examples are Kapil Raj, *Relocating Modern Science: Circulation and the Construction of Knowledge in South Asia and Europe, 1650–1900* (New York: Palgrave Macmillan, 2007); Kapil Raj, "The Historical Anatomy of a Contact Zone: Calcutta in the Eighteenth Century," *Indian Economic and Social History Review* 48, no. 1 (2011): 55–82; Bhavani Raman, *Document Raj: Writing and Scribes in Early Colonial South India* (Chicago: University of Chicago Press, 2012); E. Natalie Rothman, *Brokering Empire: Trans-Imperial Subjects between Venice and Istanbul* (Ithaca, NY: Cornell University Press, 2011); Miles Ogborn, *Indian Ink: Script and Print in the Making of the English East India Company* (Chicago: University of Chicago Press, 2007); Benjamin N. Lawrance,

Emily Lynn Osborn, and Richard L. Roberts, *Intermediaries, Interpreters, and Clerks: African Employees in the Making of Colonial Africa* (Madison: University of Wisconsin Press, 2006).

18. Antony Anghie, *Imperialism, Sovereignty and the Making of International Law* (Cambridge: Cambridge University Press, 2007); Lauren Benton, *A Search for Sovereignty: Law and Geography in European Empires, 1400–1900* (Cambridge: Cambridge University Press, 2009); Frank Trentmann, Philippa Levine, and Kevin Grant, eds., *Beyond Sovereignty: Britain, Empire and Transnationalism, c.1880–1950* (Houndmills, UK: Palgrave Macmillan, 2007); Patricia Seed, *Ceremonies of Possession in Europe's Conquest of the New World, 1492–1640* (Cambridge: Cambridge University Press, 1995).

19. Mary Dewhurst Lewis, *Divided Rule: Sovereignty and Empire in French Tunisia, 1881–1938* (Berkeley: University of California Press, 2013).

20. While this is still a dominant framework in European history, other fields have productively considered the situated, contingent construction of sovereignty. In the Indian Ocean, see Sebastian R. Prange, "Fluid Sovereignties: Maritime Claims and Contests in the Early Modern Indian Ocean" (paper presented at the Global Maritime History Conference, Huntington Library, San Marino, CA, March 4, 2016). In Ottoman history, see Gabor Kármán, "Sovereignty and Representation: Tributary States in the Seventeenth-Century Diplomatic System of the Ottoman Empire," in *The European Tributary States of the Ottoman Empires in the Sixteenth and Seventeenth Centuries*, ed. Gabor Kármán and Lovro Kunčević (Leiden, Neth.: Brill, 2013), 155–85; Joshua M. White, "Fetva Diplomacy: The Ottoman Şeyhülislam as Trans-Imperial Intermediary," *Journal of Early Modern History* 19, no. 2–3 (April 2015): 199–221.

21. In a study reflecting a dominant approach, Anthony Pagden has suggested an undivided concept of sovereignty in the early modern period that fractured into "divided" sovereignty in the modern period, in a simple chronological progression. Anthony Pagden, "Fellow Citizens and Imperial Subjects: Conquest and Sovereignty in Europe's Overseas Empires," *History and Theory* 44, no. 4 (December 2005): 28–46.

22. The royal grip was tight in the case of the French Company of the Indies but less so in the context of Mediterranean trade. On this, see Junko Thérèse Takeda, *Between Crown and Commerce: Marseille and the Early Modern Mediterranean* (Baltimore: Johns Hopkins University Press, 2011).

23. Charles Cole, *Colbert and a Century of French Mercantilism* (Hamden, CT: Archon Books, 1964); Glenn Ames, *Colbert, Mercantilism, and the French Quest for Asian Trade* (DeKalb: Northern Illinois University Press, 1996).

24. As Sanjay Subrahmanyam has noted, "The English Company, from its very inception, was not merely a commercial but a political actor." Sanjay Subrahmanyam, "Frank Submissions: The Company and the Mughals between Sir Thomas Roe and Sir William Norris," in *The Worlds of the East India Company* (Woodbridge, UK: Boydell Press, 2004), 70. Philip Stern has also suggested that the distinction between commercial and political stages in British presence in India does not reflect the reality of the English East India Company's early days. Philip J. Stern, *The Company-State: Corporate Sovereignty and the Early Modern Foundations of the British Empire in India* (New York: Oxford University Press, 2011).

25. Emily Erikson and Valentina Assenova, "Introduction: New Forms of Organization and the Coordination of Political and Commercial Actors," in *Chartering*

Capitalism: Organizing Markets, States, and Publics, ed. Emily Erikson (Bingley, UK: Emerald Group Publishing, 2015), 2–3.

26. Maxine Berg et al., "Private Trade and Monopoly Structures: The East India Companies and the Commodity Trade to Europe in the Eighteenth Century," in Ericson, *Chartering Capitalism*, 127.

27. On the background and responsibilities of the directors of the Compagnie des Indes in Paris, see Philippe Haudrère, "La direction générale de la Compagnie des Indes et son administration au milieu du XVIIIe siècle," in *Les Français dans l'océan Indien (XVIIe–XIXe siècle)* (Rennes, FR: Presses universitaires de Rennes, 2014), 51–57.

28. Sixteen percent of the initial capitalization came from merchants; 45 percent from the royal family; 19.5 percent from the nobility in the court, parliamentarians, and ministers; and 8.5 percent from financiers. Philippe Haudrère, *La compagnie française des Indes au XVIIIe siècle* (Paris: Indes savantes, 2005), 1:25. For a detailed account of the difficulties Colbert encountered in raising sufficient capital and the recurrent liquidity crises faced by the Compagnie des Indes, see Käppelin, *La Compagnie des Indes Orientales et François Martin*, esp. pt. 1, chap. 1.

29. On charter companies, see Erikson, *Chartering Capitalism*.

30. Ernestine Carreira, "La factorie française de Surat et les ports de l'Inde portugaise (1668–1778)," in *Les relations entre la France et l'Inde de 1673 à nos jours*, ed. Jacques Weber (Paris: Les Indes savantes, 2002), 23–38.

31. On Martin's relationship with Sher Khan Lodi, see G. David, "Sher Khan Lodi et François Martin ou les première relations Franco-Indiennes à Pondichéry," in *French in India and Indian Nationalism*, ed. K. S. Mathew (Delhi: B.R. Publishing Corp., 1999), 1–24.

32. L.A. Bellanger de Lespinay, *Mémoirs de L. A. Bellanger de Lespinay, Vendômois, sur son voyage aux Indes Orientales (1670–1675)* (Vendôme, FR: Typ. C. Huet, 1895), 204.

33. Historians of maritime trade in the Indian Ocean have charted the long-standing networks of exchange that connected ports such as Goa, Aden, and Aceh. More recent work has focused on how Indian Ocean communities were constituted by relationships forged both in and beyond the commercial sphere. For the importance of kinship and genealogy in Indian Ocean trade, see Engseng Ho, *The Graves of Tarim: Genealogy and Mobility across the Indian Ocean* (Berkeley: University of California Press, 2006). For linguistic exchanges in the Indian Ocean, see Pier Larson, *Ocean of Letters: Language and Creolization in an Indian Ocean Diaspora* (Cambridge: Cambridge University Press, 2009). For the binding power of religious community, see Sebastian R. Prange, "The Social and Economic Organization of Muslim Trading Communities on the Malabar Coast, Twelfth to Sixteenth Centuries" (PhD diss., University of London, 2008). On the quotidian contours of Islamic networks connecting India and Middle East, see Gagan Sood, *India and the Islamic Heartlands: An Eighteenth-Century World of Circulation and Exchange* (Cambridge: Cambridge University Press, 2016).

34. The literature on South Asian merchant communities in the Indian Ocean and their relations with European trading companies is extensive. Some foundational studies are Ashin Das Gupta, *Malabar in Asian Trade 1740—1800* (Cambridge: Cambridge University Press, 1967); Sinnappah Arasaratnam, *Merchants, Companies, and Commerce on the Coromandel Coast, 1650–1740* (New Delhi: Oxford University Press, 1986); Tapan Raychaudhuri, *Jan Company in Coromandel, 1605–1690: A Study in the Interrelations of European Commerce and Traditional Economies* ('s Gravenhage, Neth.: M. Nijhoff, 1962);

Sanjay Subrahmanyam, *Improvising Empire: Portuguese Trade and Settlement in the Bay of Bengal, 1500–1700* (New Delhi: Oxford University Press, 1990); K. N. Chaudhuri, *The Trading World of Asia and the English East India Company, 1660–1760* (Cambridge: Cambridge University Press, 1978).

35. Craig Muldrew, *The Economy of Obligation: The Culture of Credit and Social Relations in Early Modern England* (Houndmills, UK: Palgrave Macmillan, 1998); Laurence Fontaine, *The Moral Economy: Poverty, Credit, and Trust in Early Modern Europe* (New York: Cambridge University Press, 2014); Clare Haru Crowston, *Credit, Fashion, Sex: Economies of Regard in Old Regime France* (Durham, NC: Duke University Press, 2013).

36. For a review of work on intermediaries and empires, see the introduction to Rothman, *Brokering Empire*. See also Louise Bénat-Tachot and Serge Gruzinski, eds., *Passeurs culturels: Mécanismes de métissage* (Paris: Maison des sciences de l'homme, 2001); Simon Schaffer, *The Brokered World: Go-Betweens and Global Intelligence, 1770–1820* (Sagamore Beach, MA: Science History Publications, 2009).

37. Examples from South Asian historiography that do account for intermediaries are Nicholas B. Dirks, "Colin Mackenzie: Autobiography of an Archive," in *The Madras School of Orientalism: Producing Knowledge in Colonial South India*, ed. Thomas R. Trautmann (New Delhi: Oxford University Press, 2009), 29–47; Raj, *Relocating Modern Science*; Raman, *Document Raj*.

38. On the fiscal crisis of the French state, and its relationship to the War of Spanish Succession, see Guy Rowlands, *The Financial Decline of a Great Power War, Influence, and Money in Louis XIV's France* (Oxford: Oxford University Press, 2012).

39. On the *chambres de justice*, see John F. Bosher, "Chambres de Justice in the French Monarchy," in *French Government and Society 1500–1850: Essays in Memory of Alfred Cobban*, ed. John F. Bosher (London: Athlone Press, 1973), 19–40; Jean Villain, "Naissance de la Chambre de justice de 1716," *Revue d'histoire moderne et contemporaine* 35, no. 4 (1988): 544–76; Erik Goldner, "Corruption on Trial: Money, Power, and Punishment in France's Chambre de Justice of 1716," *Crime, Histoire & Sociétés/Crime, History & Societies* 17, no. 1 (May 2013): 5–28.

40. Bhaswati Bhattacharya, "The Hinterland and the Coast: The Pattern of Interaction in Coromandel in the Late Eighteenth Century," in *Politics and Trade in the Indian Ocean World: Essays in Honour of Ashin Das Gupta*, ed. Rudrangshu Mukherjee and Lakshmi Subramanian (New Delhi: Oxford University Press, 2003), 22–24.

41. G. B. Malleson, *History of the French in India, from the Founding of Pondichery in 1674 to the Capture of That Place in 1761* (London: Longmans, Green, 1868), 33.

42. Wilbert Harold Dalgliesh, *The Company of the Indies in the Days of Dupleix* (Easton, PA: Chemical Publishing Co., 1933), 154; Donald C Wellington, *French East India Companies: A Historical Account and Record of Trade* (Lanham, MD: Hamilton Books, 2006), 62.

43. Wellington, *French East India Companies*, 137–42; Käppelin, *La Compagnie des Indes Orientales et François Martin*. On the trade and impact of textiles from India in France, see Felicia Gottmann, *Global Trade, Smuggling, and the Making of Economic Liberalism: Asian Textiles in France 1680–1760* (Houndmills, UK: Palgrave Macmillan, 2016).

44. Each of the years 1712 and 1714 saw the export of nearly 150,000 pieces of cloth, with the number falling to 82,851 in 1715 and further still in 1716, the year of Nayiniyappa's arrest, down to 67,813 pieces of cloth. Wellington, *French East India*

Companies, 188. On growing investments, see Arasaratnam, *Merchants, Companies, and Commerce on the Coromandel Coast*, 203.

45. For example, the year prior to Nayiniyappa's arrest, 1715, was a fairly typical one that saw thirty-eight Dutch VOC ships, twelve English East India Company ships, and only two French ships. Haudrère, *La compagnie française des Indes au XVIIIe siècle*, 2:845.

46. Ibid., 1:214. In that census, conducted only eight years after the English mostly razed the city in 1761, the town had 27,473 residents, of whom 971 were described as *blancs*. The census is published in Société française d'histoire d'outre-mer, "Le Recensement de la population de Pondichéry en 1769," *Revue de l'histoire des colonies françaises*, 1927, 444–45.

47. A recent overview of the available demographic data is in Kévin Le Doudic, "Les Français à Pondichéry au XVIIIe siècle: Une société redessinée par sa culture matérielle," in *L'Asie, la mer, le monde: Au temps des Compagnies des Indes*, ed. Gérard Le Bouëdec (Rennes, FR: Presses universitaires de Rennes, 2014), 177–98.

48. Haudrère, *La compagnie française des Indes au XVIIIe siècle*, 1:214.

49. On Pondichéry's urbanization, see Françoise L'Hernault, "Pondicherry in the Eighteenth Century: Town Planning, Streetscapes and Housescapes," in *French in India and Indian Nationalism, 1700 A.D.–1963 A.D.*, ed. K. S. Mathew, vol. 2 (Delhi: B.R. Publishing Corp., 1999), 371–94; Jean Deloche, *Le vieux Pondichéry (1673–1824): Revisité d'après les plans anciens* (Pondichéry: Institut français de Pondichéry; École française d'Extrême-Orient, 2005); Stephen Jeyaseela, "Urban Growth of Pondicherry and the French: A Study of the Town Plans 1702–1798," in Mathew, *French in India and Indian Nationalism*, 405–22. On the mobility of Indian textile workers, see David Washbrook, "Land and Labour in Late Eighteenth-Century South India: The Golden Age of the Pariah?," in *Dalit Movements and the Meanings of Labour in India*, ed. Peter Robb (New Delhi: Oxford University Press, 1996).

50. On the close relationship between Muslim trading networks and the French company during the late seventeenth century, see Sinnappah Arasaratnam, "The Chulia Muslim Merchants in Southeast Asia, 1600–1800," in *Merchant Networks in the Early Modern World*, ed. Sanjay Subrahmanyam (Aldershot, UK: Variorum, 1996), 173–75.

51. Much work remains to be done on the topic of slaveholding in French India. Notarial and legal records indicate that domestic slave ownership was the norm among French arrivals in Pondichéry. A rich and growing vein of scholarship exists on slavery in the Indian Ocean French colonies of Réunion and Mauritus. Vaughan, *Creating the Creole Island*; Philippe Haudrère, "Projets et échecs de la Compagnie française des Indes dans le commerce des esclaves au XVIIIe siècle," in *Les Français dans l'océan Indien*; Richard B. Allen, *European Slave Trading in the Indian Ocean, 1500–1850* (Athens: Ohio University Press, 2015); Sue Peabody, *Madeleine's Children: Family, Freedom, Secrets and Lies in France's Indian Ocean Colonies, 1750–1850* (New York: Oxford University Press, forthcoming). Slaves in the French settlements in India were by and large domestic servants, but in the Mascarene islands they worked in plantation fields as artisans, manual laborers in towns and fortifications, and occasionally as sailors and soldiers. Allen, *European Slave Trading*, 19. On slavery in the South Asian context more generally, see Indrani Chatterjee, *Gender, Slavery and Law in Colonial India* (New Delhi: Oxford University Press, 2002); Indrani Chatterjee and Richard M. Eaton, eds., *Slavery in South Asian History* (Bloomington: University of Indiana Press, 2006);

Sundararaj Manickam, *Slavery in the Tamil Country: A Historical Over-View* (Madras: Christian Literature Society, 1982); Ravi Ahuja, "Labour Relations in an Early Colonial Context: Madras, C. 1750–1800," *Modern Asian Studies* 36, no. 4 (2002): 793–826.

52. Jean Deloche, *Origins of the Urban Development of Pondicherry according to Seventeenth Century Dutch Plans* (Pondicherry: Institut français de Pondichéry, 2004).

53. Kévin Le Doudic, "Encounters around the Material Object: French and Indian Consumers in Eighteenth-Century Pondicherry," in *The Global Lives of Things: The Material Culture of Connections in the Early Modern World*, ed. Anne Gerritsen and Giorgio Riello (Abingdon, UK: Routledge, 2015), 164.

54. *Procès-verbaux des délibérations du Conseil Supérieur de Pondichéry* (Pondichéry: Société de l'Histoire de l'Inde Française, 1913), 1:46.

55. Dernis, *Recueil ou collection des titres, édits, déclarations, arrêts, règlemens et autres pièces concernant la compagnie des indes orientales établie au mois d'août 1664* (Paris: Boudet, 1755). A tangible example of the company's responsibility to support missionaries was the fact that missionaries were offered free passage to the east on company ships.

56. In North America, in both French and British cases, missionaries were, as a general rule, better integrated into the state's agendas, with resettlement of the native population into colonial holdings, such as New England's "praying towns" or New France's missions, even if native converts found ways to shape their experiences. For examples of this dynamic, see Kristina Bross, *Dry Bones and Indian Sermons: Praying Indians in Colonial America* (Ithaca, NY: Cornell University Press, 2004); Emma Anderson, *The Betrayal of Faith: The Tragic Journey of a Colonial Native Convert* (Cambridge, MA: Harvard University Press, 2007). In Iberian empires, missionaries were important economic actors in ways not available to them in Asia, with large-scale agricultural holdings, as well as power exerted through institutions of the colonial state. See, for example, Irene Silverblatt, *Modern Inquisitions: Peru and the Colonial Origins of the Civilized World* (Durham, NC: Duke University Press, 2004). In India itself such variability was also evident within European enclaves: Goa was converted by the Portuguese in the sixteenth century, and the state and church were well integrated there. On the other hand, missionary work was effectively banned from holdings of the English East India Company until the very end of the eighteenth century. Penelope Carson, *The East India Company and Religion, 1698–1858* (Suffolk, UK: Boydell Press, 2012).

57. Niccolaò Manucci, *Storia do Mogur, Or, Mogul India, 1653–1708*, trans. William Irvine, Indian Texts 1 (London: J. Murray, 1906), 3:334.

58. The Conseil de la Marine, the body that supervised French colonial efforts during the Old Regime, was consistently involved in the struggle between missionary groups in Pondichéry, see for example AN, MAR, B^1/14, fols. 2–5 verso and fols. 54 verso–58 verso.

59. On this global debate, Ines G. Županov, *Disputed Mission: Jesuit Experiments and Brahminical Knowledge in Seventeenth-Century India* (New Delhi: Oxford University Press, 2001); Paolo Aranha, "The Social and Physical Spaces of the Malabar Rites Controversy," in *Space and Conversion in Global Perspective*, eds. Giuseppe Marcocci et al. (Leiden, Neth.: Brill, 2015), 214–32.

60. J. P. Daughton, *An Empire Divided: Religion, Republicanism, and the Making of French Colonialism, 1880–1914* (Oxford: Oxford University Press, 2006).

61. For historical investigations of colonial *affaires*, see, in New France, John F. Bosher, "The French Government's Motives in the Affaire du Canada, 1761–1763,"

English Historical Review 96 (1981): 59–78; in Martinique, D. G. Thompson, "The Lavalette Affair and the Jesuit Superiors," *French History* 10, no. 2 (1996): 206–39; in Louisiana, Alexandre Dubé, *The Common Goods: Political Culture of French Louisiana* (Chapel Hill: University of North Carolina Press, forthcoming); in French Guiana, Marion F. Godfroy, *Kourou, 1763: Le dernier rêve de l'Amérique française* (Paris: Vendémiaire, 2011). In metropolitan France, examples are Dale K. Van Kley, *The Damiens Affair and the Unraveling of the Ancien Regime, 1750–1770* (Princeton, NJ: Princeton University Press, 1984); Sarah C. Maza, *Private Lives and Public Affairs: The Causes Célèbres of Prerevolutionary France* (Berkeley: University of California Press, 1993). Scandals also played an important role in the politics of British empire in the eighteenth and nineteenth centuries. See Nicholas B. Dirks, *The Scandal of Empire: India and the Creation of Imperial Britain* (Cambridge, MA: Belknap Press of Harvard University Press, 2008); James Epstein, *Scandal of Colonial Rule: Power and Subversion in the British Atlantic during the Age of Revolution* (Cambridge: Cambridge University Press, 2012).

62. Historians of the Indian Ocean have long reflected on this unresolved problem: how to tell a story that does not expose exclusively the European perspective while using European archives, especially the archives of the European trading companies. Examples of recent work that examines the Indian Ocean mercantile world by relying on sources produced by non-European merchant communities in the Indian Ocean are Dirks, *The Scandal of Empire*; Epstein, *Scandal of Colonial Rule*.

63. This study owes a conceptual and methodological debt to the foundational works of microhistory situated in early modern Europe, such as Natalie Zemon Davis, *The Return of Martin Guerre* (Cambridge, MA: Harvard University Press, 1983); Carlo Ginzburg, *The Cheese and the Worms: The Cosmos of a Sixteenth-Century Miller* (Baltimore: Johns Hopkins University Press, 1980). It also follows in the footsteps of historians who have used microhistorical methods as entry into the worlds of colonized and indigenous actors, such as Allan Greer, *Mohawk Saint: Catherine Tekakwitha and the Jesuits* (New York: Oxford University Press, 2005); Anderson, *The Betrayal of Faith*. On the need to bring together global history and microhistory, see Francesca Trivellato, "Is There a Future for Italian Microhistory in the Age of Global History?" *California Italian Studies* 2, no. 1 (2011), http://escholarship.org/uc/item/0z94n9hq.

1. The Elusive Origins of a Colonial Scandal

1. The logs are held at ANOM, FM, sous-série C² (Correspondance générale de l'Inde).

2. On French India in the 1931 Colonial Exhibition, see Danna Agmon, "Failure on Display: French India, the 1931 Colonial Exhibition, and a Forgotten Historiography of Empire," in progress.

3. ANOM, INDE, série N.

4. Michel-Rolph Trouillot, *Silencing the Past: Power and the Production of History* (Boston: Beacon Press, 1995).

5. On the durability of pre-European networks, see Sinnappah Arasaratnam, *Maritime India in the Seventeenth Century* (Delhi: Oxford University Press, 1994); Christopher A. Bayly, *Rulers, Townsmen, and Bazaars: North Indian Society in the Age of British Expansion, 1770–1870* (Cambridge: Cambridge University Press, 1983); Sugata Bose,

A Hundred Horizons: The Indian Ocean in the Age of Global Empire (Cambridge, MA: Harvard University Press, 2006).

6. Michael N. Pearson, "Brokers in Western Indian Port Cities: Their Role in Servicing Foreign Merchants," *Modern Asian Studies* 22, no. 3 (1988): 427. On the importance of commercial brokers in Indian Ocean trade and South Asia see Sinnappah Arasaratnam, "Indian Intermediaries in the Trade and Administration of the French East India Company in the Coromandel (1670–1760)," in *Maritime Trade, Society and European Influence in South Asia, 1600–1800* (Aldershot, UK: Variorum, 1995), 135–44; Joseph J. Brennig, "Chief Merchants and the European Enclaves of Seventeenth-Century Coromandel," *Modern Asian Studies* 11, no. 3 (January 1977): 321–40; Ashin Das Gupta, "The Broker at Mughal Surat," *Review of Culture (Macao)* nos. 13–14 (1991): 173–80; A. J. Qaisar, "The Role of Brokers in Medieval India," *Indian Historical Review* 1, no. 2 (1974): 220–46; Michael N. Pearson, "Wealth and Power: Indian Groups in the Portuguese Indian Economy," *South Asia: Journal of South Asian Studies* 3 (1973): 36–44; G. V. Scammell, "Indigenous Assistance in the Establishment of Portuguese Power in India," *Modern Asian Studies* 14, no. 1 (1980): 1–11.

7. Pearson, "Brokers in Western Indian Port Cities." For an analysis of the creation of trust among merchant communities, using as a case study the Armenian network of Julfan merchants, see Sebouh Aslanian, *From the Indian Ocean to the Mediterranean: The Global Trade Networks of Armenian Merchants from New Julfa* (Berkeley: University of California Press, 2011), 166–201. On the issue of trust and market making among Gujarati Vāniyā merchants in the Western Indian Ocean, exchanging Indian textiles for ivory from Mozambique, see Pedro Machado, *Ocean of Trade: South Asian Merchants, Africa and the Indian Ocean, C. 1750–1850* (Cambridge: Cambridge University Press, 2014), 44–57.

8. ANOM, FM, COL, C²/70, fol. 251 verso.

9. See the entry "Dubash, Dobash, Debash" in Henry Yule, A. C Burnell, and Kate Teltscher, *Hobson-Jobson: The Definitive Glossary of British India* (Oxford: Oxford University press), 2013. On this professional group see Susan Neild-Basu, "The Dubashes of Madras," *Modern Asian Studies* 18, no. 1 (1984): 1–31. Three decades after Susan Neild-Basu noted that much still remains to be learned about this commercial cadre, her statement still holds true. Dubashes in Madras and other parts of British India have mostly been examined in light of the high-profile corruption cases involving these figures. But the English debate about the power of dubashes, described by Kanakalatha Mukund as "bordering on paranoia," did not take place until the end of the eighteenth century, when the English hold over the colony was firm, which obscured the more subtle dynamics the earlier events in Pondichéry made visible. For a discussion of dubashi-related scandal in Madras, see Kanakalatha Mukund, *The View from Below : Indigenous Society, Temples, and the Early Colonial State in Tamilnadu, 1700–1835* (New Delhi: Orient Longman, 2005), 147–48. See also Sinnappah Arasaratnam, *Merchants, Companies, and Commerce on the Coromandel Coast, 1650–1740* (Delhi: Oxford University Press, 1986), 256–63. The scholarship on the commercial agents known as banians is more plentiful than that on their South Indian counterparts. See Dilip Basu, "The Early Banians of Calcutta," *Bengal Past and Present* 90 (1971): 30–46; Dilip Basu, "The Bania and the British in Calcutta," *Bengal Past and Present* 92 (1973): 157–70; P. J. Marshall, "Masters and Banians in Eighteenth-Century Calcutta," in *The Age of Partnership: Europeans in Asia before Dominion*, ed. Blair Kling and M. N.

Pearson (Honolulu: University of Hawai'i Press, 1979), 191–213; Ranjit Sen, "A Note on the Banian, the Bengali Capitalist in the Eighteenth Century," *Indian Historical Congress Proceedings*, 1980, 563–71. Shubhra Chakrabarti has unpacked the category of middlemen or brokers in Bengal, revealing the complex hierarchy among them, from banian to dewan, contractor, gomastah, dalal, and pykar, in a descending order of status. Shubhra Chakrabarti, "Collaboration and Resistance: Bengal Merchants and the English East India Company, 1757–1833," *Studies in History* 10, no. 1 (February 1994): 107.

10. For example, ANOM, COL, C²/71, fol. 309.

11. Chakrabarti, "Collaboration and Resistance."

12. These intermediaries, working in the ports of Bombay and Calcutta, were known as "ghat serang." Shompa Lahiri, "Contested Relations: The East India Company and Lascars in London," in *The Worlds of the East India Company*, ed. H. V. Bowen, Margarette Lincoln, and Nigel Rigby (Rochester, NY: Boydell & Brewer, 2002), 171. Accusations of corruption against these maritime brokers were common, much as such accusations were frequently made against the dubashes (commercial brokers) in Madras in the late eighteenth century.

13. Michael N. Pearson, "Connecting the Littorals: Cultural Brokers in the Early Modern Indian Ocean," in *Eyes across the Water: Navigating the Indian Ocean*, ed. Pamila Gupta, Isabel Hofmeyr, and Michael Pearson (Pretoria: Unisa Press, 2010), 32.

14. Tachard, *Relation de voyage aux Indes, 1690–1699*, BNF, MF 19030, fol. 184 verso.

15. Paul Käppelin, *La Compagnie des Indes Orientales et François Martin: Etude sur l'histoire du commerce et des établissements français dans l'Inde sous Louis XIV (1664–1719)* (Paris, 1908), 67. On Marcara, see also Aslanian, *From the Indian Ocean to the Mediterranean*, 4; Ina Baghdiantz McCabe, *The Shah's Silk for Europe's Silver: The Eurasian Trade of the Julfa Armenians in Safavid Iran and India (1530–1750)* (Atlanta: Scholars Press, 1999), 309–11. A contemporaneous account of Marcara and his dealings with the French is found in the memoirs of François Martin, the company employee who became the first governor of Pondichéry. François Martin, *India in the 17th Century, 1670–1694 (Social, Economic, and Political): Memoirs of François Martin* (New Delhi: Manohar, 1981).

16. Gabriel Ranpoandro, "Un marchand arménien au service de la Compagnie française des Indes: Marcara Avanchinz," *Archipel* 17, no. 1 (1979): 100–101.

17. Ibid., 108–10.

18. Das Gupta, "The Broker at Mughal Surat."

19. Chakrabarti, "Collaboration and Resistance."

20. NAIP, eighteenth-century documents, folder 20, holds this family history, written in French by Nayiniyappa's great-nephew (or great-great nephew).

21. S. Jeyaseela Stephen, "Diaries of the Natives from Pondicherry and the Prose Development of Popular Tamil in the Eighteenth Century," *Indian Literature* 50, no. 2 (March 2006): 144–55.

22. Ananda Ranga Pillai, *The Private Diary of Ananda Ranga Pillai, Dubash to Joseph François Dupleix, Knight of the Order of St. Michael, and Governor of Pondichery. A Record of Matters Political, Historical, Social, and Personal, from 1736 to 1761* ed. J. Fredrick Price (Madras: Printed by the superintendent government press, 1904), 3:22–23.

23. French sources use a variety of spellings of the broker's name, most commonly Nainiapa or Naniapa. The spelling I employ (Nayiniyappa) is a more accurate transliteration of the name in Tamil, as it appears signed by Nayiniyappa himself on a document held at ANOM, FM, COL, C²/70, fol. 164 verso.

24. *Procès-verbaux des délibérations du Conseil Supérieur de Pondichéry* (Pondichéry: Société de l'Histoire de l'Inde Française, 1913), 1:42–44.

25. Ibid., 1:66–68.

26. On the use of the anachronistic category "Hindu," see note 7 in the introduction.

27. *Procès-verbaux des délibérations du Conseil Supérieur de Pondichéry*, 1:139–44.

28. Ibid., 1:140.

29. Ibid., 1:141.

30. Ibid., 1:142, 144.

31. ANOM, FM, COL, C²/69, fol. 103.

32. ANOM, FM, COL, C²/69, fol. 103 verso.

33. ANOM, FM, COL, C²/72, fol. 53 verso.

34. Pillai, *Private Diary*, 3:9.

35. Ibid., 2:62.

36. On the import of sedition charges in metropolitan France, see Lisa Graham, *If the King Only Knew: Seditious Speech in the Reign of Louis XV* (Charlottesville: University Press of Virginia, 2000); Jill Maciak Walshaw, *A Show of Hands for the Republic: Opinion, Information, and Repression in Eighteenth-Century Rural France* (Rochester, NY: University of Rochester Press, 2014).

37. ANOM, FM, COL, C²/70, fol. 200 verso.

38. Ibid.

39. ANOM, FM, COL, C²/70, fol. 201.

40. Ibid. The text offers another explanation for why Hébert might have turned against Nayiniyappa. When Hébert arrived in Pondichéry he was, in the broker's words, "so poor and lost" that he had to borrow significant amounts of money from the broker on three different occasions. Putting Nayiniyappa in jail was also a way to avoid repaying the debt. This account would explain why Hébert did not renege on his supposed deal with the Jesuits once he was back in Pondichéry.

41. ANOM, FM, COL, C²/70, fol. 251 verso.

42. ANOM, FM, COL, C²/70, fol. 255 verso.

43. ANOM, FM, COL, F³/238, fols. 263–267. By the seventeenth century there were few corners of the globe that had not welcomed—or rejected—Jesuit missionaries. Luke Clossey, *Salvation and Globalization in the Early Jesuit Missions* (Cambridge: Cambridge University Press, 2010).

44. Danna Agmon, "Striking Pondichéry: Religious Disputes and French Authority in an Indian Colony of the Ancien Régime," *French Historical Studies* 37, no. 3 (June 2014): 437–67.

45. ANOM, FM, COL, C²/70, fol. 251 verso.

46. ANOM, FM, COL, C²/69, fol. 91.

47. Douglas Haynes, *Rhetoric and Ritual in Colonial India: The Shaping of a Public Culture in Surat City, 1852–1928* (Berkeley: University of California Press, 1991).

48. Mukund, *The View from Below*. See especially chapter 7, "Dubashes and Patronage: Construction of Identity and Social Leadership under the Colonial State."

49. Venkata Raghotham, "Merchant, Courtier, Shipper, Prince: The Social and Intellectual World of an Eighteenth Century Tamil Merchant," *Journal of the Institute of Asian Studies* 9, no. 2 (March 1992): 14–16.

50. ANOM, INDE, série N, folder 58. Copies of the letter appear in ANOM, FM, COL, C²/70, fols. 92–92 verso, and ANOM, FM, COL, C²/70, fol. 208.

51. *Procès-verbaux des délibérations du Conseil Supérieur de Pondichéry*, 1:162.

52. ANOM, FM, COL, C²/70, fol. 208 verso.

53. ANOM, FM, C²/70, COL, fol. 209.

54. "Mémoires sur la compagnie des Indes Orientales 1642–1720," BNF, MF 6231, fol. 55 verso.

55. On the symbolic meanings of cloth in Old Regime France, see William M. Reddy, "The Structure of a Cultural Crisis: Thinking about Cloth in France before and after the Revolution," in *The Social Life of Things: Commodities in Cultural Perspective*, ed. Arjun Appadurai (Cambridge: Cambridge University Press, 1986), 261–84. On the exceptionally rich semiotic canvas provided by cloth in India, for both locals and Europeans, see C. A. Bayly, "The Origins of Swadeshi (Home Industry): Cloth and Indian Society, 1700–1930," in Appadurai, *The Social Life of Things*, 285–321; Bernard S. Cohn, "Cloth, Clothes and Colonialism: India in the Nineteenth Century," in *Colonialism and Its Forms of Knowledge: The British in India* (Princeton, NJ: Princeton University Press, 1996), 106–62.

56. On religious borrowing in this period in South India, see Susan Bayly, *Saints, Goddesses, and Kings: Muslims and Christians in South Indian Society, 1700–1900* (Cambridge: Cambridge University Press, 1989).

57. Pillai, *Private Diary*, 1:237.

58. ANOM, FM, COL, C²/71, fol. 103.

59. Sharon Kettering, "Gift-Giving and Patronage in Early Modern France," *French History* 2, no. 2 (June 1988): 131–51.

60. Alfred Albert Martineau, ed., *Résume des actes de l'Etat civil de Pondichéry* (Pondichéry: Société de l'histoire de l'Inde française, 1917), 1:ii.

61. Bayly, "The Origins of Swadeshi," 294.

62. Alexandre Dupilet, *La Régence absolue: Philippe d'Orléans et la polysynodie (1715–1718)* (Syssel, France: Champ Vallon, 2011).

63. Quoted in Isabelle Vissière and Jean-Louis Vissière, *Lettres édifiantes et curieuses des jésuites de l'Inde au dix-huitième siècle* (Paris: Publications de l'Université de Saint-Étienne, 2000), 43.

64. "Mémoires sur la compagnie des Indes Orientales 1642–1720," BNF, MF 6231, fol. 42 verso.

65. AMEP, *Lettres*, vol. 959, pp. 223–229.

66. Ibid., p. 223.

67. For the letter appointing Hébert to the position, see ANOM, FM, COL, C²/70, fols. 239–240.

68. ANOM, FM, COL, C²/69, fol. 225.

69. ANOM, FM, C²/70, COL, fol. 221. Many of the complaints that Hébert and Dulivier sent to Paris complaining against each other also appear in AN, MAR, B¹/14.

70. AN, MAR, B¹/14, fol. 5 verso.

71. ANOM, FM, COL, C²/70, fol. 252 verso.

72. ANOM, FM, COL, C²/70, fol. 221 verso.

73. ANOM, FM, COL, C²/70, fol. 222.

74. *Procès-verbaux des délibérations du Conseil Supérieur de Pondichéry*, 1:140–41.

75. Guy Rowlands, *The Financial Decline of a Great Power War, Influence, and Money in Louis XIV's France* (Oxford: Oxford University Press, 2012). In addition to the enormous debt of the state and its financial reverberations, the Compagnie des

Indes orientales was dealing with its own massive debt; in 1708, it carried a debt of 6,500,000 livres.

76. On the company's liquidity shortages, see Philippe Haudrère, *Les Français dans l'océan Indien (XVIIe-XIXe siècle)* (Rennes, FR: Presses universitaires de Rennes, 2014), 14.

These liquidity crises put the French company in a markedly different situation from that of the English East India Company, which was in a position to extend significant loans to the state. H. V. Bowen, *The Business of Empire: The East India Company and Imperial Britain, 1756–1833* (Cambridge: Cambridge University Press, 2006), 30.

77. Käppelin, *La Compagnie des Indes Orientales et François Martin*, 437; Philippe Haudrère, *La compagnie française des Indes au XVIIIe siècle* (Paris: Indes savantes, 2005), 1:25. The definitive work on the St. Malo merchant association is André Lespagnol, *Messieurs de Saint-Malo: Une élite négociante au temps de Louis XIV* (Saint Malo: Éd. l'Ancre de Marine, 1991).

78. Haudrère, *La compagnie française des Indes au XVIIIe siècle*, 1:25. On the impact of John Law's reforms on the Compagnie des Indes, see G. B. Malleson, *History of the French in India, from the Founding of Pondichery in 1674 to the Capture of That Place in 1761* (London: Longmans, Green, 1868), 39–61. On the newly organized company, see Haudrère, *La compagnie française des Indes au XVIIIe siècle*. In the existing scholarship on French India, the year 1719 acts as a watershed, with most studies devoted either to the period 1664–1719 (from the Compagnie des Indes's creation to Law's restructuring) or to the period beginning in 1719 to the end of the century. This study bridges that divide, since if the first three decades of the eighteenth century are viewed from the vantage point of Pondichéry, there is as much continuity as rupture. Most important, the same employees and relationships, Tamil and French, stayed in place and continued to inform decision making in the colony.

79. ANOM, FM, COL, C²/14, fol. 260 verso.

80. ANOM, FM, COL, C²/14, fols. 260 verso–261 verso.

81. ANOM, FM, COL, C²/14, fol. 260.

82. Ibid.

83. ANOM, FM, COL, C²/14, fol. 268.

84. AN, MAR, B¹/14, fol. 24 verso.

85. AN, MAR, B¹/15, fols. 514–514 verso and B¹/16, fols. 83–83 verso.

2. Kinship as Politics

1. Paul Olagnier, *Les jésuites à Pondichéry et l'affaire Naniapa (1705 à 1720)* (Paris: Société de l'histoire des colonies françaises, 1932).

2. Julia Adams, *The Familial State: Ruling Families and Merchant Capitalism in Early Modern Europe* (Ithaca: Cornell University Press, 2005). In the French colonial context, John Bosher has highlighted the importance of family for merchants in Canada in the same period. John Bosher, *The Canada Merchants 1713–1763* (Oxford: Oxford University Press, 1987). An important example of mercantile and family connections in the Indian Ocean is that of Armenian merchants. On the kinship networks underlying the trade of merchants with roots in New Julfa, see Sebouh Aslanian, *From the Indian Ocean to the Mediterranean: The Global Trade Networks of Merchants from New Julfa* (Berkeley: University of California Press, 2011), 144–64.

3. Julia Adams and Mounira M. Charrad, eds., *Patrimonial Capitalism and Empire* (Bingley, UK: Emerald Group Publishing, 2015). For an example of the diversity of French colonial approaches to local patrimonial power, the North African example is instructive. Mounira Charrad and Daniel Jaster have argued that in Algeria French officials tried to destroy patrimonial power and displace it with French institutions, while in Tunisia, the French tried to maintain and then co-opt these networks. Mounira M. Charrad and Daniel Jaster, "Limits of Empire: The French Colonial State and Local Patrimonialism in North Africa," in Adams and Charrad, *Patrimonial Capitalism,* 63–89.

4. Ann Laura Stoler, *Carnal Knowledge and Imperial Power: Race and the Intimate in Colonial Rule* (Berkeley: University of California Press, 2002); Ann Laura Stoler, *Race and the Education of Desire: Foucault's History of Sexuality and the Colonial Order of Things* (Durham, NC: Duke University Press, 1995).

5. Emma Rothschild, *The Inner Life of Empires: An Eighteenth-Century History* (Princeton, NJ: Princeton University Press, 2011). Rothschild's study is part of a wave of works in Atlantic and British history that examine the global mobility of families and individuals in early imperial contexts. See Alison Games, *The Web of Empire: English Cosmopolitans in an Age of Expansion, 1560–1660* (Oxford: Oxford University Press, 2008); Linda Colley, *The Ordeal of Elizabeth Marsh: A Woman in World History* (New York: Pantheon Books, 2007); Miles Ogborn, *Global Lives: Britain and the World, 1550–1800* (Cambridge: Cambridge University Press, 2008); Maya Jasanoff, *Liberty's Exiles: American Loyalists in the Revolutionary World* (New York: Knopf, 2011); Sarah M. S. Pearsall, *Atlantic Families: Lives and Letters in the Later Eighteenth Century* (Oxford: Oxford University Press, 2008).

6. David Schneider's work galvanized scholars to actively reimagine kinship beyond the limits of biological reproduction, and question the assumption that blood is thicker than water. David Murray Schneider, *A Critique of the Study of Kinship* (Ann Arbor: University of Michigan Press, 1984), 174.

7. This conjuncture of family and global structures is highlighted in Patrick Manning, "Frontiers of Family Life: Early Modern Atlantic and Indian Ocean Worlds," *Modern Asian Studies* 43, no. 1 (January 2009): 315–33. On the intersection of the "new imperial history" and the history of the family, see Kathleen Wilson, *A New Imperial History: Culture, Identity, and Modernity in Britain and the Empire, 1660–1840* (Cambridge: Cambridge University Press, 2004). For a recent consideration of the father-son tie in Islamicate Eurasia in this period, see Gagan Sood, "A Familial Order: Ties of Blood, Duty and Affect" in *India and the Islamic Heartlands: An Eighteenth-Century World of Circulation and Exchange* (Cambridge: Cambridge University Press, 2016), 79–94.

8. On "vernacular kinship" see Nara B Milanich, *Children of Fate: Childhood, Class, and the State in Chile, 1850–1930* (Durham, NC: Duke University Press, 2009), chap. 5. Originally cited in Bianca Premo, "Familiar: Thinking beyond Lineage and across Race in Spanish Atlantic Family History," *William and Mary Quarterly* 70, no. 2 (April 2013): 298.

9. Sarah Hanley, "Engendering the State: Family Formation and State Building in Early Modern France," *French Historical Studies* 16, no. 1 (April 1989): 6. On the intersection of the familial, judicial, and commercial in France on a more popular level, see Julie Hardwick, *Family Business: Litigation and the Political Economies of Daily Life in Early Modern France* (New York: Oxford University Press, 2009).

10. Sumit Guha, "The Family Feud as a Political Resource in Eighteenth-Century India," in *Unfamiliar Relations: Family and History in South Asia*, ed. Indrani Chatterjee (New Brunswick, NJ: Rutgers University Press, 2004), 78.

11. The scholarship on the French family under the Old Regime is too vast to review here, but Suzanne Desan and Jeffrey Merrick offer an excellent overview of the state of the field in their edited volume *Family, Gender, and Law in Early Modern France* (University Park: Pennsylvania State University Press, 2009), xi–xxvi. In South Asia, as the historian Indrani Chatterjee has noted, "the history of the family has long been the poor relation in the great household of South Asian history." Chatterjee, *Unfamiliar Relations*, 3. Other scholarship that has attempted to address this lack can be found in Patricia Uberoi, *Family, Kinship and Marriage in India* (New Delhi: Oxford University Press, 1993); Ákos Östör, Lina Fruzzetti, and Steve Barnett, *Concepts of Person: Kinship, Caste, and Marriage in India* (Cambridge, MA: Harvard University Press, 1982).

12. The category of caste technically encompasses that of family (castes are endogamous; members of the same kin group, as a general and widely practiced rule, belong to the same caste), but the reverse is not true (not all members of the same caste are related to one another). For an in-depth discussion of caste as a historical and particularly colonial phenomenon, see Nicholas B. Dirks, *Castes of Mind: Colonialism and the Making of Modern India* (Princeton, NJ: Princeton University Press, 2001); Sumit Guha, *Beyond Caste: Identity and Power in South Asia, Past and Present* (Leiden, Neth.: Brill, 2013). The category of caste did occasionally come into play in the course of the Nayiniyappa Affair. For example, Governor Hébert's second interrogation of Nayiniyappa in 1716 includes a line of questioning that is premised on caste divisions: the official asks Nayiniyappa why he forced a man of the right-hand castes to go and eat in the house of a man of the left-hand castes, a charge the broker denied. ANOM, FM, COL, C²/70, fol. 54.

13. *Procès-verbaux des délibérations du Conseil Supérieur de Pondichéry* (Pondichéry: Société de l'Histoire de l'Inde Française, 1913), 1:30.

14. On the arrest of the sons, see ANOM, FM, COL, C²/70, fol. 252. The arrest of sons along with their broker father had precedent in French India. In the late seventeenth century, the Compagnie des Indes employed an Armenian merchant, Marcara, to advance their interests in the Coromandel. When the Armenian fell out of favor with his French employers and was arrested in 1670, his two sons were arrested alongside him. Gabriel Ranpoandro, "Un marchand arménien au service de la Compagnie française des Indes: Marcara Avanchinz," *Archipel* 17, no. 1 (1979): 108, 110.

15. ANOM, FM, COL, C²/70, fol. 201 verso.

16. A letter by La Morandière to the directors of the company, dated January 25, 1719, ANOM, FM, COL, C²/71, fol. 58.

17. Pagodas, a gold coin currency, were minted in Pondichéry and elsewhere in India. On currencies in French India and their relative value, see Philippe Haudrère, "La monnaie de Pondichéry au XVIIIe siècle," in *Les relations entre la France et l'Inde de 1673 à nos jours*, ed. Jacques Weber (Paris: Les Indes Savantes, 2002), 39–47.

18. ANOM, FM, COL, C²/71, fol. 302.

19. For Ceylon, see Patrick Peebles, *Social Change in Nineteenth Century Ceylon* (New Delhi: Navrang in collaboration with Lake House Bookshop Colombo, 1995). For Surat, Ashin Das Gupta, *The World of the Indian Ocean Merchant 1500–1800: Collected Essays of Ashin Das Gupta* (New Delhi: Oxford University Press, 2001), 401–2.

20. Edgar Thurston, *Castes and Tribes of Southern India* (Madras: Government Press, 1909), 1:84. During one of his interrogations, when Nayiniyappa was asked to name his caste, his answer is rendered in French as "of pastoral caste." ANOM, FM, COL, C²/70, fol. 84.

21. On the joint use of the Mudali and Pillai suffixes by the Vellala caste, and the caste members' association with colonial bureaucracy in Madras and Pondichéry, see Sinnappah Arasaratnam, "Trade and Political Dominion in South India, 1750–1790: Changing British-Indian Relationships," *Modern Asian Studies* 13, no. 1 (1979): 20, 24. For more on the dubashes of Madras and their caste position, see Susan Neild-Basu, "The Dubashes of Madras," *Modern Asian Studies* 18, no. 1 (1984).

22. For a rare but incomplete discussion of this family, see Ajit Neogy, "Early Commercial Activities of the French in Pondicherry: The Pondicherry Authorities, the Jesuits and the Mudaliars," in *Mariners, Merchants and Oceans: Studies in Maritime History*, ed. K. S. Mathew (New Delhi: Manohar Publishers, 1995), 333–40.

23. Ananda Ranga Pillai, *The Private Diary of Ananda Ranga Pillai, Dubash to Joseph François Dupleix, Knight of the Order of St. Michael, and Governor of Pondichery. A Record of Matters Political, Historical, Social, and Personal, from 1736 to 1761*, ed. J. Fredrick Price (Madras: Printed by the superintendent government press, 1904), 2:150; 12:87. Eugene Irschik describes Poonamalee as a locale that "formed a base for the growth of power of many Kondaikatti vellala families"—perhaps the caste subgroup to which Lazare and his descendants belonged, since Kondaikatties were known as Mudalis. Eugene F. Irschick, *Dialogue and History: Constructing South India, 1795–1895* (Berkeley: University of California Press, 1994), 34–35.

24. *Procès-verbaux des délibérations du Conseil Supérieur de Pondichéry*, 1:67.

25. ANOM, FM, COL, C²/71, fol. 90 bis.

26. ANOM, FM, COL, C²/71, fols. 90 bis-90 bis verso.

27. Here the translation of kinship terminology into French or English does not adequately reflect the Tamil terms. The term *beau-frère*, used to refer to Tiruvangadan in French sources, might have referred to Nayiniyappa's sister's husband, his wife's brother, or a single individual who was both sister's husband and wife's brother. On Dravidian kinship terminology, see Thomas R. Trautmann, *Dravidian Kinship* (New York: Sage, 1996).On the general problem of describing South Asian kinship in English, with its relative paucity of kinship terminology, see Sylvia Vatuk, "'Family' as a Contested Concept in Early-Nineteenth-Century Madras," in Chatterjee, *Unfamiliar Relations*, 161–91.

28. ANOM, FM, COL, C²/73, fol. 23 verso.

29. *Procès-verbaux des délibérations du Conseil Supérieur de Pondichéry*, 2:104.

30. ANOM, FM, COL, C²/73, fol. 23. There is a bit of historical revisionism at play here, given that Nayiniyappa was appointed to the post in 1708 to replace Pedro's father, who was deemed incompetent.

31. ANOM, FM, COL, C²/71, fol. 117.

32. ANOM, FM, COL, C²/71, fol. 116. Another witness who had prior disagreements with Nayiniyappa was one Pautrichecli, who was said to have quarreled with Nayiniyappa over tobacco dealings and then served as a certifier for one of the testimonies against the broker. ANOM, FM, COL, C²/71, fols. 296–297 verso.

33. ANOM, FM, COL, C²/71, fol. 117 verso.

34. BNF, MF 6231, fol. 29 verso.

35. Nayiniyappa's son Guruvappa did convert to Christianity, an issue discussed in chapter 5, but subsequent family members employed by the company were not Christians.

36. Durba Ghosh has insightfully discussed both the problems posed by the "namelessness" of local women in the archives of colonial India. Durba Ghosh, *Sex and the Family in Colonial India: The Making of Empire* (Cambridge: Cambridge University Press, 2008), 15–31.

37. For a more extensive discussion of the widow Guruvappa's engagement with the French administration, see Danna Agmon, "The Currency of Kinship: Trading Families and Trading on Family in Colonial French India," *Eighteenth-Century Studies* 47, no. 2 (2014): 137–55.

38. The fact that these claims repeatedly received favorable response by French authorities speaks to the widow's position in the colony but also to the liminal status of widows in French society. In early modern France, widowed women could serve as heads of households and enjoyed the legal and economic benefits attendant on that position. Even if widows often found it difficult to take advantage of the benefits due to them in an intensely patriarchal society, as Julie Hardwick has shown, the conceptual and legal framework for their autonomy was in place. Julie Hardwick, "Widowhood and Patriarchy in Seventeenth Century France," *Journal of Social History* 26, no. 1 (1992): 133–48.

39. AMEP, *Lettres*, vol. 992, p. 2.

40. There are at least two letters in which the widow uses the first person to make her claims: AMEP, *Lettres*, vol. 992, pp. 1–3; and ANOM, FM, COL, C²/73, fols. 29–30.

41. AMEP *Lettres*, vol. 992, p. 3.

42. ANOM, FM, COL, C²/73, fol. 29.

43. ANOM, FM, COL, C²/73, fol. 29 verso.

44. AMEP, *Lettres*, vol. 992, p. 2.

45. ANOM, FM, COL, C²/73, fol. 210 verso.

46. Ibid.

47. Bhavani Raman, *Document Raj: Writing and Scribes in Early Colonial South India* (Chicago: University of Chicago Press, 2012), 27.

48. Amalia D. Kessler, *A Revolution in Commerce: The Parisian Merchant Court and the Rise of Commercial Society in Eighteenth-Century France* (New Haven: Yale University Press, 2007), 142.

49. For a fascinating account of the importance of family in advancing global early modern European commerce, see Francesca Trivellato, *The Familiarity of Strangers: The Sephardic Diaspora, Livorno, and Cross-Cultural Trade in the Early Modern Period* (New Haven: Yale University Press, 2009).

50. Catherine Manning, *Fortunes à Faire: The French in Asian Trade, 1719–48* (Aldershot, UK: Variorum, 1996), 57.

51. Paul Käppelin, *La Compagnie des Indes Orientales et François Martin: Etude sur l'histoire du commerce et des établissements français dans l'Inde sous Louis XIV (1664–1719)* (Paris, 1908), 385.

52. Colbert was responsible for the company in the period 1661–1683. The responsibility then passed to his eldest son, the Marquis de Seignelay (1683–1690). His successor was Louis Phélypeaux, Comte de Pontchartrain (1690–1699), who passed the position on to his son Jérome Phélypeaux (1693–1715).

53. Yvonne Robert Gaebelé, *Créole et grande dame: Johanna Bégum, marquise Dupleix, 1706–1756* (Paris: Leroux, 1934), 15–16.

54. ANOM, INDE, série N (exposition coloniale), folder 70. Other European trading companies in India had a similar approach to staffing. In the English company, members of only three families supplied ten members to the Council in Bengal early in the eighteenth century. Philippe Haudrère, *Les compagnies des Indes orientales: Trois siècles de rencontre entre Orientaux et Occidentaux (1600–1858)* (Paris: Desjonquères, 2006), 180. Closer still, in Madras, members of a handful of families became "dynasties of recruits" for the company over many generations. David Washbrook, "South India 1770–1840: The Colonial Transition," *Modern Asian Studies* 38, no. 3 (July 1, 2004): 489.

55. Robert Morrissey provides an analysis of godparenthood in a French colonial context, using social network analysis to determine the density of connections. Robert Michael Morrissey, "Kaskaskia Social Network: Kinship and Assimilation in the French-Illinois Borderlands, 1695–1735," *William and Mary Quarterly* 70, no. 1 (January 2013): 103–46. See also Jennifer L. Palmer, *Intimate Bonds: Family and Slavery in the French Atlantic* (Philadelphia: University of Pennsylvania Press, 2016). On the work accomplished by godparenthood in Europe in the same period, see Jürgen Schlumbohm, "Quelques problèmes de micro-histoire d'une société locale. Construction de liens sociaux dans la paroisse de Beim (XVIIe–XIXe siècles)," *Annales. Histoire, Sciences Sociales* 50, no. 4 (1995): 775–802.

56. For the Pondichéry notariat, see ANOM, INDE, série P. For the records of the Etat-civil, see Alfred Albert Martineau, ed., *Résume des actes de l'Etat civil de Pondichéry* (Pondichéry: Société de l'histoire de l'Inde française, 1917).

57. Martineau, *Résume des actes*, 1:77.

58. Ibid., 1:76.

59. Ibid., 1:93.

60. Niccolaò Manucci, *Storia Do Mogur, Or, Mogul India, 1653–1708*, trans. William Irvine, Indian Texts 1 (London: J. Murray, 1906). On Manucci's career, Sanjay Subrahmanyam, *Three Ways to Be Alien: Travails and Encounters in the Early Modern World* (Lebanon, NH: Brandeis University Press, 2011), 133–72.

61. Martineau, *Résume des actes*, 1:98.

62. Ibid., 1:108.

63. Ibid., 1:190.

64. ANOM, FM, COL, C^2/71, fol. 96 verso.

65. ANOM, FM, COL, C^2/70, fol. 201.

66. ANOM, FM, COL, C^2/71, fol. 97.

67. ANOM, FM, COL, C^2/71, fol. 101.

68. ANOM, FM, COL, C^2/71, fol. 293 verso.

69. ANOM, FM, COL, C^2/71, fol. 83 verso.

70. ANOM, FM, COL, C^2/70, fol. 204.

71. ANOM, FM, COL, C^2/71, fol. 57 verso.

72. ANOM, FM, COL, C^2/71, fol. 299 verso.

73. ANOM, FM, COL, C^2/71, fol. 58.

74. ANOM, FM, COL, C^2/71, fols. 299 verso–300 verso.

75. ANOM, FM, COL, C^2/67, fol. 272. Another account of this arrest appears in BNF, MF 6231, fol. 30.

76. Danna Agmon, "Striking Pondichéry: Religious Disputes and French Authority in an Indian Colony of the Ancien Régime," *French Historical Studies* 37, no. 3 (June 2014): 458–61.

77. Manuel is described in a letter Dulivier sent to the Marine Council as "the catechist who served as clerk" during Nayiniyappa's interrogation. AN, MAR, B¹/27, folio 65.

78. ANOM, FM, COL, C²/71, fol. 292 verso.

79. A. Lynn Martin, "Jesuits and Their Families: The Experience in Sixteenth Century France," *Sixteenth Century Journal* 13, no. 1 (April 1982): 3–24.

80. Quoted ibid., 5.

81. "Lettre du Père Martin, missionnaire de la Compagnie de Jésus aux Indes: Au Père de Villette de la même Compagnie," in Jesuits, *Lettres édifiantes et curieuses, écrites des missions étrangères* (Paris: Chez Nicolas Le Clerc, 1703), 9:173.

82. Ibid.

83. "Lettre du Père Martin, missionnaire de la Compagnie de Jésus, au Père Le Gobien de la même Compagnie," Camien-naiken-patty, Madurai, June 1, 1700, in Jesuits, *Lettres édifiantes*, 5:94.

84. Jesuits, *Lettres édifiantes*, 9:173.

85. Ibid., vol. 9, preface.

86. ANOM, FM, COL, C²/69, fol. 18 verso.

87. "Le paganisme des Indiens, nommés Tamouls," BNF, NAF 2627, p. 582.

88. Ibid., p. 583.

89. Pillai, *Private Diary*, 1:21.

90. Raman, *Document Raj*.

3. The Denial of Language

1. The description in these opening paragraphs is compiled from Nayiniyappa's own account of his first interrogation, in ANOM, FM, COL, C²/70, fol. 252, and from the official transcribed record of this interrogation prepared by the governor's secretary, in ANOM, FM, COL, C²/70, fols. 48 verso–52.

2. ANOM, FM, COL, C²/70, fol. 252.

3. Even Marcara, the Armenian merchant who led the French efforts to establish commerce in Coromandel in 1699–1670 and had lived in Europe, was described by his employer, François Caron, as "not very well versed in French." ANOM, FM, COL, C²/62, fol. 37. Cited in Gabriel Ranpoandro, "Un marchand arménien au service de la Compagnie française des Indes: Marcara Avanchinz," *Archipel* 17, no. 1 (1979): 113n22.

4. ANOM, FM, COL, C²/71, fol. 302. The fact that Hébert spoke Portuguese fluently was also attested to in a letter sent by Hébert's rival Dulivier. AN, MAR, B¹/27, fol. 65.

5. Michael Pearson, *The Indian Ocean* (New York: Routledge, 2003), 156.

6. ANOM, INDE, Série M/25.

7. See, for example, the French-speaking dubash David Moutou, employed by a French officer in India. Mautort, *Mémoires du Chevalier de Mautort: Capitaine au régiment d'Ausrasie Chevalier de l'ordre royal et militaire de Saint-Louis (1752–1802)* (Paris: Librairie Plon, 1895), 207. Nayiniyappa's nephew, Ananda Ranga Pillai, who was chief

commercial broker in Pondichéry in the mid-eighteenth century, also spoke French with his employers.

8. ANOM, FM, COL, C²/70, fol. 252.

9. Well into the seventeenth century, extreme linguistic diversity was a defining feature of French society. Paul Cohen, *Kingdom of Babel: The Making of a National Language in France, 1400–1815* (Ithaca, NY: Cornell University Press, forthcoming). Cohen has also demonstrated how polyglossia—the use of French, Latin, and regional languages—was the norm in French courts of law. Prior to 1789, judges, lawyers, and scribes all accommodated linguistic diversity in the courts. Paul Cohen, "Judging a Multilingual Society: The Accommodation of Linguistic Diversity in French Law Courts, Fifteenth to Eighteenth Centuries" (paper presented at the American Historical Association Annual Meeting, Boston, January 2011).

10. S. Arokianathan has found some evidence of French influence on the form of Tamil spoken in Pondichéry in the eighteenth century. S. Arokianathan, "Influence of French in 18th Century Pondicherry Tamil Dialect," in *French in India and Indian Nationalism*, ed. K. S. Mathew (Delhi: Distributed by BRPC, 1999), 2:357–63.

11. BNF, NAF 6557, fol. 64 verso.

12. Ibid.

13. The need to examine polylingual scenarios was also raised in Michael N. Pearson, "Connecting the Littorals: Cultural Brokers in the Early Modern Indian Ocean," in *Eyes across the Water: Navigating the Indian Ocean*, ed. Pamila Gupta, Isabel Hofmeyr, and Michael Pearson (Pretoria: Unisa Press, 2010), 32–47.

14. Johannes Fabian, *Language and Colonial Power: The Appropriation of Swahili in the Former Belgian Congo, 1880–1938* (Berkeley: University of California Press, 1991), 3.

15. Legal scholars have increasingly paid attention to the role of language in constituting legal and sovereign power. John M. Conley and William M. O'Barr, *Just Words: Law, Language, and Power*, 2nd ed. (Chicago: University of Chicago Press, 2005). Anthropologists and historians alike have contributed to this strand of scholarship by demonstrating the centrality of language to the making of jurisdiction, and by extension sovereignty, in legal contexts. For an excellent review of this scholarship, see Justin B. Richland, "Jurisdiction: Grounding Law in Language," *Annual Review of Anthropology* 42, no. 1 (2013): 209–26. The intersection of law and language has been studied in the specific context of colonialism in Kathryn Burns, *Into the Archive: Writing and Power in Colonial Peru* (Durham, NC: Duke University Press, 2010).

16. Ines G. Županov, *Missionary Tropics: The Catholic Frontier in India (16th–17th Centuries)* (Ann Arbor: University of Michigan Press, 2005), 14.

17. "Lettre du Père Martin, Missionnaire de la Compagnie de Jésus, au P. de Villette, de la même Compagnie," Balassor, Royaume de Bengale, January 30, 1699, in Jesuits, *Lettres édifiantes et curieuses, écrites des missions étrangères* (Paris: Chez Nicolas Le Clerc, 1703), vol. 1:1–29.

18. "Lettre du Père Tachard, Missionnaire de la Compagnie de Jésus, au R. P. du Trevou, de la même Compagnie, confesseur de S.A.R. Monseigneur de Duc d'Orléans," Chandenagore, January 18, 1711, in Jesuits, *Lettres édifiantes*, 12:366–442. Also quoted in Isabelle Vissière and Jean-Louis Vissière, *Lettres édifiantes et curieuses des jésuites de l'Inde au dix-huitième siècle* (Paris: Publications de l'Université de Saint-Étienne, 2000), 42.

19. 1703 letter by P. Paul Vendôme, BC, manuscript 92, fol. 158 verso.

20. Quoted in Stephen Neill, *A History of Christian Missions* (New York: Penguin, 1986), 153–54.

21. "Le paganisme des Indiens, nommés Tamouls," BNF, NAF 2627, p. 15. On Jesuit struggles with Tamil, see also Ines G. Županov, "Twisting a Pagan Tongue: Portuguese and Tamil in Sixteenth-Century Jesuit Translations," in *Conversion: Old Worlds and New*, ed. Kenneth Mills and Anthony Grafton (Rochester, NY: University of Rochester Press, 2003).

22. "Lettre du Père Mauduit, missionnaire de la compagnie de Jésus, au Père Le Gobien de la même compagnie," Carouvepondi, Carnat, January 1, 1702, in Jesuits, *Lettres édifiantes*, 6:4–5.

23. "Lettre du P. Bouchet, missionnaire de la compagnie de Jésus, à Monsieur Cochet de Saint-Valliér, président des requétes du palais à Paris," in Jesuits, *Lettres édifiantes*, 11:7.

24. "Lettre du Père Martin, missionnaire de la compagnie de Jésus, au Père Le Gobien de la même compagnie," Camien-naiken-patty, Madurai, June 1, 1700, in Jesuits, *Lettres édifiantes*, 5:92–93.

25. Ibid.

26. Ibid., 5:94.

27. Ibid., 5:93.

28. Simon de La Farelle, *Deux officiers français au XVIIIe siècle: Mémoires et correspondance du chevalier et du général de La Farelle* (Paris: Berger-Levrault et cie, 1896), 85.

29. The Tamil broker Ananda Ranga Pillai described Jeanne Dupleix performing this service for her husband on several occasions. Pillai, *The Private Diary of Ananda Ranga Pillai, Dubash to Joseph François Dupleix, Knight of the Order of St. Michael, and Governor of Pondichery. A Record of Matters Political, Historical, Social, and Personal, from 1736 to 1761* (Madras: Printed by the superintendent government press, 1904), ed. J. Fredrick Price, 3:96.

30. ANOM, FM, COL, C²/70, fol. 251 verso.

31. ANOM, FM, COL, C²/71, fol. 86.

32. ANOM, FM, COL, C²/71, fols. 88 verso–89.

33. ANOM, FM, COL, C²/71, fol. 129 verso.

34. Quoted in Marcel Thomas, *Le Conseil Supérieur de Pondichéry, 1702–1820: Essai sur les Institutions Judiciaires de l'Inde Française* (Paris: L'auteur, 1953), 104.

35. Scholars of medieval and early modern Europe have examined the transmission of data from scribal and printed forms to oral ones and vice versa. See M. T. Clanchy, *From Memory to Written Record: England 1066–1307* (Chichester, UK: Wiley-Blackwell, 2012); Natalie Zemon Davis, "Printing and the People," in *Society and Culture in Early Modern France: Eight Essays* (Stanford: Stanford University Press, 1975), 189–226.

36. Gnanou Diagou, *Arrêts du Conseil supérieur de Pondichéry* (Pondichéry: Bibliothèque publique, 1935), 8:126.

37. *Procès-verbaux des délibérations du Conseil Supérieur de Pondichéry* (Pondichéry: Société de l'Histoire de l'Inde Française, 1913), 1:163–64.

38. ANOM, FM, COL, C²/70, fol. 255.

39. Only the French version would be archived. Manuel's statement is cited here from ANOM, FM, COL, C²/71, fols. 293 verso–294 verso. The same text is also reproduced in C²/71, fol. 82, as well as C²/71, fol.156. The multiple appearance of the

testimony in the French archives is further evidence of the centrality of interpretation in the Nayiniyappa Affair.

40. ANOM, FM, COL, C²/71, fol. 293 verso.

41. Writing on palm leaves remained a common medium for Tamil writing until the end of the nineteenth century. Stuart H. Blackburn, *Print, Folklore, and Nationalism in Colonial South India* (Delhi: Permanent Black, 2006), 21–23.

42. ANOM, FM, COL, C²/71, fol. 293 verso.

43. Ibid.

44. Ibid. Xaveri Moutou was likely the Christian who had been appointed co-broker with Nayiniyappa in 1714; see chapter 1.

45. ANOM, FM, COL, C²/70, fol. 255. The law in question appears in section 14, article II of the 1670 Criminal Ordinance, discussed in the next chapter. Nayiniyappa's appeal cites here from Philippe Bornier, *Conférences des nouvelles ordonnances de Louis XIV roy de France et de Navarre, avec celles des rois predecesseurs de Sa Majesté, le droit écrit, & les arrêts*, Nouvelle édition reveuë, corrigée & augmentée (A Paris chez les associez choisis par ordre de Sa Majesté pour l'impression de ses nouvelles ordonnances. M. D C C. Avec privilege du roy, 1700).

46. For example, the testimony of Nicolas Piri was thus heard by the council in 1739. Diagou, *Arrêts du Conseil supérieur de Pondichéry*, 1:68.

47. ANOM, FM, COL, C²/71, fols. 292 verso–293.

48. ANOM, FM, COL, C²/71, fol. 294 verso.

49. For mentions of Cordier and his biography, see ANOM, FM, COL, C²/71, fol. 292 verso and C²/71, fol. 82. Cordier the elder arrived in India as a *sous-marchand* in 1686 and was the chief official of a small French presence in Caveripatam (Kaveripakkam). Paul Käppelin, *La Compagnie des Indes Orientales et François Martin: Etude sur l'histoire du commerce et des établissements français dans l'Inde sous Louis XIV (1664–1719)* (Paris, 1908), 252.

50. ANOM, FM, COL, C²/71, fol. 292 verso.

51. The denial of shared language in interrogations has more often been studied in modern context; see Susan Berk-Seligson, *Coerced Confessions: The Discourse of Bilingual Police Interrogations* (Berlin: Mouton de Gruyter, 2009).

52. ANOM, FM, COL, C²/71, fol. 110 verso.

53. There is no discernible pattern to the shift in the eighteenth century between the two nomenclatures used for this institution. Henri Joucla, *Le Conseil supérieur des colonies et ses antécédents, avec de nombreux documents inédits et notamment les procès-verbaux du Comité colonial de l'Assemblée constituante* (Paris: Les Editions du monde moderne, 1927), 15. The term "Sovereign Council" appears to be more common in the early eighteenth century, with "Superior Council" coming to be the more common term later in that century. I use the two terms interchangeably, as do the primary sources.

54. See the dossiers held in ANOM, INDE, série M.

55. ANOM, FM, COL, C²/71, fol. 294.

56. Ibid.

57. Diagou, *Arrêts du Conseil supérieur de Pondichéry*, 8:95–96.

58. *Procès-verbaux des délibérations du Conseil Supérieur de Pondichéry*, 1:191.

59. ANOM, FM, COL, C²/71, fol. 56 verso.

60. ANOM, FM, COL, C²/71, fol. 61.

61. Ibid.

62. See, for example, in ANOM, FM, COL, C²/70, fol. 59 verso.

63. The Nayiniyappa Affair was not the only case heard by Pondichéry's Sovereign Council in which Tamil witnesses deposed by the council claimed that they had signed documents in French without understanding their contents. In a case heard in 1729, regarding the forging of Tamil receipts, the Brahman Vingayen testified that only after he had signed a certain French document was it read to him. ANOM, INDE, série M/25.

64. ANOM, FM, COL, C²/70 fol. 202.

65. ANOM, FM, COL, C²/70, fol. 252 verso.

66. ANOM, FM, COL, C²/70, fol. 205 verso.

67. ANOM, FM, COL, C²/70, fol. 202.

68. ANOM, FM, COL, C²/70, fol. 252 verso.

69. ANOM, FM, COL, C²/70, fol. 89.

70. ANOM, FM, COL, C²/71, fol. 296 verso.

71. ANOM, FM, COL, C²/71, fol. 296.

72. Ibid.

73. ANOM, FM, COL, C²/70, fol. 254.

74. ANOM, FM, COL, C²/71, fol. 295.

75. Ibid.

76. ANOM, FM, COL, C²/71, fol. 299.

77. For a description of the Hundi system, see François Martin, *India in the 17th Century, 1670–1694 (Social, Economic, and Political): Memoirs of François Martin* (New Delhi: Manohar, 1981), vol. 1, app. 2. See also Lakshmi Subramanian, *Indigenous Capital and Imperial Expansion: Bombay, Surat, and the West Coast* (Delhi: Oxford University Press, 1996). Originally cited in Claude Markovits, Jacques Pouchepadass, and Sanjay Subrahmanyam, eds., *Society and Circulation: Mobile People and Itinerant Cultures in South Asia, 1750–1950* (Delhi: Permanent Black, 2003), 5. For a critical evaluation of the system, focusing on recent usage but providing historical background, see Marina Martin, "Hundi/Hawala: The Problem of Definition," *Modern Asian Studies* 43, no. 4 (July 2009): 909–37. On the use of Hundi among Gujarati merchants in the Western Indian Ocean, see Pedro Machado, *Ocean of Trade: South Asian Merchants, Africa and the Indian Ocean, C. 1750–1850* (Cambridge: Cambridge University Press, 2014), 65–67. For a discussion of signing practices in the Tamil region in India in the modern period, see Francis Cody, "Inscribing Subjects to Citizenship: Petitions, Literacy Activism, and the Performativity of Signature in Rural Tamil India," *Cultural Anthropology* 24, no. 3 (November 2012): 347–80.

78. Pillai, *Private Diary*, 1:3.

79. ANOM, FM, COL, C²/71, fol. 296.

80. ANOM, FM, COL, C²/71, fol. 296 verso.

81. ANOM, FM, COL, C²/71, fol. 61.

82. ANOM, FM, COL, C²/71, fol. 108.

83. ANOM, FM, COL, C²/71, fol. 60 verso.

84. François Pouillon, *Dictionnaire des Orientalistes de Langue Française* (Paris: Karthala Editions, 2008), 348–49.

85. Alfred Albert Martineau, ed., *Correspondance du Conseil supérieur de Pondichéry et de la Compagnie [des Indes]* (Pondichéry: Société de l'histoire de l'Inde française, 1920), 1:165.

86. Ibid.

87. Two centuries later, French colonial administrators in Africa were still facing very similar problems and were prompted to "learn the language of the country that they govern." Emily Lynn Osborn, "Interpreting Colonial Power in French Guinea: The Boubou Penda-Ernest Noirot Affair of 1905," in *Intermediaries, Interpreters and Clerks: African Employees in the Making of Colonial Africa*, ed. Benjamin N. Lawrance, Emily Lynn Osborn, and Richard L. Roberts (Madison: University of Wisconsin Press, 2006), 56–76.

88. Pillai, *Private Diary*, 3:266.

4. Conflict at Court

1. ANOM, FM, COL, C^2/71, fol. 130.

2. David Parker, "Sovereignty, Justice, and the Function of the Law in Seventeenth-Century France," *Past and Present* 122 (1989): 36–74. For an example of this dynamic at work in provincial France, see Zoë A. Schneider, *The King's Bench: Bailiwick Magistrates and Local Governance in Normandy, 1670–1740* (Rochester, NY : University of Rochester Press, 2008). In a colonial context, Éric Wenzel has argued that Québec's Superior Council in the same period was a tool used by local elites to shape legal and social realities, bypassing the central authority of the metropolitan state. Éric Wenzel, *La justice criminelle en Nouvelle-France (1670–1760): Le grand arrangement* (Dijon, FR: Editions universitaires de Dijon, 2012), 27–29. An important difference between the two cases is that local elites in New France were a much better established and stronger group than the employees of the Compagnie des Indes in Pondichéry in the first decades of the eighteenth century, who held a much weaker position in relation to the state.

3. On French legal terms and procedures in the period, a useful reference tool is Claude de Ferrière, *Dictionnaire de droit et de pratique* (Paris: V. Brunet, 1769). On French criminal procedure, see Arlette Lebigre, *Les Institutions de l'Ancien Régime* (Paris: Les Cours de droit, 1976); Benoît Garnot, *Crime et justice aux XVIIe et XVIIIe siècles* (Paris: Imago, 2000). For a review of the growing field of early modern French legal social history, see Michael Breen, "Law, Society, and the State in Early Modern France," *Journal of Modern History* 83, no. 2 (June 2011): 346–86.

4. The minutes describing this decision, made on February 7, 1718, are in AN, MAR, B^1/27, fols. 102–112 verso. A copy of the decision is reproduced in ANOM, FM, COL, F^3/238, fols. 381–387.

5. The declaration of Nayiniyappa's innocence, made on January 20, 1719, appears in ANOM, FM, COL, C^2/71, fols. 190–191.

6. This order was made on September 10, 1720. ANOM, FM, COL, F^3/238, fols. 391–410.

7. On such uses of the legal arena in medieval Marseille, see Daniel Lord Smail, *The Consumption of Justice: Emotions, Publicity, and Legal Culture in Marseille, 1264–1423* (Ithaca, NY: Cornell University Press, 2003).

8. Lauren Benton, *Law and Colonial Cultures: Legal Regimes in World History, 1400–1900* (Cambridge: Cambridge University Press, 2002); Lauren Benton, *A Search for Sovereignty: Law and Geography in European Empires, 1400–1900* (Cambridge: Cambridge University Press, 2009). See also Eric Lewis Beverley, "Frontier as Resource: Law, Crime, and Sovereignty on the Margins of Empire," *Comparative Studies in Society*

and History 55, no. 2 (2013): 241–72; Brian Owensby, *Empire of Law and Indian Justice in Colonial Mexico* (Stanford, CA: Stanford University Press, 2008).

9. Katherine A. Hermes, "Jurisdiction in the Colonial Northeast: Algonquian, English and French Governance," *American Journal of Legal History* 43, no. 1 (January 1999): 52.

10. Laurie M. Wood discusses the global legal regime of the First Empire in "Archipelago of Justice: Law in France's Early Modern Empire" (unpublished manuscript in progress). The work on law and crime in the French empire has been especially rich in the context of New France. See Wenzel, *La justice criminelle en Nouvelle-France*; Elise Frêlon, *Les pouvoirs du Conseil souverain de la Nouvelle France dans l'édiction de la norme, 1663–1760* (Paris: L'Harmattan, 2002); A. J. B. Johnston, *Control and Order in French Colonial Louisbourg, 1713–1758* (East Lansing: Michigan State University Press, 2001); David Gilles, "Les acteurs de la norme coloniale face au droit métropolitain: De l'adaptation à l'appropration (Canada, XVIIe–XVIIIe siècles)," *Clio@Themis* 4 (2011): 1–41; André Lachance, *Vivre, aimer et mourir: Juger et punir en Nouvelle-France* (Montreal: Libre Expression, 2004).

11. In the French context, see Malick W. Ghachem, *The Old Regime and the Haitian Revolution* (Cambridge: Cambridge University Press, 2012); Sue Peabody, *"There Are No Slaves in France": The Political Culture of Race and Slavery in the Ancien Régime* (New York: Oxford University Press, 1996); Brett Rushforth, *Bonds of Alliance: Indigenous and Atlantic Slaveries in New France* (Chapel Hill: University of North Carolina Press, 2012). The scholarship on the intersection of slavery and law in colonial contexts more generally is expansive. For a review, see David S. Tanenhaus, "Law, Slavery, and Justice: A Special Issue," *Law and History Review* 29, no. 4 (November 2011): v.

12. Lauren A. Benton and Richard Jeffrey Ross, eds., *Legal Pluralism and Empires, 1500–1850* (New York: NYU Press, 2013).

13. Voltaire quoted in Suzanne Desan, "'War between Brothers and Sisters': Inheritance Law and Gender Politics in Revolutionary France," *French Historical Studies* 20, no. 4 (October 1997): 602.

14. David Avrom Bell, *Lawyers and Citizens: The Making of a Political Elite in Old Regime France* (New York: Oxford University Press, 1994), 23.

15. In addition to these two judicial forums, a tribunal of the admiralty was created in 1717 in Pondichéry, to deal with maritime matters and sailors, and a *conseil de guerre* in 1729, for military affairs and soldiers.

16. The two terms were used interchangeably to describe this institution throughout the eighteenth century.

17. This and similar decrees were modeled after a 1645 royal decree creating a sovereign council in French island holdings in the New World. Joucla, *Le Conseil supérieur*, 12. See also Jean Gingast, *De l'oeuvre et du rôle des gouverneurs coloniaux* (Rennes: Imprimerie Rennaise, 1902), 56.

18. "25 Septembre 1702, Création du Conseil souverain de Pondichéry." Reproduced in *Lettres* du Centre d'information et de documentation de l'Inde francophone, no. 36, http://cidif.go1.cc/index.php?option=com_content&view=article&id=364:25-septembre-1702-creation-du-conseil-souverain-de-pondichery&catid=40:lettre-nd36&Itemid=3.

19. Joucla, *Le Conseil supérieur*, 24. In Québec, for example, some of the councillors were respected members of the local commercial society with no legal experience,

but others had arrived from France with formal legal instruction. Wenzel, *La justice criminelle en Nouvelle-France*, 37.

20. On the making of the various *coutumes*, see Martine Grinberg, *Écrire les coutumes. Les droits seigneuriaux en France (XVIe–XVIIIe siècle)* (Paris: Presses universitaires de France, 2006). On the use of the *coutume* in a colonial context, see Jerah Johnson, "La Coutume de Paris: Louisiana's First Law," *Louisiana History: The Journal of the Louisiana Historical Association* 30, no. 2 (April 1989): 145–55.

21. For an example in which the rules of the 1670 ordinance were disregarded in cases involving indigenous populations in New France, see Jan Grabowski, "French Criminal Justice and Indians in Montreal, 1670–1760," *Ethnohistory* 43, no. 3 (July 1996): 405–29. On the impact of the ordinance in New France, see Wenzel, *La justice criminelle en Nouvelle-France*, 63–112.

22. In British India, the early colonial period was one of great legal variability, and even once India came largely under British control, the Raj did not implement a universal codified body of law until the implementation of the Code of Criminal Procedure in 1861. Elizabeth Kolsky, "Codification and the Rule of Colonial Difference: Criminal Procedure in British India," *Law and History Review* 23, no. 3 (October 2005): 631–83.

23. Gagan D. S. Sood, "Sovereign Justice in Precolonial Maritime Asia: The Case of the Mayor's Court of Bombay, 1726–1798," *Itinerario* 37, no. 2 (August 2013): 48.

24. Much more work is needed on the Pondichéry Chaudrie. Its surviving records are held at NAIP. The most important current work, as well as a published selection of cases, is in Jean-Claude Bonnan, *Jugements de la tribunal de la Chaudrie de Pondichéry 1766–1817* (Pondicherry: Institut française de Pondichéry, Ecole française d'Extrême Orient, 2001). See also Joseph Minattur, *Justice in Pondicherry* (Mumbai: N. M. Tripathi, 1973); Joseph Minattur, "Tribunal de la Chaudrie, 1728–1827," *Revue historique de Pondichéry* 12 (1974–75): 12–18; Jaganou Diagou, "The Judicial Set-up in Pondicherry between 1701 and 1819," *Revue Historique de Pondichéry* 11 (1973): 71–72; Jean-Claude Bonnan, "L'organisation judiciare de Pondichéry au 18ème siècle: L'example du tribunal de la Chaudrie," in *French in India and Indian Nationalism*, ed. K. S. Mathew (Delhi: BRPC, 1999), 2:535–52.

25. Allan Christelow, *Muslim Law Courts and the French Colonial State in Algeria* (Princeton, NJ: Princeton University Press, 1985).

26. Richard White, *The Middle Ground: Indians, Empires, and Republics in the Great Lakes Region, 1650–1815* (Cambridge: Cambridge University Press, 1991).

27. Grabowski, "French Criminal Justice."

28. Wenzel, *La justice criminelle en Nouvelle-France*, 50.

29. Sood, "Sovereign Justice," 46.

30. James Jaffe, *Ironies of Colonial Governance: Law, Custom and Justice in Colonial India* (Cambridge: Cambridge University Press, 2015); Amrita Shodhan, "The East India Company's Conquest of Assam, India, and 'Community' Justice: Panchayats/ Mels in Translation," *Asian Journal of Law and Society* 2, no. 2 (November 2015): 357–77. For the British legal setup in the early colonial period, see Charles Fawcett, *The First Century of British Justice in India: An Account of the Court of Judicature at Bombay, Established in 1672, and of Other Courts of Justice in . . . to the Latter Part of the Eighteenth Century* (Darmstadt, Ger.: Clarendon Press, 1934).

31. The records of the interrogation are themselves copies made by the council in 1718 as a result of the reinvestigation of the Nayiniyappa Affair. They appear

in ANOM, FM, COL, C² 70, fols. 48 verso–75 verso. In Nayinoyappa's 1717 appeal, the mediated account of the interrogations appears in ANOM, FM, COL, C²/70, fols. 251–256.

32. Owensby, *Empire of Law and Indian Justice*, 53.

33. ANOM, FM, COL, C²/70, fols. 51–51 verso.

34. ANOM, FM, COL, C²/70, fols. 68 verso–69.

35. ANOM, FM, COL, C²/70, fol. 253.

36. Gnanou Diagou, *Arrêts du Conseil supérieur de Pondichéry* (Pondichéry: Bibliothèque publique, 1935), 1:xiv. Later on the use of lawyers in French India was both allowed and regulated. An 1818 ordinance aimed at the French-run tribunal in Bengal serving locals (the equivalent of the Pondichéry Chaudrie) noted that the parties appearing before this tribunal always had the right to be represented by "Moktayers, or *procureurs*," except in cases where the judge ordered otherwise. Indian defendants could choose to be represented by a gentile (Hindu) or a Moor (Muslim). In cases in which either a European or a métis (known in French India as *gens à chapeau*) was the plaintiff, the defendant could choose to be represented by a European or a métis. Article 39 of "11 mars 1818—Tribunal de la cacherie de Chandernagor." Reproduced in *Lettres du* Centre d'information et de documentation de l'Inde francophone, no. 36, http://cidifoliogo1.cc/index.php?option=com_content&view=article&id=315:11-mars-1818-tribunal-de-la-cacherie-de-chandernagor&catid=40:lettre-nd36&Itemid=3.

37. Gene Edwin Ogle, "Policing Saint Domingue: Race, Violence, and Honor in an Old Regime Colony" (PhD diss., University of Pennsylvania, 2003), 179.

38. My thanks go to Alexandre Dubé for his insights on this issue.

39. ANOM, FM, COL, C²/71, fol. 109.

40. ANOM, FM, COL, C²/70, fol. 202.

41. ANOM, FM, COL, C²/70, fol. 252 verso.

42. ANOM, FM, COL, C²/70, fol. 255.

43. ANOM, FM, COL, C²/70, fol. 252.

44. Criminal Ordinance of 1670, article 8 of title 14. On rights due to the accused under the Old Regime, see Antoine Astaing, *Droits et garanties de l'accusé dans le procès criminel de l'Ancien Régime, XVIe et XVIIe siècle: Audace et pusillanimité de la doctrine pénale française* (Aix-en-Provence: Presses Universitaires d'Aix-Marseille, 1999).

45. ANOM, FM, COL, C²/70, fol. 252 verso.

46. ANOM, FM, COL, C²/70, fol. 254.

47. ANOM, FM, COL, C²/70, fols. 13–48 verso.

48. The confrontations are at ANOM, FM, COL, C²/70 fols. 77 verso–83 verso. On witnesses in the French legal system in this period, see Éric Wenzel, "Forcer les témoignages : Le délicat recours au monitoire sous l'Ancien Régime," in *Les témoins devant la justice : Une histoire des statuts et des comportements*, ed. Benoît Garnot (Rennes: Presses universitaires de Rennes, 2015), 83–90.

49. ANOM, FM, COL, C²/71, fol. 299.

50. ANOM, FM, COL, C²/70, fol. 254.

51. ANOM, FM, COL, C²/70, fol. 252 verso.

52. ANOM, FM, COL, C²/70, fol. 253 verso.

53. ANOM, FM, COL, F/³/238, fol. 394.

54. ANOM, FM, COL, C²/71, fol. 299. The inquest is reprinted along with other supporting evidence in an appeal filed by Nayiniyappa's heirs in 1720. ANOM, FM,

COL, C²/71, fols. 282–302. Other reprinted evidentiary materials that I have been able to compare with the earlier original sources have been accurately reproduced in this appeal, so there is no reason to doubt the accuracy of the testimony of the judges reproduced here.

55. ANOM, FM, COL, C²/71, fols. 300–300 verso.

56. ANOM, FM, COL, C²/71, fol. 300 verso.

57. La Prévostière's suggestions for sentencing, dated May 16, 1716, are at ANOM, FM, COL, C²/70, fols. 75 verso–76.

58. ANOM, FM, COL, C²/71, fol. 299 verso.

59. ANOM, FM, COL, C²/70, fols. 76–77 verso.

60. ANOM, FM, COL, C²/70, fol. 76 verso.

61. Ibid.

62. ANOM, FM, COL, C²/70, fol. 77.

63. Ghachem, *The Old Regime and the Haitian Revolution*; Nasser Hussain, *The Jurisprudence of Emergency: Colonialism and the Rule of Law* (Ann Arbor: University of Michigan Press, 2003); Elizabeth Kolsky, *Colonial Justice in British India: White Violence and the Rule of Law*, repr. ed. (Cambridge: Cambridge University Press, 2011). On the rejection of state law through the use of private violence, see Sumit Guha, "Wrongs and Rights in the Maratha Country: Antiquity, Custom and Power in Eighteenth-Century India," in *Changing Concepts of Law and Justice in South Asia*, ed. Michael Anderson and Sumit Guha (New Delhi: Oxford University Press, 1997), 14–29.

64. Diagou, *Arrêts du Conseil supérieur de Pondichéry*, 8:28.

65. ANOM, FM, COL, C²/71, fol. 110 verso.

66. The record of Nayiniyappa's brief interrogation by the judges is at ANOM, FM, COL, C²/70, fols. 83 verso–84.

67. ANOM, FM, COL, C²/71, fol. 299 verso.

68. Ibid.

69. Nayiniyappa's sentencing is at ANOM, FM, COL, C²/70, fols. 84 verso–85.

70. ANOM, FM, COL, C²/70, fol. 84 verso.

71. ANOM, FM, COL, C²/70, fol. 252.

72. ANOM, FM, COL, C²/71, fol. 301.

73. ANOM, FM, COL, C²/71, fols. 300–300 verso.

74. ANOM, FM, COL, C²/71, fol. 301.

75. ANOM, FM, COL, C²/71, fol. 301 verso.

76. *Procès-verbaux des délibérations du Conseil Supérieur de Pondichéry* (Pondichéry: Société de l'Histoire de l'Inde Française, 1913), 1:104.

77. ANOM, FM, COL, C²/71, fol. 251.

78. ANOM, FM, COL, C²/70, fol. 89.

79. Hébert's letter naming La Morandière as the author is ANOM, FM, COL, C²/71, fol. 255 verso; La Morandière's admission is in ANOM, FM, COL, C²/71, fol. 54.

80. ANOM, FM, COL, C²/71, fol. 59.

81. ANOM, FM, COL, C²/71, fol. 54.

82. Diagou, *Arrêts du Conseil supérieur de Pondichéry*, 8:95.

83. ANOM, FM, COL, C²/71, fols. 50–53; and fols. 54–65.

84. ANOM, FM, COL, C²/71, fol. 59 verso. One of these Portuguese manifestos appears in the French archive, in ANOM, FM, COL, C²/70, fols. 155–166. Its translation into French is at ANOM, FM, COL, C²/70 fols. 200–207 verso.

85. ANOM, FM, COL, C²/71, fol. 83.

86. ANOM, FM, COL, C²/71, fol. 59 verso.

87. ANOM, FM, COL, C²/71, fol. 61.

88. ANOM, FM, COL, C²/70, fol. 138.

89. La Morandière's reference to finding the records is in ANOM, FM, COL, C²/71, fol. 60. The actual exchange between Hébert and Father Turpin, to which he is referring, is at ANOM, FM, COL, C²/70 fols. 138–139 verso, and is a reproduction made in the course of the 1718 inquiry into Nayiniyappa's conviction.

90. On the Malabar Rites controversy in Pondichéry, Paolo Aranha's work is key. See Paolo Aranha, "'Glocal' Conflicts: Missionary Controversies on the Coromandel Coast between the XVII and the XVIII Centuries," in *Evangelizzazione e Globalizzazione: Le Missioni Gesuitiche Nell'età Moderna Tra Storia e Storiografia*, ed. Michael Catto, Guido Mongini, and Silvia Mostaccio (Castello, It.: Società Editrice Dante Alighieri, 2010), 79–104; Paolo Aranha, "Les meilleures causes embarassent les Juges, si elles manquent de bonnes preuves: Père Norbert's Militant Historiography on the Malabar Rites Controversy," in *Europäische Geschichtskulturen um 1700 zwischen Gelehrsamkeit, Politik und Konfession*, ed. Thomas Wallnig, Thomas Stockinger, Ines Peper, and Patrick Fiska (Berlin: De Gruyter, 2012), 239–68; Paolo Aranha, "The Social and Physical Spaces of the Malabar Rites Controversy," in *Space and Conversion in Global Perspective*, ed. Giuseppe Marcocci, Aliocha Maldavsky, Wietse de Boer and Ilaria Pavan (Leiden, Neth.: Brill, 2015)." Another account of the Pondichéry context of the Malabar Rites controversy appears in K. S. Mathew, "Missionaries from the Atlantic Regions and the Social Changes in French Pondicherry from the Seventeenth to Nineteenth Centuries," in *Les relations entre la France et l'Inde de 1673 à nos jours*, ed. Jacques Weber (Paris: Les Indes savantes, 2002). On the Malabar Rites conflict at its point of origin in seventeenth-century Madurai, the definitive work is Ines G. Županov, *Disputed Mission: Jesuit Experiments and Brahminical Knowledge in Seventeenth-Century India* (New Delhi: Oxford University Press, 2001).

91. ANOM, FM, COL, C²/71, fol. 60 verso.

92. ANOM, FM, COL, C²/71, fol. 58 verso.

93. Ibid.

94. ANOM, FM, COL, C²/71, fols. 63 verso–64.

95. Cuperly's letters are at ANOM, FM, COL, C²/70, fols. 86–88.

96. ANOM, FM, COL, C²/70, fol. 86.

97. ANOM, FM, COL, C²/70, fol. 86 verso.

98. ANOM, FM, COL, C²/71, fol. 261.

99. AN, MAR, B¹/27, folio 62–67 verso.

100. Dale K. Van Kley, *The Damiens Affair and the Unraveling of the Ancien Regime, 1750–1770* (Princeton, NJ: Princeton University Press, 1984), 101.

101. ANOM, FM, COL, C²/70, fols. 88–88 verso.

102. ANOM, FM, COL, C²/70, fol. 88 verso.

103. An analysis of Bouchet's letter is in Ludo Rocher, "Father Bouchet's Letter on the Administration of Hindu Law," in *Studies in Hindu Law and Dharmasastra*, ed. Donald R. Davis Jr. and Richard W. Lariviere (London: Anthem Press, 2012), 111–14.

104. The Padroado was the legal and political arrangement by which the Portuguese Crown exercised authority over the Catholic Church in India (and other colonial holdings). Under the Padroado, bishops in India were appointed by the Portuguese

Crown; other figures of religious authority were vicars apostolic, who were appointed by the papal Propaganda Fide, with authority similar to bishops' but without territorial powers. For this distinction and the power struggles it entailed, see Stephen Neill, *A History of Christianity in India: 1707–1858* (Cambridge: Cambridge University Press, 2002), 436–38. On the Capuchins' and other missionaries' relationships with the bishopric of Mylapore see Mathew, "Missionaries from the Atlantic Regions," 353–57.

105. For example, Diagou, *Arrêts du Conseil supérieur de Pondichéry*, 8:38–42.

106. Ibid., 8:40.

107. Ibid., 8:41.

108. Ibid., 8:60.

109. Ibid.

110. Ibid., 8:61.

111. Ibid., 8:61–62.

112. *Procès-verbaux des délibérations du Conseil Supérieur de Pondichéry*, 1:176.

113. Ibid.

114. Diagou, *Arrêts du Conseil supérieur de Pondichéry*, 8:36.

115. Ibid., 8:43.

116. Ibid., 8:44.

117. *Procès-verbaux des délibérations du Conseil Supérieur de Pondichéry*, 1:232–33.

118. ANOM, FM, COL, $C^2/71$, fol. 190.

119. Ibid.

120. ANOM, FM, COL, $C^2/71$, fol. 58.

121. ANOM, FM, COL, $C^2/71$, fol. 58 verso.

122. Niels Brimnes, "Beyond Colonial Law: Indigenous Litigation and the Contestation of Property in the Mayor's Court in Late Eighteenth-Century Madras," *Modern Asian Studies* 37, no. 3 (July 2003): 517.

123. Alexis De Tocqueville, *The Old Regime and the French Revolution* (New York: Doubleday, 2010), 117, cited in Bell, *Lawyers and Citizens*, 21.

5. Between Paris and Pondichéry

1. For a representative example, see Steve Clark's introduction to *Travel Writing and Empire: Postcolonial Theory in Transit*, ed. Steve Clark (London: Zed Books, 1999), where he refers to colonists as belonging to "the mobile culture." Mary Louise Pratt, in her definition of "contact zones," similarly refers to colonizers and colonized, or travelers and "travelees," a formulation that opposes the condition of being colonized to the act of traveling. Mary Louise Pratt, *Imperial Eyes: Travel Writing and Transculturation* (London: Routledge, 1992), 7.

2. For a review of the Annales school's tendency to overlook mobility in the study of French history, see the special issue of *French Historical Studies* devoted to the subject, especially Carla Hesse and Peter Sahlins, "Introduction," *French Historical Studies* 29, no. 3 (July 2006): 347–57. Two influential works in the field of French mobility studies are James B. Collins, "Geographic and Social Mobility in Early-Modern France," *Journal of Social History* 24, no. 3 (April 1, 1991): 563–77; Daniel Roche, *Humeurs vagabondes: De la circulation des hommes et de l'utilité des voyages* (Paris: Fayard, 2003). For a similar attempt to overturn the assumption of stability in

premodern South Asian history, see David Ludden, "History outside Civilisation and the Mobility of South Asia," *South Asia: Journal of South Asian Studies* 17, no. 1 (June 1994): 1–23; David Ludden, "Presidential Address: Maps in the Mind and the Mobility of Asia," *Journal of Asian Studies* 62, no. 4 (November 2003): 1057–78.

3. Claude Markovits, Jacques Pouchepadass, and Sanjay Subrahmanyam, eds., *Society and Circulation: Mobile People and Itinerant Cultures in South Asia, 1750–1950* (Delhi: Permanent Black, 2003).

4. Tony Ballantyne and Antoinette M. Burton, *Moving Subjects: Gender, Mobility, and Intimacy in an Age of Global Empire* (Urbana: University of Illinois Press, 2009).

5. Stephen Greenblatt, *Cultural Mobility: A Manifesto* (Cambridge: Cambridge University Press, 2010), 250.

6. On French commercial efforts in the Mascareignes in the eighteenth century, see Auguste Toussaint, *Le mirage des îles: Le négoce français aux Mascareignes au XVIIIe siècle, suivi de la correspondance du négociant lyonnais Jean-Baptiste Pipon* (Aix-en-Provence: Édisud, 1977), 19–46.

7. "Observations sur l'Etablissement d'une nouvelle Compagnie des Indes," AN, Ancien régime séries administrative, M/1026, fols. 4–5.

8. ANOM, FM, COL, C²/72, fol. 10 verso.

9. Alfred Albert Martineau, ed., *Correspondance du Conseil supérieur de Pondichéry et de la Compagnie [des Indes]* (Pondichéry: Société de l'histoire de l'Inde française, 1920), 1:33.

10. ANOM, FM, COL, C²/70, fol. 173.

11. NAIP, eighteenth-century documents, folder 20, fol. 2.

12. ANOM, FM, COL, C²/70, fol. 173.

13. Ibid.

14. NAIP, eighteenth-century documents, folder 20, fol. 4.

15. *Procès-verbaux des délibérations du Conseil Supérieur de Pondichéry* (Pondichéry: Société de l'histoire de l'Inde Française, 1913), 1:234–35.

16. Ananda Ranga Pillai, *The Private Diary of Ananda Ranga Pillai, Dubash to Joseph François Dupleix, Knight of the Order of St. Michael, and Governor of Pondichery. A Record of Matters Political, Historical, Social, and Personal, from 1736 to 1761* (Madras: Printed by the superintendent government press, 1904), 1:35–36.

17. NAIP, eighteenth-century documents, folder 20, fols. 11–12.

18. Ibid., fols. 8–9.

19. Ibid., fol. 9.

20. ANOM, FM, COL, C²/71, fols. 123–123 verso.

21. ANOM, FM, COL, C²/71, fol. 123 verso.

22. BNF, MF 6231, fol. 56 verso.

23. ANOM, FM, COL, C²/71, fol. 124.

24. ANOM, FM, COL, C²/71, fols. 124–124 verso.

25. ANOM, FM, COL, C²/71, fol. 125.

26. Quoted in Yvonne Gaebelé, "Du nouveau sur la famille d'Ananda Ranga Poulle—Dubash de Dupleix," *Revue Historique de l'Inde Française* 8 (1952), 129–31.

27. ANOM, INDE, N/61, fol. 2.

28. For mention of Guruvappa's British-enabled itinerary, see ANOM, INDE, N/61, fols. 1–2, and NAIP, eighteenth-century documents, folder 20, fol. 3. Mention of Guruvappa's trip to Paris also appears in AMEP, *Lettres*, vol. 991, pp. 783–85.

29. AMEP, *Lettres*, vol. 960, p. 115.

30. Ibid., vol. 992, p. 2.

31. Ibid., vol. 960, p. 116.

32. Adrien Launay, *Histoire des missions de l'Inde* (Paris: Indes savantes, 2000), 1:xxxv. The Pillai family memoir in Pondichéry has the duchesse du Berry serving as the godmother. NAIP, eighteenth-century documents, folder 20, fol. 3.

33. ANOM, FM, DPPC, GR/675.

34. ANOM, FM, COL, F³/238, fols. 391–410.

35. ANOM, FM, COL, C²/71, fols. 313–328.

36. Jean Luquet, *Considérations sur les missions catholiques et voyage d'un missionnaire dans l'Inde* (Paris: Au bureau de l'Université catholique, 1853), 306.

37. NAIP, eighteenth-century documents, folder 20, p. 3.

38. Pillai, *Private Diary*, 1:21.

39. A letter from Ananda Ranga Pillai, dated November 17, 1757. Printed in "Enfance et Adolescence d'Ananda Rangapoullé," *Revue historique de l'état de Pondichéry* 9 (1955): 99.

40. Ibid., 100.

41. All French governors of the colony, beginning with François Martin, were made knights of the order of Notre dame de mont carmel et de St. Lazare de Jérusalem.

42. Luquet, *Considérations sur les missions catholiques*, 307n1.

43. For the discussion of Guruvappa's Christian descendants, see ibid., 306. For the widow Guruvappa's profession of faith, see AMEP, *Lettres*, vol. 992, p. 2.

44. Alfred Albert Martineau, ed., *Résume des actes de l'Etat civil de Pondichéry* (Pondichéry: Société de l'histoire de l'Inde française, 1917), 1:269.

45. H. de Closets d'Errey, *Précis chronologique de l'histoire de l'Inde française (1664–1816), suivi d'un relevé des faits marquants de l'Inde française au XIXe siècle* (Pondichéry: Librairie E. Léroux, 1934), 20.

46. Luquet, *Considérations sur les missions catholiques*, 307.

47. Ibid., 307n1 (quoting the eighteenth-century missionary Mathon).

48. ANOM, FM, COL, C²/73, fol. 40 verso.

49. The supercargo on French voyages was always French except on the yearly voyage to Manila. Catherine Manning, *Fortunes à Faire: The French in Asian Trade, 1719–48* (Aldershot, UK: Variorum, 1996), 144.

50. ANOM, INDE, série M/ 91.

51. On Indians living in France during the eighteenth century, see Erick Noël, "Les Indiens en France au XVIIIe siècle," in *Les relations entre la France et l'Inde de 1673 à nos jours*, ed. Jacques Weber (Paris: Les Indes savantes, 2002), 203–19. Noël's account relies on the French census of 1777, and most of the India-born residents of France he identified were domestic servants. Much earlier, at the beginning of the eighteenth century, another instance of an Indian traveling from Pondichéry to Paris demonstrates how such travels were shared with missionaries and could be framed as touristic expeditions. In a 1702 letter written, in French, by a young Indian convert to an unnamed Jesuit, the writer mentions seeing St. Cloud, on the outskirts of Paris, and the Notre Dame Cathedral. See "Rélations et lettres de Jésuites de l'Inde (1699–1740): Missions dans le Maduré, journaux de voyages dans l'Inde par les P. Martin, Lalanne, Barbier, de Bourses [sic], de la Breville etc etc. [sic]. 1699 à 1740," BNF, NAF 11168, *Manuscrits et lettres autographes*, fols. 53–54 verso. A better-known example

of an Indian in France is of the Pondichéry-born slave Francisque, who demanded his freedom based on the "Free Soil Principle" in 1759, as described by Sue Peabody in *"There Are No Slaves in France": The Political Culture of Race and Slavery in the Ancien Régime* (New York: Oxford University Press, 1996), 57–71. An interesting example of a European but locally born woman making such a trip is the wife of M. Dumas, who would become governor of Pondichéry. She was a Lutheran named Marie Gertaude Van Zyll, who converted to Catholicism in 1724. Martineau, *Résume des actes de l'Etat civil de Pondichéry*, 1:198, 260. The Indian-born, Dutch-bred Madame Dumas was quite cosmopolitan, having lived for several years in France. She was described by one French observer as "possessing all the charm one could find among the fair sex in Paris." Simon de La Farelle, *Deux officiers français au XVIIIe siècle: Mémoires et correspondance du chevalier et du général de La Farelle* (Paris: Berger-Levrault et cie, 1896), 90.

52. Vanves, fond Brotier, vol. 80, fol. 127.

53. ANOM, FM, COL, C²/70, fol. 254 verso. Clearly, Nayiniyappa had an interest in claiming that Manuel's return to Pondichéry was tied to Hébert's reinstallment in the colony, but it is also possible the two events were unrelated.

54. ANOM, FM, COL, C²/70, fol. 197 verso.

55. Other colonial servants traveled with Jesuits to France. In fact, Father Tachard not only took a gardener with him from Siam to Paris but then brought this Siamese gardener with him to India. BNF, MF 19030, fol. 185. For British examples, see Michael H. Fisher, *Counterflows to Colonialism: Indian Travellers and Settlers in Britain, 1600–1857* (Delhi: Permanent Black, 2004).

56. The Danish Tranquebar mission provides an example analogous to Manuel's global travels: Peter Maleiappen (1700–1730), who taught Tamil to the Protestant missionaries there, went with the head of the mission, the German missionary Bartholomaüs Zeigenblag, to Europe in 1714–1716. Heike Liebau, "Country Priests, Catechists, and Schoolmasters as Cultural, Religious, and Social Middlemen in the Context of the Tranquebar Mission," in *Christians and Missionaries in India: Cross-Cultural Communication since 1500, with Special Reference to Caste, Conversion, and Colonialism*, ed. Robert Eric Frykenberg and Alaine M. Low (Grand Rapids, MI: Eerdmans, 2003), 87. See also Heike Liebau, *Cultural Encounters in India: The Local Co-Workers of the Tranquebar Mission, 18th to 19th Centuries*, trans. Rekha V. Rajan (New Delhi: Social Science Press, 2013).

57. "Lettre du Père Martin, Missionnaire de la Compagnie de Jésus, au P. de Villette, de la Même Compagnie," Balassor, Royaume de Bengale, January 30, 1699, in Jesuits, *Lettres édifiantes et curieuses, écrites des missions étrangères* (Paris: Chez Nicolas Le Clerc, 1703), 1:13.

58. For an account of dramatic instance of conflict between French Jesuits and their catechists in the Nayaka-ruled city of Madurai, see Danna Agmon, "Conflicts in the Context of Conversion: French Jesuits and Tamil Religious Intermediaries in Madurai, India," in *Intercultural Encounter: Jesuit Mission in South Asia, 16th–18th Centuries*, ed. Anand Amaladass and Ines G. Županov (Bangalore, India: Asian Trading Company, 2014), 179–98.

59. "Lettre du Père Pierre Martin, missionnaire de la Compagnie de Jésus, au Père Le Gobien de la même Compagnie," Aour, Madurai, December 11, 1700, in Jesuits, *Lettres édifiantes et curieuses*, 6:180–81.

60. "Lettre du Père Le Gac, missionnaire de la Compagnie de Jésus, à Monsieur le Chevalier Hébert, Gouverneur de Pondichéry," Chruchsnabouram, December 10, 1718, in Jesuits, *Lettres édifiantes*, 16:176–77.

61. Ibid., 16:178–79.

62. Ibid., 16:179.

63. Ibid., 16:188–90.

64. Ibid., 16:190.

65. BNF, MF 19030, fol. 137 verso.

66. Vanves, fond Brotier, vol. 80, fols. 124–161.

67. Ibid., fols. 124–124 verso.

68. Ibid., fols. 125–127 verso.

69. Ibid., fol. 128 verso.

70. Ibid., fols. 130 verso–131.

71. Ibid. fol. 131 verso.

72. Ibid., fols. 146 verso–147.

73. Georges Roques, *La manière de négocier aux Indes, 1676–1691: La Compagnie des Indes et l'art du commerce*, ed. Valérie Bérinstain (Paris: Ecole française d'Extrême Orient, 1996), 33.

6. Archiving the Affair

1. ANOM, FM, COL, C^2/71, fol. 101 verso.

2. ANOM, FM, COL, C^2/ 71, fols. 113–113 verso.

3. Ann L. Stoler, *Along the Archival Grain: Epistemic Anxieties and Colonial Common Sense* (Princeton, NJ: Princeton University Press, 2009), 19–20.

4. For a review of this scholarship, see Matthew S. Hull, "Documents and Bureaucracy," *Annual Review of Anthropology* 41, no. 1 (2012): 251–67. On scribal culture in the context of American capitalism, see Michael Zakim, *Accounting for Capitalism: The Business Clerk as Social Revolutionary* (Chicago: University of Chicago Press, 2016). On the fashioning of identity more generally through practices of writing, see Brinkley Messick, *The Calligraphic State: Textual Domination and History in a Muslim Society* (Berkeley: University of California Press, 1992).

5. Early influential work on the construction of historical narrative through archives is Natalie Zemon Davis, *Fiction in the Archives: Pardon Tales and Their Tellers in Sixteenth-Century France* (Stanford, CA: Stanford University Press, 1987). See also Paul Ricoeur, "Archives, Documents, Traces," in *Time and Narrative*, vol. 3 (Chicago: University of Chicago Press, 1988), 116–26. Recent reflexive work by historians about archives includes Antoinette Burton, *Archive Stories: Facts, Fictions, and the Writing of History* (Durham, NC: Duke University Press, 2005); Nicholas B. Dirks, "Annals of the Archive: Ethnographic Notes on the Sources of History," in *From the Margins: Historical Anthropology and Its Futures*, ed. Brian Keith Axel (Durham, NC: Duke University Press, 2002), 47–65; Carolyn Kay Steedman, *Dust: The Archive and Cultural History* (New Brunswick, NJ: Rutgers University Press, 2002); Stoler, *Along the Archival Grain*. On the so-called archival turn in multiple disciplines, see Renisa Mawani, "Law's Archive," *Annual Review of Law and Social Science*, no. 8 (2012): 337–65.

6. This focus on documentary practices contributes to historians' efforts to look not only *through* papers but *at* them. Ben Kafka, "Paperwork: The State of the Discipline," *Book History* 12, no. 1 (2009): 340–53. On documentary practices in bureaucratic regimes, see Annalise Riles, *Documents: Artifacts of Modern Knowledge* (Ann Arbor: University of Michigan Press, 2006). In India, for work that has considered the role of organizing paper in colonial rule, see Bhavani Raman, *Document Raj: Writing and Scribes in Early Colonial South India* (Chicago: University of Chicago Press, 2012).

7. David Zeitlyn, "Anthropology in and of the Archives: Possible Futures and Contingent Pasts. Archives as Anthropological Surrogates," *Annual Review of Anthropology* 41 (January 2012): 461–80.

8. On archives and colonialism in the South Asian context, see Tony Ballantyne, "Archive, Discipline, State: Power and Knowledge in South Asian Historiography," *New Zealand Journal of Asian Studies* 3, no. 2 (2001): 87–105; Antoinette M. Burton, *Dwelling in the Archive: Women Writing House, Home, and History in Late Colonial India* (New York: Oxford University Press, 2003); Nicholas B. Dirks, "Colin Mackenzie: Autobiography of an Archive," in *The Madras School of Orientalism: Producing Knowledge in Colonial South India*, ed. Thomas R. Trautmann (New Delhi: Oxford University Press, 2009), 29–47; Saloni Mathur, "History and Anthropology in South Asia: Rethinking the Archive," *Annual Review of Anthropology* 29, no. 89 (2000), 89–106.

9. These archives are mostly held in the Archives nationales d'outre-mer over a wide range of different archival series. A good finding guide to these collections is Philippe Le Tréguilly and Monique Morazé, *L'Inde et la France: Deux siècles d'histoire commune, XVIIe–XVIIIe siecles: Histoire, sources, bibliographie* (Paris: CNRS editions, 1995). A not insignificant portion of these materials was also published at the beginning of the twentieth century by French colonial administrators in India who were devoted historians, chief among them Alfred Martineau and Edmond Gaudart. Their efforts are the topic of an ongoing research project about the meaning and uses of the eighteenth century for twentieth-century French colonial administrators. Danna Agmon, "Failure on Display: French India, the 1931 Paris Exhibition, and a Forgotten Historiography of Empire," journal article in progress.

10. Ananda Ranga Pillai, *The Private Diary of Ananda Ranga Pillai, Dubash to Joseph François Dupleix, Knight of the Order of St. Michael, and Governor of Pondichery. A Record of Matters Political, Historical, Social, and Personal, from 1736 to 1761*, ed. J. Fredrick Price (Madras: Printed by the superintendent government press, 1904), 3:38.

11. Miles Ogborn, *Indian Ink: Script and Print in the Making of the English East India Company* (Chicago: University of Chicago Press, 2007), xvii. For more on documentary practices of the British East Indies Company, see H. V. Bowen, *The Business of Empire: The East India Company and Imperial Britain, 1756–1833* (Cambridge: Cambridge University Press, 2006), 151–81.

12. On the early modern "relation" as genre, artifact, and practice, see Thomas V. Cohen and Germaine Warkentin, "Things Not Easily Believed: Introducing the Early Modern Relation," *Renaissance and Reformation/Renaissance et Réforme* 34, no. 1–2 (2011): 7–23.

13. Alfred Albert Martineau, ed., *Correspondance du Conseil supérieur de Pondichéry et de la Compagnie [des Indes]* (Pondichéry: Société de l'histoire de l'Inde française, 1920), 1:2n2.

14. Colonies in the French Atlantic in the same period had less independence from metropolitan authority because news from Paris arrived there with greater rapidity.

15. On distance, empire, and paperwork, see Sylvia Sellers-García, *Distance and Documents at the Spanish Empire's Periphery* (Stanford, CA: Stanford University Press, 2013).

16. ANOM, FM, COL, C²/71, fol. 12 verso. The St. Malo complaint they mention and the directors' response are at ANOM, FM, COL, C²/14, fols. 260–270.

17. ANOM, FM, COL, C²/71, fols. 12 verso–13.

18. ANOM, FM, COL, C²/71, fol. 12 verso.

19. Martineau, *Correspondance du Conseil supérieur*, 1:24–25. Letter written in Paris on December 28, 1726.

20. Ibid. Letter written in Pondichéry, October 8, 1727.

21. ANOM, FM, COL, C²/71, fol. 12.

22. The analysis here has been informed by Donna Merwick, "A Genre of Their Own: Kiliaen van Rensselaer as Guide to the Reading and Writing Practices of Early Modern Businessmen," *William and Mary Quarterly*, 3rd ser., 65, no. 4 (October 2008): 669–712. A work that demonstrates the potential of mercantile archives for crafting global narratives of the early modern world is Francesca Trivellato, *The Familiarity of Strangers: The Sephardic Diaspora, Livorno, and Cross-Cultural Trade in the Early Modern Period* (New Haven: Yale University Press, 2009).

23. Merwick, "A Genre of Their Own," 671.

24. Ibid., 672–73.

25. The Jesuit letters were collected and disseminated in the multivolume *Lettres édifiantes et curieuses, écrites des missions étrangères* (Paris: Chez Nicolas Le Clerc, 1703). The lesser-known but still voluminous correspondence of the MEP missionaries is held at the order's archives in Paris on Rue de Bac. Scholarly and historical works written by French missionaries in India in this period were authored by members of all three orders active in Pondichéry.

26. Gnanou Diagou, *Arrêts du Conseil supérieur de Pondichéry* (Pondichéry: Bibliothèque publique, 1935), 8:104–5.

27. Ibid., 8:105–6.

28. Irina Paperno, "What Can Be Done with Diaries?," *Russian Review* 63, no. 4 (October 2004): 561–73, cited in Heather Beattie, "Where Narratives Meet: Archival Description, Provenance, and Women's Diaries," *Libraries & the Cultural Record* 44, no. 1 (January 2009): 83. On diaries, see also Lynn Z. Bloom, "'I Write for Myself and Strangers': Private Diaries as Public Documents," in *Inscribing the Daily: Critical Essays on Women's Diaries*, ed. Suzanne Bunkers (Amherst: University of Massachusetts Press, 1996), 23–37; Thomas Mallon, *A Book of One's Own: People and Their Diaries* (St. Paul, MN: Hungry Mind Press, 1995).

29. Pillai, *Private Diary*, 1:1.

30. Ibid., 1:xii; 2:300.

31. Ibid., 1:17.

32. Ibid., 1: 98–99, 101.

33. Ibid., 1:177–78.

34. Ibid., 1:67–68.

35. The translators of the diary from Tamil to English suggested that this unnamed writer was the dubash's nephew, who went on to keep his own diary, also published. Ibid., 12:402n1.

36. Ibid., 12:408.

37. Rangappa Thiruvengadam Pillai, *The Diary of Rangappa Thiruvengadam Pillai: 1761–1768*, ed. S. Jeyaseela Stephen (Pondicherry: IIES, 2001). On the Tamil diaries of the eighteenth century and the significance of these texts for the development of a prose style in Tamil, see S. Jeyaseela Stephen, "Diaries of the Natives from Pondicherry and the Prose Development of Popular Tamil in the Eighteenth Century," *Indian Literature* 50, no. 2 (March 2006): 144–55.

38. S. Jeyaseela Stephen provides the following account of diarists and their period of activity: Ananda Ranga Pillai (diary of 1736–1760), Rangappa Thiruvengadam Ananda Ranga Pillai (1760–1781), Veera Nayakar (1778–1792), and Muthu Vijaya Thiruvengadam Pillai (1794–1796). Stephen, "Diaries of the Natives from Pondicherry," 148. A different list appears in M. Gobalakichenane's account of the diarists' lineage: Vijaya Tirouvengadapillai (diary 1760–1791) and Muttu Vijaya Tirouvengadapillai (1791–1799). M Gobalakichenane, "La relation du siège de Pondichéry de 1778 et son auteur," in *Les relations entre la France et l'Inde de 1673 à nos jours*, ed. Jacques Weber (Paris: Les Indes savantes, 2002), 103.

39. The manuscript is held at NAIP, eighteenth-century documents, folder 20. The text makes reference to the existence of this document also in Tamil (p. 13), but the archive doesn't hold this version.

40. For his appointment to this post, see NAIP, French Correspondence of the Eighteenth Century, file 54.

41. NAIP, eighteenth-century documents, folder 20, p. 1.

42. Ibid., p. 2.

43. Ibid.

44. Ibid., p. 3.

45. ANOM, FM, COL, C²/71, fol. 164 verso.

46. ANOM, FM, COL, C²/71, fol. 129 verso.

47. ANOM, FM, COL, C²/71, fol. 301 verso.

48. ANOM, FM, COL, C²/71, fol. 61 verso.

49. ANOM, FM, COL, C²/71, fol. 300.

50. ANOM, FM, COL, C²/73, fol. 210.

51. The notion of an archive acting as a "monument" to the colonial state's power is introduced and then elaborated in, respectively, Ann Laura Stoler, "Colonial Archives and the Arts of Governance," *Archival Science* 2, no. 1–2 (March 2002): 87–109, and Stoler, *Along the Archival Grain*.

52. The family relationship is not mentioned in the contemporaneous French sources but is revealed in the family history written by Tiruvangadan's grandson later in the eighteenth century, which refers to "Nainiapapoullé, brother-in-law to Tirouvengadanpopoullé, my grandfather." NAIP, eighteenth-century documents, folder 20, p. 1. Later in the text Nayiniyappa is referred to by the author as "my grand uncle." Ibid, p. 2. The author was a son of Ananda Ranga Pillai's younger brother.

53. ANOM, FM, COL, C²/70, fol. 173.

54. ANOM, FM, COL, C²/70, fol. 173 verso.

55. ANOM, FM, COL, C²/70, fol. 173 verso–174.

56. ANOM, FM, COL, C²/70, fol. 174.

57. Ibid.

58. Ibid.

59. ANOM, FM, COL, C²/70, fol. 174 verso.

60. ANOM, FM, COL, C²/70, fol. 175.

61. ANOM, FM, COL, C²/70, fol. 176 verso.

62. ANOM, FM, COL, C²/70, fols. 176 verso177.

63. Tiruvangadan's description of this is in ANOM, FM, COL, C²/70, fol. 177; the French translation of Pedro's very brief letter in Tamil is in ANOM, FM, COL, C²/70, fol. 192.

64. ANOM, FM, COL, C²/70, fols. 177–177 verso; Pedro's three letters are in ANOM, FM, COL, C²/70, fols. 192–192 verso.

65. ANOM, FM, COL, C²/70, fol. 192 verso.

66. ANOM, FM, COL, C²/70, fol. 192.

67. Ibid.

68. ANOM, FM, COL, C²/70, fol. 192 verso.

69. The letters to de Nyons are at ANOM, FM, COL, C²/70, fols. 181–184 and fols. 184–184 verso.

70. On the early modern prison as a site for the production of texts, albeit literary instead of legal, see Molly Murray, "Measured Sentences: Forming Literature in the Early Modern Prison," *Huntington Library Quarterly* 72, no. 2 (June 2009): 147–67.

71. Pillai, *Private Diary*, 1:viii.

72. *Procès-verbaux des délibérations du Conseil Supérieur de Pondichéry* (Pondichéry: Société de l'Histoire de l'Inde Française, 1913), 1:118–19.

73. Paul Käppelin, *La Compagnie des Indes Orientales et François Martin: Etude sur l'histoire du commerce et des établissements français dans l'Inde sous Louis XIV (1664–1719)* (Paris, 1908), 619.

74. *Procès-verbaux des délibérations du Conseil Supérieur de Pondichéry*, 1:119.

75. Käppelin, *La Compagnie des Indes Orientales*, 619n7.

76. *Procès-verbaux des délibérations du Conseil Supérieur de Pondichéry*, 1:192–93.

77. There are hints that indicate that the removal of Hébert from office might not have been tied solely to his mistreatment of Nayiniyappa. Dulivier wrote to the Marine Council multiple times in 1715 and 1716 to complain about Hébert. In one of these letters, he wrote that he had been working on a potentially lucrative deal, regarding the purchase of a large amount of pepper, but that Hébert was holding up the negotiations. When this complaint was inscribed in the Marine records in January 1717, a marginal comment noted tersely, "M. Hébert said nothing of this [in his letter.]" AN, MAR, B¹/14, fol. 6 verso.

78. The order installing la Prévostière as the new governor of Pondichéry was dated January 1, 1718, but its execution was delayed by the time of travel from France to India. The order is reproduced in Diagou, *Arrêts du Conseil supérieur de Pondichéry*, 8:111–113. In fact, the king had ordered a company employee stationed in Bengal, d'Hardencourt, to serve as governor, but his death led to La Prévostière's being sworn in as interim governor. *Procès-verbaux des délibérations du Conseil Supérieur de Pondichéry*, 1:192–194.

79. *Procès-verbaux des délibérations*, 1:195.

80. Ibid., 1:204–5.
81. Ibid., 1:205.
82. Ibid., 1:205–6.
83. Ibid., 1:206.
84. ANOM, FM, COL, C²/71, fol. 256.
85. Ibid.
86. ANOM, COL, FM, C²/71, fol. 258.
87. ANOM, FM, COL, C²/71, fol. 262.
88. ANOM, FM, COL, C²/71, fol. 59.
89. Ibid.
90. ANOM, FM, COL, C²/71, fol. 255.
91. Ibid.
92. Ibid.
93. ANOM, FM, COL, C²/71, fol. 255 verso.
94. Ibid.
95. Ibid.
96. Ibid.
97. ANOM, FM, COL, C²/71, fol. 256.
98. ANOM, FM, COL, C²/70, fol. 252 verso.
99. ANOM, FM, COL, C²/71, fol. 256.
100. The officials of the Compagnie des Indes also sent a report to Paris in 1718, complaining about Hébert's refusal to hand over his papers. ANOM, FM, COL, C²/71, fol. 19.
101. ANOM, FM, COL, C²/71, fol. 257 verso.
102. ANOM, FM, COL, C²/71, fol. 255 verso.
103. Ibid. Hébert was referring here mainly to his rival La Prévostière, who replaced him as governor.
104. ANOM, FM, COL, C²/71, fol. 117 verso.
105. ANOM, FM, COL, C²/71, fol. 56 verso.
106. ANOM, FM, COL, C²/71, fol. 57.
107. ANOM, FM, COL, C²/71, fol. 256 verso.
108. Ibid.
109. ANOM, FM, COL, C²/71, fol. 257.
110. ANOM, FM, COL, C²/71, fols. 262–262 verso.
111. Some materials were left in Pondichéry and are currently housed at NAIP—for example, the original records of the Chaudrie court. The process by which this decision was made—which sources belonged in France, which did not—merits further scholarly examination.
112. A reminder of this fact, and a discussion of the historiographic legacy from von Ranke on down that has tended to obscure the processes by which archives are created, is in Filippo De Vivo, "How to Read Venetian 'Relazioni,'" *Renaissance and Reformation / Renaissance et Réforme* 34, no. 1–2 (2011): 25–59.
113. A list of the goods brought to France by the *Jason* and sold in 1715 is at ADN, série HH 201, item 44.
114. "Journal de bord de navires le Mercure, le Jason et la Vénus," ADLA, série C, 875. The journal is not paginated, but the entries about the wedding are for the dates May 30, 1714; May 31, 1714; and June 1, 1714.

115. Ibid., entry for May 30, 1714.

116. Ibid.

117. Ibid., entries for May 31 and June 1, 1714.

118. I am indebted to Natalie Rothman for highlighting this point. An important meditation on the intersection of power and archives is Michel-Rolph Trouillot, *Silencing the Past: Power and the Production of History* (Boston: Beacon Press, 1995).

Epilogue

1. Letter to Paris from Beauvollier de Courchant, ANOM, FM, COL, C²/73, fol. 23.

2. Ibid.

3. Ibid.

4. ANOM, FM, COL, A/20, fol. 76 verso.

5. James Pritchard has considered the relationship of absolutism to colonialism in the Atlantic but concluded that absolutism failed in the colonial context—a formulation that assumes that empire requires hegemony and subscribes to the paradigm of French "failure" that has also informed much of the work on India. James Pritchard, *In Search of Empire: The French in the Americas, 1670–1730* (Cambridge: Cambridge University Press, 2004). The scholarship on absolutism in France is vast; for an influential account of the provincial limits on the Crown, see William Beik, *Absolutism and Society in Seventeenth-Century France: State Power and Provincial Aristocracy in Languedoc* (Cambridge: Cambridge University Press, 1985).

6. William H. Sewell, "Historical Events as Transformations of Structure," in *Logics of History: Social Theory and Social Transformation* (Chicago: University of Chicago Press, 2005), 226.

7. A similar point is made in Nicholas B. Dirks, *The Scandal of Empire: India and the Creation of Imperial Britain* (Cambridge, MA: Belknap Press of Harvard University Press, 2008).

8. It has been suggested that when Dupleix incorporated the notion of territorial expansion in India into French colonial policy, he changed the dynamic and practice of European presence in the subcontinent, thereby ushering in a new era of modern imperialism. Jay Howard Geller, "Towards a New Imperialism in Eighteenth-Century India: Dupleix, La Bourdonnais and the French Compagnie des Indes," *Portuguese Studies* 16 (January 2000): 240–41.

9. Arlette Farge and Jacques Revel, *The Vanishing Children of Paris: Rumor and Politics before the French Revolution* (Cambridge, MA: Harvard University Press, 1991), 4. For further reflections on this methodological strategy, and the suggestion that a "case" is neither general nor singular, see Jean-Claude Passeron and Jacques Revel, "Penser par cas: Raisonner à partir de singularités," in *Penser par cas*, ed. Jean-Claude Passeron and Jacques Revel (Paris: Éditions de l'École des Hautes Études en Sciences Sociales, 2005), 9–44. On the necessity of simultaneously employing multiple scales of analysis, see the programmatic suggestions in Michael Werner and Bénédicte Zimmermann, "Beyond Comparison: Histoire Croisée and the Challenge of Reflexivity," *History and Theory* 45, no. 1 (February 2006): 30–50; Jacques Revel, ed., *Jeux d'échelles. La micro-analyse à l'expérience* (Paris: Seuil, 1998).

10. Few historians of the eighteenth century are so fortunate as to meet the descendants of their research subjects and walk into their homes. I am immensely grateful to Dr. Parasuraman of the Pondicherry Institute of Linguistics and Culture for making the introductions.

11. Gérard Le Bouëdec and Brigitte Nicolas, eds. *Le goût de l'Inde* (Rennes, FR.: Presses Universitaires de Rennes, 2008).

12. For a meditation on the processes by which imperial pasts continue to structure postcolonial presents, which Ann Stoler terms "ruination," see the essays in Ann Laura Stoler, ed., *Imperial Debris: On Ruins and Ruination* (Durham, NC: Duke University Press, 2013).

INDEX

Page numbers in italics indicate illustrations.

CPSIA information can be obtained
at www.ICGtesting.com
Printed in the USA
LVOW12*2122261017

553948LV00002B/24/P